Loving All

Loving All

Stories from My Life, My Teachers, and the Path of Compassion

A Commentary on Gyalse Tokme Zangpo's
Thirty-Seven Practices of Bodhisattvas

TULKU PEMA RIGTSAL

Translated by LAURA SWAN
Foreword by MATTHIEU RICARD

SHAMBHALA

Shambhala Publications, Inc.
2129 13th Street
Boulder, Colorado 80302
www.shambhala.com

Cover art: "Accepting Flower Culture" by Lama Tashi Norbu
Cover design: Daniel Urban-Brown

9 8 7 6 5 4 3 2 1

First Edition

Printed in the United States of America

Shambhala Publications makes every effort to print on acid-free, recycled paper.

Shambhala Publications is distributed worldwide by Penguin Random House, Inc., and its subsidiaries.

LIBRARY OF CONGRESS CATALOGING-IN-PUBLICATION DATA
Names: Padma-rig-rtsal, Sprul-sku, 1963-, author | Swan, Laura, translator
Title: Loving all: Stories from my life, my teachers, and the path of compassion / Tulku Pema Rigtsal; translated by Laura Swan.
Description: Boulder: Shambhala, 2026. | Includes bibliographical references.
Identifiers: LCCN 2025033084 | ISBN 9781645474760 trade paperback
Subjects: LCSH: Thogs-med-bzang-po, Rgyal-sras, 1295-1369. Rgyal-sras lag len so bdun ma. English | Enlightenment (Buddhism)—Requisites | Spiritual life—Buddhism
Classification: LCC BQ4399.R463 P33 2026 | DDC 294.3/444—dc23/eng/20260114
LC record available at https://lccn.loc.gov/2025033084

The authorized representative in the EU for product safety and compliance is eucomply OU, Pärnu mnt 139b-14, 11317 Tallinn, Estonia, hello@eucompliancepartner.com.

Contents

Foreword

With *Loving All*, Tulku Pema Rigtsal offers a lively and deeply inspiring commentary on *The Thirty-Seven Practices of Bodhisattvas*. With warmth and great skill, he interweaves uplifting and instructive stories about his revered teachers and masters of the past with classical quotations from the great luminaries of Buddhism, together with insights drawn from his own experience as both a scholar and a meditator. Rather than a dry commentary, this book is a living dialogue with the Dharma—at once practical and deeply motivating for us to engage in the practice.

Uniting erudition with practical guidance and heartfelt immediacy, Tulku Pema Rigtsal encourages readers to mingle their minds with the Dharma, to free themselves from worldly concerns, and to go into the heart of contemplative practice—progressing, step-by-step, toward liberation from samsara and, ultimately, to inner freedom and the ultimate fruit of buddhahood.

Tulku Pema Rigtsal is dedicated to preserving the Himalayan Buddhist tradition, having, among other things, established an active monastery, Namkha Khyung Dzong, in the Humla district in Nepal, near the Nepal-Tibet border, where he is taking care of more than five hundred monks and nuns who are upholding the lineage's tradition of study and practice.

The Thirty-Seven Practices of Bodhisattvas, composed by the great master Ngulchu Tokme Zangpo (1295–1369), occupies a unique place in Tibetan Buddhist literature. Though concise in form, it distills the vast and profound teachings of the Mahayana into clear instructions that guide practitioners on the bodhisattva path. In thirty-seven verses, Tokme Zangpo elucidates the essential attitudes and practices required to transform one's ordinary habits into the path of liberation, making it one of the most widely studied, memorized, and practiced texts across all schools of Tibetan Buddhism.

The work presents the bodhisattva path not through elaborate philosophical reasoning but through direct, heartfelt counsel. Each verse addresses a specific challenge that practitioners face—attachment to possessions, pride in learning, anger and resentment toward adversaries, clinging to loved ones, or despair at hardship—and offers practical methods to turn such obstacles into opportunities for progress. Because the verses are easy to memorize, they can be recalled in moments of difficulty, serving as a constant companion and guide for one's daily life.

The text also encapsulates the essence of bodhichitta, the altruistic aspiration to attain enlightenment for the benefit of all beings. Every verse is infused with this spirit of compassion and selflessness, reminding practitioners that true progress lies not in self-concern but in cultivating an unshakable commitment to the welfare of others. By embodying this perspective, one gradually erodes the roots of self-cherishing that bind beings to suffering, while nurturing the qualities of generosity, ethical discipline, patience, diligence, meditative concentration, wisdom, and unconditional loving-kindness and compassion.

The enduring importance of this work is reflected in its universality. In its relevance to everyone—beginners as well as advanced practitioners—it transcends sectarian biases and has thus been revered by masters of all Tibetan traditions, who have composed numerous commentaries and taught it to generations of disciples.

In essence, Ngulchu Tokme's *Thirty-Seven Practices of Bodhisattvas* is not merely a literary jewel but a road map to unconditional compassion. For this reason, along with Shantideva's *Entering the Way of the Bodhisattva* (*Bodhicharyavatara*), Langri Tangpa's *Eight Verses of Training the Mind*, Shabkar Tsogdruk Rangdrol's *Emanated Scriptures of the Bodhisattvas*, Minyak Kunzang Sonam Chokyi Trakpa and Dzatrul Ngawang Tenzin Norbu's commentaries on these *Thirty-Seven Practices*, as well as Shechen Gyaltsab Pema Namgyal's detailed commentary on mind training, *The Vase of Exquisite Honey*—it remains an indispensable guide for anyone who sincerely aspires to walk the bodhisattva's path.

Gelong Konchog Tenzin (Matthieu Ricard)
Shechen Tennyi Dargyeling Monastery, Nepal
2025

About the Author

Tulku Pema Rigtsal Rinpoche was born in 1964. His father was the second Degyal Rinpoche, Pema Jigme Namgyal, and his mother was Kyabma Tsering. At the age of three, he was recognized by Kyabje Dudjom Rinpoche as the reincarnation of Chime Rinpoche, a renowned emanation of the Indian siddha Padampa Sangye and head lama of the Riwo Gedenpa monastery Shepel Ling in Purang, Ngari, who later on became one of the finest heart disciples of the first Degyal Rinpoche.

Until the age of nineteen, Tulku Pema Rigtsal studied Tibetan reading, writing, composition, and so forth and the sadhana practices and ritual traditions of the Dudjom Tersar under his father, Degyal Rinpoche. He then accompanied Khenchen Dazer Rinpoche to East Tibet where, for more than ten years, he studied and contemplated the thirteen major treatises and the teachings of Rongzompa, Longchenpa, Mipham Rinpoche, Jigme Lingpa, Ngari Panchen, and others under the guidance of Khenchen Dazer Rinpoche and Khenchen Chokhyab Rinpoche.

In 1985, in Yalbang Purbachen, Humla, in the far northwest of Nepal, Pema Rigtsal Rinpoche established Namkha Khyung Dzong Monastery, building a temple housing statues, stupas, scriptures, and so on. To the 150 monks[1] who now reside at the monastery, Rinpoche teaches without cease the thirteen major treatises and other scriptures of sutra and tantra, with a special emphasis on the wisdom system of All-Knowing Mipham

Rinpoche. He has stayed in retreat to read the Collected Words of the Buddha and the Collection of Nyingma Tantras. He has also completed a three-year retreat, a six-month retreat, and so on.

In service of the Humla people in general and the monastic and lay practitioners from Ngari—to all those with sincere interest—Rinpoche teaches the Sater Ngondro (Khandro Nyingtik Preliminary Practices), *The Words of My Perfect Teacher*, *Entering the Way of the Bodhisattva*, *Mountain Dharma*, *Buddhahood Without Meditation: A Visionary Account Known as Refining One's Perception (Nang Jang)*, *The Self-Arising Natural State (Neluk Rangjung)*, and so on, and thus continues to teach and propagate the profound teachings of the Dudjom Tersar tradition.

He has received empowerments, transmissions, and instructions primarily from Kyabje Dudjom Rinpoche, Kyabje Dilgo Khyentse Rinpoche, Kyabje Dodrup Rinpoche, Kyabje Penor Rinpoche, Khenchen Dazer Rinpoche, and so on. He also includes my name among his gurus, for which I am thankful.

In any case, considering present circumstances, Pema Rigtsal Rinpoche does not lack the noble qualities of learning and righteousness, and in my own experience, the presence of all such noble qualities depends upon the absence of the demon of conceit. Therefore, may all those with the eyes of wisdom constantly watch over him. I pray with whatever prayers I know that he may live long and that the great waves of benefit he generates for Buddha's teaching in general, and for the study and practice of the Kama and Terma teachings of the Nyingma tradition in particular, may expand like oceans in the summertime!

Dungse Thinley Norbu Rinpoche

Translator's Note

Loving All is primarily based on two sets of teachings, both given in 2019. In October 2019, Tulku Pema Rigtsal Rinpoche taught Gyalse Tokme's *Thirty-Seven Practices of Bodhisattvas* to a small group of Australian students at his monastery in Humla, Nepal. I was fortunate to be one of those students, as well as the interpreter. Earlier that year, Rinpoche also taught the text in Taiwan, using a variety of stories to illustrate each of the thirty-seven points. With their evocative stories and their focus on a contemporary context, I and several other students thought these teachings could benefit a wider audience, and so I began the process of compiling them into a book.

In addition to these 2019 teachings, I drew from recordings of teachings that Rinpoche gave on *The Thirty-Seven Practices* between 2014 and 2024 in Humla, Kathmandu, and Toronto, and in 2024 I requested Rinpoche to elaborate on some of the stories and clarify various points.

Although there are already several excellent English translations of Gyalse Tokme's *Thirty-Seven Practices of Bodhisattvas*, I found myself making a new translation to complement Rinpoche's commentary and bring out the crisp and candid character of the text. I am grateful to the Padmakara Translation Group, Adam Pearcey, and Heidi I. Koppl for their previous translations to which my own is much in debt.

Finally, my deepest thanks to Dharma siblings in Australia, Taiwan, and Nepal, who assisted by sharing recordings of previous teachings and transcribing those given in Humla in 2019. Most of all, my profound gratitude to our teacher Tulku Pema Rigtsal Rinpoche for his wisdom and love.

Laura Swan
Namkha Khyung Dzong Monastery, Humla
2025

Preface

Introducing Myself

I was born in 1964, on the fifteenth day of the second Tibetan month, in Sendeu in India. My father was Pema Jikme Namgyal, the reincarnation of Kyabgon Pema Dewe Gyalpo, and my mother was Kyabma Tsering. At the age of three, following the prophecies of the deity Dorje Yudronma and the guru Kyabje Dudjom Jigdral Yeshe Dorje, I was recognized as the reincarnation of Chime Rinpoche, a renowned emanation of the Indian *siddha* Padampa Sangye.

My father and my uncle Namgyal taught me to read and write the Tibetan script. Then, for several years I attended the Tibetan government's Namgyal School and Durbar High School in Kathmandu, where I studied up to sixth grade. After that, I studied the ritual practices of my lineage, Namkha Khyung Dzong—the melodies, liturgical chanting, and so forth.

From a young age, due to the strong presence of Dharma in my environment, I felt unshakable faith in Kyabje Dudjom Jigdral Yeshe Dorje and his son Dungse Thinley Norbu Rinpoche. I also felt great faith and respect for the sacred Dharma itself. When I was nineteen, Pema Kundrol Rinpoche, the son of my predecessor Chime Rinpoche, had a sudden stroke and died. This triggered within me an intense disenchantment, and I became determined to practice the Dharma properly.

Soon afterward, I met Khenchen Dawe Ozer Rinpoche, a teacher who showed me indescribable kindness. For the next ten years, I stayed by Khen Rinpoche's side, following him to India, Nepal, Bhutan, Sikkim, East Tibet, and various other places. At his feet, I studied the sutras and tantras and the general sciences. For the duration of my time with him, I focused on my studies and cast aside all concern for food, clothing, and reputation. I joyfully assumed responsibility for my own needs and embraced all the hardships this involved. This pleased the guru greatly, and so my efforts became great clouds of offerings.

Khen Rinpoche told me that I must teach the scriptures and make this one of the main focuses of my life. To honor this command, from 1993 until the present day, I have been teaching a group of fifty or more monks and nuns daily, almost without break. During these years, I have also completed one three-year retreat and several yearlong retreats. In this way, I have stayed put at my monastery, Namkha Khyung Dzong in Humla, striving to the best of my ability to uphold our Dharma lineage through the unity of study and practice. I have also sponsored the construction of several statues and *stupas*, which are considered in Buddhism to be supports for awakened body, speech, and mind.

At present, there are more than five hundred monks and nuns at Namkha Khyung Dzong Monastery and Nunnery. They are upholding the lineage's tradition of practice, and they offer *puja* on the tenth and twenty-fifth days every month, without fail.[2]

My Teachers

My greatest fortune is that all the teachers I have met in this life have been buddhas in human form. Their awakened deeds cannot be fathomed by someone like me, but nevertheless the conduct and lifestyles of each one of them seem to me to be wondrous and unique. I have trained under thirteen or fourteen teachers so far this life, and there are several more with whom I have made Dharma connections.

My main gurus are Kyabje Dudjom Jigdral Yeshe Dorje Rinpoche, a master who was Guru Rinpoche in the flesh and who was prophesied in the treasure teachings as being able to lead all those connected with him through sight and sound to the continent of Chamara;[3] Kyabje Dilgo Khyentse Rinpoche; Kyabje Dodrupchen Rinpoche; Kyabje Trulshik Rinpoche; Kyabje Dungse Thinley Norbu Rinpoche; Kyabje Drubwang Penor Rinpoche; Kyabje Domang Yangtang Rinpoche; Khenchen Pema Tsewang Rinpoche; my father, the second Pema Dewe Gyalpo, Pema Jigme Namgyal Rinpoche; my paternal uncle Tsewang Rinpoche; Khenchen Dawe Ozer Rinpoche; and Khenchen Pema Choying Khyabdal Rinpoche.

Khenpo Choying Khyabdal Rinpoche (Khenpo Chokhyab Rinpoche)

Long before I met Khen Rinpoche, I had heard that he was a real *jadralwa*, a pure renunciate and totally carefree. But when I actually met him, I saw that he was even more of a pure renunciate, more *jadral*, than I could have possibly imagined. When I met him, he was old, thin, and a little frail. His room was a weather-worn wooden hut just one arm-span square, containing nothing more than a small wooden box that served as his seat and bed. In front of this was a small stove and just enough space for an attendant to sit cross-legged while making tea. He was wearing old grimy woolen robes, and there was not even five hundred rupees worth of possessions in the room. I had heard people talk about Khen Rinpoche's austere living conditions and how he had lived this way his entire life, but I had struggled to believe it. Once I witnessed it with my own eyes, I had no choice but to believe.

Having offered three prostrations, I presented a ceremonial scarf, or *kata*,[4] and the letter Khenpo Dazer Rinpoche had sent with me—a letter in which he introduced me and requested Khenpo Chokhyab Rinpoche to grant me teachings on Rongzom Mahapandita's *Entering the Way of the Great Vehicle*.[5] When I explained why and how I had come to meet him, he paid little attention. He responded to all my talk with a scolding that was in fact a precious instruction exposing my hidden faults. He glanced at the envelope containing Khenpo Dazer Rinpoche's letter and then tossed it aside.

"I used to call him Long Ears. I've never called him Khenpo," he said, and he seemed displeased when I called him Khen Rinpoche.

When I think about it now, I can see that Khenpo Chokhyab Rinpoche was totally different from worldly people. In general, people like being praised and dislike being criticized, but it was not that way with Khen Rinpoche. If one of us said, "Oh, Khen Rinpoche, everyone is saying wonderful things about you!" he would appear livid and say, "If people see some good qualities in me, they can develop those qualities in themselves! I have no need for praise—I know very well what I'm like. I have no need of criticism—I know very well what I'm like." When he spoke like this, I felt like a debater sitting in front of Noble Nagarjuna.[6] I had no idea what to say and could do nothing more than sit and stare.

The practice instructions teach us that we should perceive the guru as the Buddha and cultivate pure perception. When I was with Khenpo Chokhyab Rinpoche, this perception would come about naturally, effortlessly. Just sitting in his presence would reduce me to tears. I came to see that his rebuke of Khenpo Dazer Rinpoche was in fact a skillful way of felling my own pride. In short, his mere presence and lifestyle imparted to me the futility of samsara and the necessity of discarding self-grasping and the eight worldly concerns.

When granting instructions and the like to us students, he would sometimes point to a particular student's conduct and display anger and other emotions. However, it was clear that he was always in the state of the Great Perfection:[7] in the four modes of natural rest,[8] his three gates—body, speech, and mind—wide open and at ease.[9]

One time, while receiving teachings on *Entering the Way of the Great Vehicle*, due to the tremendous blessing of the text itself and the extraordinary skill and erudition of Khen Rinpoche, from the first day of the teaching until the very last, I felt as if I had arrived in a totally new world. Previously, the assertions of the various tenet systems and the different presentations of the great scholars had seemed conflicting to me, and this perceived conflict was like a cancerous tumor eating away at me. But now, through the blessings of this teaching and the kindness and compassion of the teacher himself, I felt like this tumor had been removed from my body, offering a tremendous sense of lightness and relief.

From then on, I understood that all the teachings of the sutras and the various classes of tantra are contained in the Great Perfection and that the nine graded vehicles[10] all stem from the Great Perfection, the pinnacle and source. When that understanding dawned in me, I felt an impartial, far-reaching faith in the vast ocean of teachings pertaining to the sutras and tantras—a faith unlike anything I had felt before. I came to understand that all the various teachings are stepping stones leading us to the path of the Great Perfection. I had previously been able to parrot the words of the Great Perfection with a superficial kind of understanding, but then I really understood, deep down, how all the vehicles of Dharma are contained in the Great Perfection. I understood why and how the vital point of all practice boils down to the Great Perfection. As a result, a deep-seated conviction dawned in me, and I developed unshakable, wholehearted faith in the teaching and teacher.

At times I would have a vivid, visceral sense that all these present appearances are illusory and unreal. In the fifth chapter of *Entering the Way of the Great Vehicle*, we came to this quotation from *The Omnipotent Monarch*:

> Since neither faults nor qualities are generated,
> No matter what marks of conceptualization arise,
> They are uncontrived, unfabricated, and luminous in and of themselves,
> Unobstructed, naturally arising, unpursued, and naturally at peace.[11]

When explaining this quotation, Khen Rinpoche's meditative experience seemed to blaze forth, and I found myself in a state of naked awareness unlike anything I had experienced before. Subsequently, I gained certainty as stable as a mountain in the fact that there is nothing more to resolve and nothing more to comprehend.

Khen Rinpoche Dawe Ozer

Khenpo Dazer Rinpoche was a great scholar of the Buddhist scriptures and a perfect monk. Moreover, he practiced the Great Perfection unceasingly, day and night. He was untouched by the eight worldly concerns and always took delight in adhering to solitude, where he planted the victory banner of spiritual accomplishment. He was a renunciate and hidden yogi.

Whatever teaching and advice Khen Rinpoche gave, it was always deeply moving. For example, one day when Khen Rinpoche was speaking about the benefits of Longchenpa's *Seven Treasuries*, I was flooded with such intense faith that my hair stood up on end, my eyes filled with tears, and I said to Khen Rinpoche that I would vow, in his presence, to commission a copy of the *Seven Treasuries* written in gold.[12] He replied, "That's a great thing to do, but the most important thing is to put into practice what these *Seven Treasuries* teach. And if you can also commission wooden printing blocks for them, that would be excellent."

Similarly, one day Khen Rinpoche was talking about Khunu Lama Tenzin Gyaltsen[13]—how for thirteen years Khunu Lama wandered from place to place, meeting teachers, going on pilgrimage, listening, contemplating, and meditating on an ocean of teachings, and always staying in places where he was totally unknown. As Khen Rinpoche was extolling this kind of lifestyle, I felt so inspired. I told him, "I want to live like that myself. In your presence, I want to make a pledge to that end." Khen Rinpoche replied, "That is an admirable aspiration. But you know, those who can succeed will succeed regardless of whether they're on the move or whether they stay put. And for people like us, it is best not to travel around too much. It is better to stay put. So, just stay in one place and practice the Dharma there." As everyone knows, I am not impulsive nor easily moved, but Khen Rinpoche's words were like proclamations of truth. They had such a profound and transformative effect on me. This was one of his special qualities.

In short, the little knowledge and understanding I have and the fact that I at least have the semblance of a Dharma practitioner is all thanks to Khenpo Dazer Rinpoche, directly and indirectly. He was one of my root gurus, a guru who showed me the three types of kindness, and he has influenced me more than anyone else in my life. His kindness is indescribable. I will never forget it.

As for how I received the pointing-out instructions of the Great Perfection from Khen Rinpoche, when Khen Rinpoche was teaching us Longchenpa's *Treasury of the Dharmadhatu*, I said to him, "Khen Rinpoche, we're already about halfway through the text, but so far, even though I understand the words, I don't have even the slightest understanding or experience of the real meaning of *rigpa*, the true nature of mind. What should I do?" Khen Rinpoche said,

> That's not a problem. Just pray to Longchenpa wholeheartedly and chant the root text daily. Then at some point, due to some trigger or condition, you will come to recognize.
>
> Think of the great scholar and undisputed reincarnation Patrul Rinpoche.[14] Although he'd been following genuine, qualified teachers for many years, it was only later in life that he recognized rigpa. One day, he was coming down from Shri Singha and bumped into Do Khyentse Yeshe Dorje.[15] Do Khyentse was wearing a sheepskin chuba and had a sword fastened to his belt. Patrul Rinpoche didn't lack faith in Do Rinpoche, but nevertheless he thought to himself, *Would it hurt him to dress in accord with the Dharma?!* Do Khyentse knew what he was thinking, and all of a sudden he grabbed him by the throat and shook him back and forth, shouting, "Old dog! Old dog!" It was at that very moment that Patrul Rinpoche recognized rigpa.
>
> Likewise, even when the famous Khenpo Tubten was enthroned as Khenchen and was teaching the sutras and tantras to huge groups of students, he still had not recognized the nature of mind. But one day he was walking to a village to perform some prayers, and while walking over a small bridge he slipped and fell into the river below—at that very moment, he found himself in the state of rigpa and recognized the nature of mind.

By telling me these and other stories, Khen Rinpoche changed my outlook, and from then on I was always wondering when something like this might happen to me. A few days later,

I dreamed I was in an empty open cave, like the road tunnels they build through mountains these days. In the middle of the cave was a stone trough full of blood, both fresh and old. I thought it must be a place where Hindus make blood sacrifices, like the Goddess Kali temple in Dakshinkali, Kathmandu. I was terrified and revolted, and I thought, *I must exorcise these malicious spirits!* Assuming the divine pride of Vajrakilaya, I recited the fourfold HUNG mantra and threw white mustard seeds to drive out the obstacle-making spirits. At the same time, the awesome sounds of ritual horns, drums, thigh-bone trumpets, and so on filled the air. My mind then merged with space and I found myself in the state of rigpa and my fear and revulsion vanished without trace. The next morning, when I told Khen Rinpoche my dream, he said, "Well, what was the state of rigpa like?" I did not know how to reply. Then Khen Rinpoche said, "Exactly, that's it!" and he was really pleased. I knew then that my dream had been the guru's blessing.

Dungse Thinley Norbu Rinpoche

Dungse Thinley Norbu Rinpoche lived as a hidden yogi, a secret adept who had realized samsara and nirvana to be of equal taste in the *dharmakaya* and for whom all appearances dawned as instructions. He had very special ways of bestowing upon his fortunate disciples the pith instructions of the Great Perfection.

One day in 1997, Rinpoche made a pilgrimage to the Swayambhu and Boudhanath stupas with a large group of students. In the evening, after returning to his residence, he sat down with us and began giving us some Dharma instruction and advice. Rinpoche was drinking wine and acting a little tipsy, and he started giving very direct and candid pointing-out instructions in quite an unusual way. He was telling us, using his own experience, how to sustain rigpa with great naturalness in the very midst of ordinary attachment and aversion. I thought to myself, *All those gathered here today must have all recognized rigpa. How incredibly fortunate we are!* and I was overcome with joy and delight.

Another time I went to see Rinpoche in California, and in the evening, while we were making a feast offering[16] and Rinpoche was teaching, he scolded me.

"It's true that you're learned, but you're polluted by pride," he said, and he made lots of jokes about me.

One day he said, "It's no use being a great scholar. You need to practice well. If you're proud of your learning, that will damage your practice, so it would probably be best if you stopped teaching scholarly texts." Rinpoche said this not just once but again and again. This made me think I should make a pledge, in Rinpoche's presence, to practice, so I asked Rinpoche, "Should I do a yearlong togal retreat or a yearlong retreat reciting the Collection of Nyingma Tantras? Please tell me which would be best."

"Both would be excellent, so do both," Rinpoche replied. Then I said, "But it'll be difficult to do them both at the same time, so which one should I do first?" Rinpoche did not seem very pleased when I asked this.

The next day, Rinpoche said again and again that my teaching scholarly texts had polluted me. I then thought to myself, *In the past, when I knew nothing at all and Khenpo Dazer Rinpoche told me to teach the scriptures, I said, "But I don't know anything, so how can I teach?" Khen Rinpoche replied, "When I first came to India and started teaching, I don't think I was as learned as you are now." In that way, he encouraged me and boosted my confidence. As a result, for about seventeen years now, I have been teaching fifty or so monastics almost daily without break. It seems that I've fulfilled Khen Rinpoche's command to teach, and now it's time to fulfill Dungse Rinpoche's command.* And so I said to Rinpoche, "From now on, I vow to not teach even a single verse of Dharma to a single soul!" For a little while, Rinpoche remained silent. Then he said, "If I tell you not to teach the Dharma, I'll be creating negative karma. I'm not saying that. What I'm saying is that you need to rid yourself of pride in your learning."

Later that evening, after we had finished the feast offering and I was back in my room, I lay on my bed thinking, *What happened today was quite shocking. What would my life look like if Rinpoche had really made me vow not to teach anymore? If I were to give up teaching the Dharma, it would be like my life's work had come to an end. Our monastery is supported financially by students in Taiwan and other countries. And when I go to those countries, I go there to teach the Dharma. So if I stopped teaching, I would have no reason to travel overseas anymore. Likewise, if I were to stop teaching the monks and nuns up at the monastery, there would be no real point in my being there. I'd also have to stop giving teachings and advice to the lay students at our annual vajra-guru mantra accumulations and so on. I'd have no work. It would be like I were retired. From today on, I'd have nothing to do except stay alone in retreat, and I'd be committed to staying there for the rest of my entire life.*

Pondering what would have happened if Rinpoche had accepted my vow, I stayed awake for many hours. Thinking about all this made me very anxious, and when I looked carefully at that anxiety I saw that, just as Rinpoche had said, I really did have a very strong attachment to the scriptures. Even though I did not think I was proud about my learning in the way Rinpoche had said I was, I realized that I was incredibly attached to the scriptures, so much so that I could not bear to part from them. As a result, I came to understand that whether it is attachment to virtue or vice, attachment is attachment and it obscures the dharmakaya, the natural state. From then on, with this newfound awareness of my own faults, my attachment to the scriptures gradually lessened. This ability of Dungse Rinpoche to see into the depths his students' minds was one of his extraordinary qualities.

Dodrupchen Rinpoche

Dodrupchen Rinpoche is one of the main gurus from whom I received empowerments, transmissions, and instructions. I have also felt his blessings in my dreams and so on.

For instance, during my three-year retreat, when I was close to completing the practice of Vajrakilaya I had a dream of Rinpoche. Rinpoche was sitting on a throne in a small shrine room. He was chanting a liturgy and playing the ritual drum, or *damaru*,[17] and bell. Me and a few other monks were sitting there, and at one point during the liturgy Rinpoche said, "Now it's time to pay homage, so make the mudras!" Then all of a sudden I was naked. I fell to the floor, and my two legs wrapped all the way around my back and reappeared at the front, my right leg on my left thigh and my left leg on my right thigh, and then they stretched out so that an incredibly tight knot formed at my waist and I was transformed into Vajrakilaya. When I woke up, it was like I had no waist, and for a long time I experienced my body as empty form.

In another dream during that three-year retreat, Dodrupchen Rinpoche was sitting in a tent on a hill carpeted with green grass and colorful wildflowers. I told Rinpoche that I had completed various recitation practices during my three-year retreat, and in response he said, "Now you need to recite one million one hundred thousand ARAPATSA (Manjushri) mantras. That will help you swiftly bring all activities to completion."

Later on, when I told Dodrupchen Rinpoche about those dreams, he said they were very auspicious. I said, "Rinpoche, I want to practice Manjushri, but there are so many different Manjushri *sadhanas*. Which one should I use for my practice?"

Rinpoche then said, “My guru is Yukhok Jadral,[18] and he considered the Manjushri sadhana of the tantric system to be very precious, so do the entire mantra recitation—the approach and accomplishment—for that.”[19]

I then began a recitation retreat for peaceful Manjushri according to the tantric system. It took about three months to complete. The number of mantras one has to accumulate for this practice is one million, plus an additional one hundred thousand as amendment, making a total of exactly one million one hundred thousand. When I realized this, I felt that the Dodrupchen Rinpoche who had appeared in my dream and told me to do this mantra recitation really was no different from the Dodrupchen Rinpoche in person who had told me to do this specific practice. I felt confident then that the guru really had come in person to my dream.

Domang Yangtang Rinpoche

In the Vajra Vehicle in general, and in the Great Perfection in particular, the student sees their root guru as the Buddha in person, as the sovereign of the *mandala*, and reveres their commands above all else. This is a crucial point demonstrating that the blessings of the wisdom lineage come through the guru and the guru alone. I came to understand this through the life story of Yangtang Rinpoche and the way he honored his own guru’s commands.

In 1959, when the troubles erupted in Tibet, the great teachers, monasteries, and teaching centers were subjected to grave harm. Nevertheless, honoring the command of his root guru Lingtrul Rinpoche, Yangtang Rinpoche stayed put in his monastery, even though he knew his life was at risk and even though he had the chance to flee to India.

Though Rinpoche was free of even the slightest fault, he took upon himself all the hardships of the Cultural Revolution.

For twenty years, he was incarcerated in Dardo Ranga prison. During this time, the government arrested most high-ranking lamas, *tulkus*, and *khenpos*, and the majority of high-standing laypeople, and imprisoned them in appalling conditions.[20] They set out to "reeducate" them in the values of the Cultural Revolution, and they lied to them endlessly, telling them that very soon they would all be given various positions and assets and be released. Some people then pretended to have faith in the Cultural Revolution, and they denigrated the Dharma and the gurus. For the nonreligious this behavior was abhorrent, and for the religious it was distressing and sad.

Throughout this entire period, Yangtang Rinpoche remained steadfast, like a mountain amid a snowstorm. He overcame all obstacles, and no matter how much they tortured and abused him, he remembered his guru's command and devoted himself to training in the Great Perfection. In secret, he took Sera Yangtrul Rinpoche,[21] a fellow prisoner, as a teacher and shared his experience and realization with him. There were many indications of his experience and realization flourishing—indications that are still legendary in the area.

Rinpoche's teachings were in fact mind treasures, some of which he wrote down in the form of compositions.[22] From among these, his *Instructions on the Great Perfection: A Brief Presentation of View, Meditation, and Action* is an inconceivably precious and potent teaching. It is commensurate with Patrul Rinpoche's *The Three Statements That Strike the Vital Point*, the essential practice of hundreds of scholars and thousands of siddhas.

Although I was born in this dark age, where the five degenerations are rampant, having met with and been blessed by teachers like Yangtang Rinpoche, who are in true possession of the realization of the Great Perfection, I regard myself as incredibly fortunate.

Introduction

OM SVASTI! It was from his wondrous *bodhichitta*, arisen many
eons ago,
That the Blessed Buddha, King of Shakyas, was born.
To bodhichitta, essence of the profound and vast Dharma,
With firm and fervent faith, I bow down.

O Ngulchu Tokme Zangpo, magical emanation of
The *mahasattva* Shantideva,
Your every deed skillfully displays the excellent path to
buddhahood.
To *The Thirty-Seven Practices of Bodhisattvas*, I pay obeisance.

When we study the Dharma, it is imperative that we do so with the correct motivation and conduct. These points are traditionally expounded at the beginning of oral teachings, but they must also be applied when reading and studying on our own.

Our motivation should be the vast heart of bodhichitta—the thought, *I will establish all mother-beings, who are as limitless in number as the vast reaches of space, at the level of perfect unsurpassable awakening! To this end, I will now study the Dharma and apply it accordingly.* All beings have been our mother in one or other of our countless past lives, and when they were our mothers, they took care of us with tremendous love and care. They put our well-being before their own and endured suffering and hardship for our sake. Just look at the way mothers love their children. We see this even in animals, in the way a tigress cares for her cubs, in the way a mother bird cares for her chicks. Every single being has shown us great love and kindness in the past, and now those very same beings are suffering. They are suffering endlessly, despite longing for nothing but happiness. Our "mothers," not recognizing that happiness stems from virtue and suffering stems from non-virtue, unwittingly sow the seeds for their own suffering and obstruct their own happiness.

At present, we have attained a precious human birth, we have encountered the sacred Dharma, and we have met with genuine teachers. This is an extremely fortunate and rare situation. Without encountering the Dharma and without encountering a spiritual guide, we would remain in the dark—we would remain ignorant of what to accept and reject. We would not recognize the downfalls of samsara nor the benefits of awakening. To lead all beings—our kind parents of this life, together with all other mother-beings—to awakening, the state of ultimate happiness, we must make use of this precious opportunity and study the authentic Dharma. Then we must reflect on the Dharma we have studied and internalize it through meditation.

Without the motivation of bodhichitta, one's study, reflection, and meditation will not, and cannot, become the Great Vehicle path. And without the Great Vehicle path, there is no Vajra Vehicle path. Our motivation must be pure—it must be free of worldly concerns for this fleeting life.

As the Indian sage Padampa Sangye said,

> Listen to the teachings like a deer listening to music;
> Contemplate them like a northern nomad shearing sheep;
> Meditate on them like a dumb person savoring food;
> Practice them like a hungry yak eating grass;
> Reach their result, like the sun coming out from behind
> the clouds.[23]

We need to view the teachings as pith instructions—as practical advice for transforming ourselves. Khenpo Dazer Rinpoche would often say that these days there are many people receiving the pith instructions but there are very few people who know how to do so. You should receive pith instructions in the same way you look in a mirror, he would say. You search your reflection for imperfections, dirt, and dust, and then you clean yourself up. Likewise, when you listen to and study the Buddhist teachings, you need to take a close look at yourself. You need to ask, "Do I really conduct myself as it's taught here? Is my outlook in accord with this instruction?" If the answer is yes, you should rejoice. And if the answer is no, then feel regret, confess your shortcomings, and do whatever you can to change.

Regarding the conduct, there are certain points we must adopt and certain points we must avoid. The conduct to avoid includes the three defects of the pot, the six stains, and the five wrong ways of remembering. The conduct to adopt includes the four metaphors, the six *paramitas*,[24] and other modes of conduct. The four metaphors are taught in *The Sutra Arranged Like a Tree*:

> Noble one, you should think of yourself as someone
>   who is sick,
> Of the Dharma as the remedy,
> Of your spiritual friend as a skillful doctor,
> And of diligent practice as the way to recovery.[25]

You can learn more about these points of conduct from *The Words of My Perfect Teacher* and other texts.

The Five Principal Considerations

In the Noble Land of India, there were two main seats of Buddhist learning: the glorious monasteries of Nalanda and Vikramashila. When transmitting the Buddhadharma to the Snowy Land of Tibet, the Tibetan translators (*lotsawas*), scholars (*panditas*), and practitioners chose to follow the long-standing tradition of Glorious Nalanda. At Nalanda, the words of the Buddha were taught by means of the five perfections, while the treatises (commentaries on the words of the Buddha) were explained by means of the five principal considerations. *The Thirty-Seven Practices of Bodhisattvas* is a treatise, so we will discuss it in terms of the five principal considerations:

1. Who is the author? The author of this text is Gyalse Tokme.
2. What is the main theme of the text? The main theme is relative bodhichitta and ultimate bodhichitta. Alternatively, we could say the main theme is how to generate bodhichitta and train in the six paramitas.
3. From which scriptures does the text draw? It draws upon the three baskets, or *pitakas*,[26] of the Great Vehicle teachings, and specifically the Great Vehicle sutras.
4. To which category does it belong? From among the two main vehicles, the Lesser Vehicle and the Great Vehicle, it belongs to the Great Vehicle. Within the Great Vehicle, from among the two categories of sutra and mantra, it belongs to the category of sutra.
5. For whose benefit and for what purpose was it composed? It was composed for the benefit of all those seeking awakening, for by putting these teachings into practice we can attain genuine awakening.

The Author

Gyalse Tokme was a Kadampa geshe.[27] Within the Kadampa tradition there are two subtraditions: the New Kadampa and the Old Kadampa. The Old Kadampa tradition begins with the eleventh-century Indian master Atisha's disciple Dromton Gyalwe Jungne and continues until Gyalse Tokme, while the

New Kadampa tradition begins with the fourteenth-century Tibetan master Je Rinpoche (Tsongkhapa) and continues to the present. Therefore, Gyalse Tokme was one of the last geshes of the Old Kadampa traditions. Not only was he a great and renowned scholar, but he was also an extraordinary practitioner. He spent much of his later life in retreat, living for the most part in a cave called Ngulchu Rinchen Puk. (This is why he is often called Gyalse Ngulchu Tokme.) Gyalse Tokme composed more than one hundred texts, but *The Thirty-Seven Practices of Bodhisattvas* is the most renowned of all his works.

Gyalse Tokme was born in 1295 in a place called Puljung Drakya in Sakya, Tibet. At birth, he was named Konchok Zangpo and later on became known as Gyalse Tokme. From a young age, he demonstrated bodhichitta. For instance, when he was three years old, he went outside to relieve himself. It was the middle of winter, and winters in Tibet are extremely harsh. When the young Konchok Zangpo came back inside, he was naked. His mother was shocked. "Where on earth are your clothes?" she said.

"There was a man outside and he had no clothes. He was really cold, so I gave him mine," he replied.

When his mother went out to look for this man, she found her son's clothes draped over a mound of straw. This mound, with tufts of grass resembling hair growing out from the top, did indeed look like a person huddled up in the snow, to a child's eye at least. This is just one example of the uncontrived compassion Gyalse Tokme demonstrated from his earliest years. There are also accounts of him assuming the meditation posture and entering a state of equipoise at the tender age of two or three, without anyone prompting him. These are clear signs of having trained on the bodhisattva path in past lives.

Gyalse Tokme's mother, Bumdron, died when he was just three years old, and his father, Konchok Pal, died two years later. From then on, he was raised by his other relatives. He spent his time herding the family's livestock. Each winter, several livestock would be slaughtered, since they needed meat to survive the cold. Each winter, Gyalse Tokme would beg his family to spare the animals. Even though he was just a child, he would try to intervene. He felt so much compassion for the animals that he would faint from distress when they were killed.

At the age of nine, he entered a monastery called Samling and began his formal education. At the age of fifteen, he began studying seminal scriptures such as Asanga's *Compendium of Abhidharma*, the five treatises of Asanga, *Entering the Way of the Bodhisattva*, and the six major treatises of the Madhyamaka. Due to his learning and accomplishment in past lives, he gained a deep understanding of these teachings almost effortlessly. He quickly became an adept scholar learned in all five genres of scripture,[28] and in particular the five treatises of Asanga (also known as the five treatises of Maitreya). That is in fact how he acquired the name Tokme, which is the Tibetan translation of Asanga, meaning "unimpeded." Later on, he was also given the name Gyalse, meaning "heir of the victorious ones," or "bodhisattva," and so became known as Gyalse Tokme.

In his twenties, he began to teach and soon became renowned for his great learning and excellent qualities. He was invited to many monasteries and centers, and a community of many thousands of disciples gathered around him. At one point, Gyalse Tokme was invited to teach at the monastic seat of Botong Tamche Khyenpa. The monastic community there were struggling financially, so they asked Gyalse Tokme for advice. No doubt they were expecting him to advise them to start farming their land, to sell some of the monastery's assets, or seek out some new sponsors. Instead he told them, "If you are really followers of Buddha Shakyamuni and you really want my advice, then engage in these thirty-seven practices of bodhisattvas. This is the appropriate action to take." This is how this precious teaching came about.

Later on, Gyalse Tokme went to a place called Toka to finalize his composition. One day, as he was working on the text, a great gale suddenly rose up and tore the sheets of paper from his hand. Before he knew it, his writing was carried far away, scattered in all directions. At first, he felt alarmed but soon realized that he knew the entire text by heart. So, without difficulty, he was able to write it down again. In hindsight, he saw this to be a prophecy of sorts—a sign that this teaching would spread as far as the reaches of the wind. And indeed, this prophecy has been fulfilled. For there is no teaching to be found in India, China, or in any of Tibet's four main schools—Kagyu, Geluk, Sakya, or Nyingma—that is more widely taught and unanimously revered than this.

The great waves of benefit this text has brought about, and continues to bring, stem from Gyalse Tokme's accomplishment as a bodhisattva and the strength of his bodhichitta and aspiration prayers. The activities of noble bodhisattvas have vast reach and enduring benefit. Look, for example, at Patrul Rinpoche's *The Words of My Perfect Teacher*. There are hundreds of compositions similar to *The Thirty-Seven Practices of Bodhisattvas* and *The Words of My Perfect Teacher* but none that effect the mind so powerfully, none that have had such enduring benefit.

Gyalse Tokme lived to the age of seventy-five. When he passed away, he was welcomed by deities and gurus while rainbows and orbs of light filled the sky and fragrant scents permeated the air. Such are the wondrous signs that accompany the passing of great bodhisattvas.

Transmission

I received teachings on *The Thirty-Seven Practices of Bodhisattvas* at least ten times from my root guru Khenpo Dazer Rinpoche. When he taught this text, he would do so through his personal experience—what we call *nyamtri*, "instructing through experience." He had put these teachings into practice and developed these bodhisattva qualities within himself. He did not teach from mere knowledge, the way people like me teach these texts. Khenpo Dazer Rinpoche was not only a great scholar—he was not skilled merely in the words of these texts. He was a true bodhisattva who had gained direct experience and realization and embodied the very meaning of the words he taught.

Of course, as a student it is a failing, not to mention negative karma, to search for flaws in one's spiritual teachers. Nevertheless, say you were to search for flaws—say you searched day and night, scrutinizing each and every action of teachers such as Khenpo Dazer Rinpoche. Still, you would not find a single thing to criticize. I spent ten years with Khenpo Dazer Rinpoche, receiving teachings from him almost every day, and yet there was not a single action, gesture, or word that I could find fault with. It was an inconceivable fortune to receive these bodhisattva teachings from him.

Over the centuries, many teachers have written commentaries on this precious text. From among them, the most extensive, at least to my knowledge, is that composed by Minyak Kunso,[29] an outstanding scholar and a student of both the Nyingma and Geluk traditions. He began his education at the Geluk monasteries Sera and Drepung, where he became renowned for his great learning. Later on, he became a close disciple of Patrul Rinpoche and studied at his feet for many years. At some point, seeing the sharpness of his mind, Patrul Rinpoche advised him to go to Sershu, a Geluk monastery.

"Continue your studies there for a while, then return to me," he said.

But for various reasons, Minyak ended up staying there. Later on, Patrul Rinpoche said, "I made two mistakes in my life. One was sending Minyak Kunso to Sershu Monastery. If I'd kept him here, he would have been a great aide to Mipham Rinpoche." It is not that Patrul Rinpoche had sectarian bias. After all, he was one of the leading figureheads of the nonsectarian, or *rime*, movement. However, it seems that if Minyak Kunso had stayed with Patrul Rinpoche, he could have been of great service to the Nyingma teachings, as much as Mipham Rinpoche.[30]

I had the good fortune to receive the oral transmission and brief teachings on Minyak Kunso's commentary from Minyak Khenpo Tsering Nyima. And as I said, I received *The Thirty-Seven Practices of Bodhisattvas* from Khenpo Dazer Rinpoche many times. He received it from his guru Bopa Tulku Dongak Tenpe Nyima, who received it from Khenpo Kunpal Rinpoche, who received it directly from the peerless Patrul Rinpoche, who is universally acknowledged to be an emanation of the bodhisattvas Shantideva and Gyalse Tokme, among others. In this way, the transmission I hold for this precious text is very short and very blessed. Furthermore, since in the Nyingma tradition the transmission of *The Thirty-Seven Practices*, and *Entering the Way of the Bodhisattva* as well, descends from Patrul Rinpoche, we can feel truly confident that we have a blessed line of transmission for these bodhisattva teachings.

The Text

The content of *The Thirty-Seven Practices of Bodhisattvas* is none other than the conduct of bodhisattvas taught by Buddha Shakyamuni in the Great Vehicle sutras and condensed into practical instructions by the great bodhisattva Shantideva in *Entering the Way of the Bodhisattva. Entering the Way of the Bodhisattva* lays out the entire bodhisattva path—the path to perfect awakening—in one thousand stanzas organized in ten chapters.

There are many commentaries on *Entering the Way of the Bodhisattva*, including a commentary by Gyalse Tokme himself. However, one of the most widely used commentaries is Khenpo Kunpal Rinpoche's *The Nectar of Manjushri's Speech*.[31] It is profound, eloquent, and detailed, consisting of more than three hundred folios. Most especially, it follows the explanatory tradition of Patrul Rinpoche, and Patrul Rinpoche was arguably the most supreme bodhisattva to ever appear in Tibet. Of course, a host of amazingly learned and accomplished masters, both male and female, have appeared in Tibet over the centuries. Nevertheless, most teachers agree that none of them match Patrul Rinpoche. Patrul Rinpoche was said to be an emanation of Gyalse Tokme as well as an emanation of the bodhisattva Shantideva and other masters. He taught *Entering the Way of the Bodhisattva* so many times—more frequently and extensively than it had ever been taught in Tibet.

It takes several months to study *Entering the Way of the Bodhisattva* in any kind of detail, and it is very difficult for modern people to find the time and circumstances to do this. And yet, without studying the bodhisattva path from beginning to end, there is no way to reach awakening. *The Thirty-Seven Practices of Bodhisattvas* condenses the entire meaning of Shantideva's *Entering the Way of the Bodhisattva* into thirty-seven succinct, accessible verses. It is as if Gyalse Tokme composed this text specifically for beings of these degenerate times, those who want and need to practice the bodhisattva path but lack the time to study more extensive texts.

As Patrul Rinpoche said, "A text like *Entering the Way of the Bodhisattva* is not found in China or Tibet. Without practicing this, there is no way to attain buddhahood!" We could just as well say, "Without practicing *The Thirty-Seven Practices of Bodhisattvas*, there is no way to attain buddhahood!"

Nevertheless, as you read through this text, you might find yourself wondering if it is really possible to practice like this. Some of the practices, or perhaps a lot of them, might seem unrealistic or unattainable—for an ordinary person at least.

I have seen many students, from various backgrounds, react to the bodhisattva teachings like this, and it is understandable. If you are not yet familiar with the benefits of bodhichitta; the faults of samsara; the extraordinary qualities of awakened body, speech, and mind; and so on, these teachings could well seem far-fetched. However, as you come to understand the wondrous qualities of buddhahood and the endless shortcomings of samsara, these teachings will start to make sense. You will realize the truth of the statement that without training in the practices of the bodhisattvas, it is impossible to reach buddhahood. You will develop the heartfelt aspiration to train on the bodhisattva path, and you will find the courage to begin.

The Benefits of Using a Structural Outline

When teaching the text, I make use of the structural outline from Minyak Kunso's commentary. It provides an excellent framework, and it is more authentic and blessed to follow his existing outline than to try to create my own.

There are many benefits to using a structural outline when teaching or studying a text. That said, in the Noble Land of India, there was no tradition of using structural outlines, only annotations that indicate how the various parts of a text relate to one another. The structural outline was a Tibetan innovation—and a very helpful one.

A structural outline is like a map. Around ten years ago, a group of foreign trekkers visited our monastery in Humla, Nepal. One of them asked a local, "How many kilometers is it from here to Yangar, the neighboring village?" This person did not know, so they just gave a wild guess.

"Oh, I think it's nine or ten kilometers," they said.

The trekker promptly replied, "No, no, you're completely wrong! It's only one and a half kilometers from here. You can see clearly on the map." Even though these trekkers were new to the area, they had a clear overview of the entire district, thanks to the map and their map-reading skills.

In the same way, a structural outline gives you a thorough and clear overview of the teaching from beginning to end. Traditionally, when teaching a text, the outline will be reiterated on an almost daily basis. The purpose of this is to refresh your memory of the text's topics and how those topics relate to one another, and to pinpoint where you are in the text, a bit like pinpointing where you are on a map. When we have this kind of aerial view, the teachings are easier to comprehend and also easier to retain.

The Virtuous Beginning

The Introduction

CHAPTER 1

The Title

As Buddha taught in the *Lankavatara Sutra*,

> If things were left unnamed,
> Worldly folk would be confused.
> Therefore, Lord Buddha, skilled in means,
> Assigned names to things.

In order to communicate, we need to give things names. If an author does not give their composition a title, we will not know how to identify it or how to talk about it. The names we give people, objects, medicines, and so on work in the same way. They allow us to identify who and what we are talking about. They allow us to communicate effectively. It is for this reason that titles are given to texts.

It is taught that practitioners of the highest capacity can intuit the entire meaning of a text through its title alone. For those of middling capacity, the title gives them a clear idea of what the text is about and to which category it belongs. For those of the lowest, or modest, capacity, the title at least enables them to locate the text on a bookshelf.

A title can be given according to various criteria, such as the text's meaning, range, or function, or a related place, time, person, or metaphor. In this instance, the title reflects the text's meaning, or subject matter: the thirty-seven practices of bodhisattvas.

Thirty-Seven

"Thirty-Seven" refers to the number of verses that make up the main body of the text. These thirty-seven verses are preceded by an opening verse of homage and the author's pledge to compose, and they are followed by three concluding verses explaining the reasons for composing the text, demonstrating the thirty-seven practices to be free of confusion, and expressing humility and requesting forgiveness. This makes a total of forty-two verses. However, the main body of the text is composed of the thirty-seven verses that distill for us the vast conduct of the buddhas and bodhisattvas and teach the ground, path, and fruition of the bodhisattva path.

Practices

"Practices" means practical application. The buddhas and bodhisattvas seek to establish all beings in perfect buddhahood. Their every word, thought, and deed is devoted to this. But how is buddhahood achieved, for oneself and for others? It is by engaging in, or implementing, the practices taught in this precious text.

Bodhisattvas

The Tibetan term *gyalse* is translated here as "bodhisattva" for ease of understanding. A more literal translation would be "the victorious ones and their offspring." Thus, the term *gyalse* includes the buddhas as well. "The victorious ones" refers to the buddhas, who are so called because they reign victorious over the four *maras*: the mara of the afflictions, the mara of the aggregates, the mara of death, and the mara of the divine son.[32] It is because we are ensnared, or intimidated, by these four maras that we remain bound in samsara. On the other hand, it is by defeating them that perfect awakening is attained. It is only the perfect buddhas who are truly triumphant over these four maras. Forget about ordinary beings—even noble bodhisattvas on the tenth *bhumi*[33] are yet to gain complete victory over them.

The victorious one, Buddha Shakyamuni, has offspring of body, speech, and mind. The offspring of his body was Rahula, his physical son, and the offspring of his speech are the *shravakas* and *pratyekabuddhas*.[34] The offspring of Buddha's mind are the male and female bodhisattvas. From among these three types of offspring, here we are referring to the bodhisattvas, the offspring of the victorious one's mind.

Therefore, we could translate the title as *The Thirty-Seven Practices of the Victorious Ones and Their Heirs*, or *The Thirty-Seven Practices of Buddhas and Bodhisattvas*. However, for the sake of ease we will stick with the existing, well-known translation: *The Thirty-Seven Practices of Bodhisattvas*. Nevertheless, remember that the practices taught here are not only the practices of the bodhisattvas; they are also the practices of the buddhas who, even after attaining perfect awakening themselves, continue to display the way of bodhisattvas in order to guide beings on the path.

CHAPTER 2

The Opening Homage

The Concise Homage

> Namo lokeshvaraye (Homage to Avalokiteshvara!)

The text opens with a line of homage in Sanskrit: *namo lokeshvaraye*. *Namo* means to "pay homage" or "prostrate." *Loke*, or *loka*, means "the world." Then, "shvara" represents the word *ishvara*, meaning "sovereign" or "lord," and *ye* represents the grammatical declension meaning "to." So, all together this line reads "Homage to the Lord of the World," an epithet for Avalokiteshvara.

You might wonder why this opening homage is written in Sanskrit when the author, who was Tibetan, wrote the remainder of the text in Tibetan. There is a long-standing tradition in the Snowy Land of Tibet to write the opening homage (and also the title) in Sanskrit—it is not an idiosyncrasy of Gyalse Tokme—and there are several reasons for this.

First, making the opening homage in Sanskrit indicates that the teaching originates from the Noble Land of India, the wellspring of the Buddhadharma, thereby inspiring the reader with confidence in its authenticity. Second, by expressing the homage in Sanskrit, the primary and supreme of the four canonical languages of India, we receive the blessings of this divine tongue. Third, it makes a positive imprint in our minds. Since the Dharma will be taught again in Sanskrit by future buddhas, this imprint will be of benefit to us. Fourth, rendering the homage in Sanskrit reminds us of the kindness of the translators who translated the Dharma from Sanskrit and other languages into Tibetan—and also into Chinese and other languages.

In general, there are many reasons for opening a treatise with an homage. As Nagarjuna explains,

> The writer of a treatise who pays homage to the Buddha
> Cannot fail to have success.
> For he is stimulating faith and interest
> Both toward the Buddha and the text itself.[35]

The act of paying homage dispels obstacles that might prevent the author from completing the work. Second, the homage—or rather, the object of the homage—indicates to the reader that this is a treatise of authentic content. For example, when you pick up a text and on the first page you see, "Homage to Avalokiteshvara, Lord of the World," as someone seeking liberation and awakening, you can be confident that this text is worth your time, that it is not a mundane treatise concerned merely with worldly affairs. It is for these and other reasons that Dharma texts begin with an homage.

The Expanded Homage

> You see that all things are beyond coming and going,
> Yet still you strive solely for wandering beings' sake.
> To the supreme guru, inseparable from Lord Avalokita,
> I offer constant, respectful homage with body, speech,
> and mind.

"You" refers to Avalokiteshvara, who is inseparable with Gyalse Tokme's root guru. "All things" refers to all phenomena from form up to omniscience.[36] "Beyond coming and going" refers to emptiness, the abiding nature of all things, as taught in *The Heart of the Perfection of Wisdom Sutra*:

> Form is empty. Emptiness is form. Emptiness is not other than form, and form is also not other than emptiness. In the same way, feeling, perception, formation, and consciousness are empty.[37]

In short, all perceiving subjects, whether they be conceptual or nonconceptual, whether they pertain to primary mind or subsidiary mental states, and all perceived objects—the five sense objects of form, sound, smell, taste, and touch, as well as mental objects—are "beyond coming and going." They are emptiness, beyond concepts and extremes. As Nagarjuna states in the opening verse of *The Root Stanzas of the Middle Way*, and as Buddha states in *The Diamond-Cutter Sutra*,

> Everything that arises interdependently
> Is unceasing and unborn,
> Neither nonexistent nor everlasting,
> Neither coming nor going,
> Neither multiple nor single.
> To this teaching that pacifies all concepts and duality,
> The most sacred speech of the fully enlightened Buddha,
> We pay homage![38]

The meaning of all twenty-seven chapters of Nagarjuna's *Root Stanzas of the Middle Way*, and indeed the meaning of all sixteen large volumes of Prajnaparamita (Perfection of Wisdom) sutras, are contained in these opening lines. Likewise, their entire meaning is contained in the short phrase "beyond coming and going," which describes the emptiness of all things. If we can realize this, we will have realized the meaning of the entire corpus of Buddha's teaching.

Some people might think of *The Thirty-Seven Practices of Bodhisattvas* as a simple teaching, but in fact it contains tremendous depths. The Buddhist teachings are like elastic in this way: they can be stretched out wide and explained in great detail, and they can also be condensed and explained in a simple, succinct way. As such, a great scholar could explain this phrase "beyond coming and going" in such breadth and depth, making reference to seminal treatises such as *The Root Stanzas of the Middle Way*, *Introduction to the Middle Way*, and *The Precious Beacon of Certainty* and using supportive quotations from the sutras and so on. They could teach on these four words for as long as nine or ten days. Such is the depth and breadth of meaning this phrase contains. A single word of Dharma, if you really delve into it, contains an incredible wealth of meaning.

As followers of Buddha's teaching, it is important that we know this—that we know just how profound and vast Buddha's teachings are. This knowledge strengthens our confidence in the teachings, even if we are not engaged in in-depth study ourselves. When we become confused or doubtful, we need not worry. We can be sure that if we make the effort to study the teachings, we will find all the answers there.

Khenpo Dazer Rinpoche would often say that if you correctly understand one scripture from one genre of Buddha's teachings, you will understand all others by virtue of that. In the past, a humble monk met with a renowned scholar.

"Have you studied the scriptures?" the scholar asked the monk.

"I've studied a little bit, but I really don't know much," the monk replied.

"Oh well, that's a shame. But tell me, which scriptures are you most familiar with? What do you know best?"

"Well, I studied the *prajnaparamita* a little bit, but like I said, I really don't know much."[39]

"I see, I see. You don't know *The Treasury of Abhidharma* then?" the scholar said condescendingly.

"Well, *abhidharma* explains the evolution of the world and beings, does it not?" the monk replied.[40]

The scholar was slightly taken aback by this astute answer. "So, you know abhidharma then, clearly. But what about *pramana*? Have you studied that?" he said.[41]

"Pramana teaches the reasonings of the prajnaparamita, does it not?" the monk replied.

"Well, how about the *madhyamaka* teachings? Have you studied them?"[42]

"The madhyamaka teaches the view of the prajnaparamita, does it not?" the monk replied.

"Well, yes, indeed," the scholar said. He was feeling somewhat affronted by now! "What about the vinaya then? Do you know that?" he said.[43]

"The vinaya teaches the conduct related to the prajnaparamita, does it not?"

This exchange shows how a thorough comprehension of just one of the five genres of Buddha's teachings will give you an understanding of all other genres of Buddha's teaching as well. This is even more so when it comes to the Great Perfection. As Omniscient Longchenpa states in *The Treasury of Dharmadhatu*, the Great Perfection is like mounting the summit of a mountain range; from this vantage point, all phenomena from form to omniscience and all nine vehicles of Buddha's teachings are clearly seen and understood. The very same thing is taught by Omniscient Jigme Lingpa:[44]

> Since all the sublime teachings of the vast and
> perfect path
> Are solely for the cleansing of the mind,

> The three vows, six perfections, generation and
> perfection, and the rest—
> All are steps that lead us to the path of Great Perfection.[45]

Thus, when you truly understand the Great Perfection, you will automatically understand the sutras and tantras in their entirety. Such are the extraordinary qualities of Buddha's teachings, as my teacher Khenpo Dazer Rinpoche would explain.

Avalokiteshvara sees that "all things are beyond coming and going," that ultimately all phenomena are the single sphere of simplicity. *Coming* and *going* are relative terms. Without a notion of going, we cannot speak of coming, and vice versa. These two are posited in dependence upon one another. They are concepts that exist in relation to one another—and *only* in relation to one another. The same applies to the rest of the eight extremes. This is established with great precision in the Middle Way teachings and will be explained in more detail later in the text. In short, all phenomena are ultimately beyond, or void of, coming and going and all other extremes. The realization of this is ultimate bodhichitta.

The root text then says, "Yet still you strive solely for wandering beings' sake." This line describes relative bodhichitta, the wish to establish all beings in buddhahood. This might seem to be a contradiction in terms. If the ultimate nature of all things is emptiness, why strive for others' benefit? Why do anything at all? All phenomena are originally empty, but emptiness is not a blank, inert state. It is infused with the natural glow of compassion that, like sunrays streaming forth from the sun, benefits beings ceaselessly in vast and varied ways. We talk about emptiness and compassion as if they are separate things. As sentient beings blinkered by duality, we have no choice but to discuss them in this way. However, in reality they are not separate; emptiness and compassion are a natural unity.

Whether one follows the path of sutra or tantra, there is no way to reach buddhahood without bodhichitta. As Nagarjuna taught,

> Emptiness with a core of compassion—
> This is the sole route to awakening.

And as Saraha said,

> Those who train in emptiness void of compassion
> Have not found the supreme path.
> But if you train in compassion alone,
> You will remain stuck in samsara—liberation will not be attained.

Emptiness must be infused with compassion; compassion must be infused with emptiness. The natural unity of emptiness and compassion is the awakened state.

Avalokiteshvara sees that all things are emptiness. At the same time, he sees that beings are suffering endlessly, and needlessly, as they wander through samsara. Perceiving true existence where there is none, beings become trapped in the dualistic perception of self and other, which proliferates into a plethora of ever-coarser concepts and afflictions, such as enemy and friend, pleasure and pain, and gain and loss, which in turn generate a stream of karma that produces the endless suffering of samsara's three realms.[46] This all stems from not recognizing the way things are. The perception of sentient beings is in discord with reality. We are like someone suffering from jaundice who perceives a conch as yellow instead of white. This misperception is called confusion. This is the state of sentient beings.

In Buddhist art and iconography, Avalokiteshvara is often depicted standing to the right of Buddha Amitabha. His standing posture illustrates his pledge to work ceaselessly for others' benefit. Although he has attained buddhahood, he has vowed to remain in the form of a tenth-bhumi bodhisattva in order to benefit all countless beings. The Tibetan translation of Avalokiteshvara is Chenrezik, which means "always looking with open eyes." He is always—throughout past, present, and future—looking upon beings with eyes of great compassion and love.

Lord Atisha had numerous gurus, one of whom was Guru Serlingpa, with whom Atisha stayed for twelve years. Whenever the names of any one of his gurus was mentioned, Atisha would join his palms at his heart, but whenever Guru Serlingpa's name was mentioned, he would join his hands at the crown of his head. When his disciples asked him about this, Atisha explained that although his teachers were all equal in qualities, Guru Serlingpa had shown him superior kindness. For it was through Guru Serlingpa's guidance that bodhichitta dawned in him. The kindness of the teacher who grants you the bodhisattva vow and helps you to generate the precious mind of bodhichitta is unparalleled.

In the Vajra Vehicle, it is understood that the guru is inseparable from the *yidam* deity.[47] It is understood that the guru is the buddha in person and that, as students training on the path, we need to cultivate this perception. If we see the guru as a buddha, we will receive the blessings of a buddha. If we see the guru as a realized being, we will receive the blessings of a realized being. And if we perceive the guru as an ordinary human, we will receive the blessings of an ordinary human, which is to say there will be no blessings! Here, Gyalse Tokme is paying homage to his guru with the knowledge that he is inseparable from Avalokiteshvara.

He offers "constant" (meaning continuous and unwavering) and "respectful" homage "with body, speech, and mind." He expresses his respect with his body by bowing down, with his speech by reciting words of homage, and with his mind by regarding his teacher with faith, confidence, and delight.

CHAPTER 3

The Author's Commitment to Compose

> The perfect buddhas, source of benefit and joy,
> Come from accomplishing the sacred Dharma,
> And this, in turn, stems from knowing how to practice it.
> Therefore, I shall now explain the bodhisattva practices.

It is said that pledges made by the wise are like carvings in stone, while pledges made by the foolish are like drawings in water. When a wise person makes a pledge, they do so carefully. They honor their promises and ensure they are fulfilled. In contrast, the pledges of the foolish (meaning "ordinary people") are as changeable as writing on water. Such people make promises casually and often break them without a second thought.

Even in mundane situations, it is important to honor our promises if we want to achieve any kind of success. Whether we are engaged in business, agriculture, politics, or whatever it is, we need to be honest and reliable. Otherwise, our endeavors will be compromised. We will not be trusted and we will not achieve success.

Here, Gyalse Tokme is pledging to compose the text. He is declaring his intentions and stating that he will follow the task through to the end. "Perfect" describes the state of consummate buddhahood in which all obscurations have been perfectly, or completely, eliminated and one has realized perfectly, or completely, that the personal self and all phenomena lack reality. The perfect buddhas are the source of all benefit and joy, both temporal and ultimate, both secular and spiritual.

Temporal, or secular, benefit and joy refer to mundane success, personal fulfillment, social harmony, good health, economic prosperity, and so on—even the simple pleasure of getting a good night's sleep. In short, it refers to all short-term happiness experienced in this and future lives. You might wonder how the buddhas are the source of these secular benefits and pleasures. The buddhas embody bodhichitta, and when someone has bodhichitta, they automatically benefit others. Their mere presence brings others joy. You can read the first chapter "Explaining the Benefits of Bodhichitta" in *Entering the Way of the Bodhisattva* to learn more about its incredible benefits.

Ultimate, or spiritual, benefit and joy is the lasting, consummate happiness of liberation and omniscience.[48] The source of this too is the perfect buddhas. Buddha Shakyamuni, the fourth guide of this Excellent Eon,[49] turned the Dharma Wheel three times. The first turning took place in Deer Park, Sarnath, where Buddha taught the four noble truths. The second turning on the absence of characteristics took place at Vulture Peak in Rajgir, where Buddha taught the Prajnaparamita, and the third, or final, turning of complete revelation took place in Vaishali and other places. As it is taught,

> The buddhas do not wash away sins with water,
> They do not wipe away beings' pain with their hands,
> They do not transfer their realization to others—
> They free beings by revealing the true nature of things.

By accomplishing the Dharma—by studying, reflecting, and meditating upon Buddha's teachings, which teach us the true nature of phenomena, both relative and ultimate—we too can become perfect buddhas, source of all benefit and joy.

The word *dharma* has so many different meanings. However, in this instance, *Dharma* refers to the sacred Dharma, the teachings of Buddha, and primarily to bodhichitta. Without cultivating bodhichitta, it is simply impossible to achieve buddhahood. Cultivating bodhichitta was the highway to awakening for all the buddhas of the past; it is the highway to awakening for all the buddhas of the present; it will likewise be the highway to awakening for all the buddhas of the future. It is for this reason that Chandrakirti[50] opens his seminal treatise *Introduction to the Middle Way* with an homage to compassion:

> Of buddhahood's abundant crop, compassion is the seed.
> It is like moisture bringing increase and is said
> To ripen as the state of lasting happiness.
> Therefore to begin, I celebrate compassion![51]

Since the perfect buddhas arise from bodhichitta, we need to learn how to cultivate bodhichitta ourselves and how to engage in the practices of the bodhisattvas. The word *practice* here means practical application. We are not talking about mere knowledge or exposition but direct application—applying the teachings in one's own experience and internalizing them. It is these bodhisattva practices, the source of awakening, that Gyalse Tokme pledges to now explain.

The Virtuous Middle

The Main Body of the Treatise

CHAPTER 4

The Preliminaries

Entering the Dharma

The heart of the sacred Dharma is bodhichitta, and the source of buddhahood is bodhichitta. But what does *bodhichitta* actually mean? In *Entering the Way of the Bodhisattva*, Shantideva defines bodhichitta as a mind focused on sentient beings with compassion and focused on perfect awakening with wisdom. Similarly, Maitreya's *Ornament of Clear Realization* states,

> The generation of bodhichitta is, for the welfare of others,
> The desire for completely perfect enlightenment.[52]

And *The Ornament of the Mahayana Sutras* teaches,

> The bodhisattva's intention
> Is the mental factor associated with two aims.[53]

From the outset, we need to have a clear and correct understanding of what bodhichitta is. These days, the term is bandied about a lot. You often hear people describing someone who does a lot of charity work, for example, as having great bodhichitta, but that is not necessarily the case. Bodhichitta is more than benevolence. It is a mind endowed with two aspects, or qualities: compassion focused on all beings and wisdom focused on perfect awakening.

The benefits of bodhichitta are literally immeasurable. As Buddha taught in *The Questions of the Householder Viradatta*,

> If the merits of the resolve for awakening [*bodhichitta*]
> Were to assume physical form,
> They would fill the whole expanse of space
> And exceed even that.[54]

Think of how vast outer space is. Our entire solar system, not to mention billions of other planets, are all contained in space. There are entire galaxies, not to mention black holes, which range from one hundred thousand to more than sixty billion times our Sun's mass,[55] which itself is one hundred times larger than the Earth. All of this is contained in space, yet the merit of bodhichitta is so immense that, if it were given form, it would overflow even the infinity of space. The attainment of buddhahood is the outcome of purification and accumulation, and bodhichitta is the most powerful method of purification and the most effective way to gather merit.[56]

Dudjom Rinpoche explained that, from among the eighty-four thousand teachings of Buddha, the most profound of all is bodhichitta. By maintaining bodhichitta, both relative and ultimate, one upholds the united intent of sutra and mantra. As such, all practices of Secret Mantra—such as deity generation, mantra recitation, and training in the subtle channels and winds—must be grounded in pure bodhichitta.

How do we give rise to this inconceivably precious mind, this heart of awakening? To begin with, we need to gather various causes and conditions. This is what the first seven verses explain.

CHAPTER 5

Making Meaningful These Freedoms and Advantages That Are So Difficult to Attain

> 1. Now that you have this great ship of freedoms
>   and advantages, so difficult to attain,
> You must free yourself and others from the ocean of samsara.
> To this end, to study, reflect, and meditate
> Without distraction, day and night, is the practice of
>   bodhisattvas.

Bodhichitta does not arise on its own; it is born from causes and conditions. These causes and conditions are composed of physical supports and mental supports. Gyalse Tokme begins by identifying three physical supports, the first of which is a human birth endowed with the eight freedoms and ten advantages.

The Eight Freedoms

The eight freedoms refer to being free from eight unfree states in which one lacks the leisure, or ability, to engage with the sacred Dharma. They are enumerated by Nagarjuna as follows:

> Being born in the hells, in the *preta* realm,
> As an animal, a long-lived god, or a barbarian,

> Having wrong views, being born when there is no
> buddha,
> Or being born deaf and mute—these are the eight states
> without freedom.[57]

If you are born in the hot, cold, or ephemeral hells, you are tortured by such intense heat, cold, and other physical torments that you cannot reflect on the Dharma for a single instant. If you are born as a *preta*, or hungry ghost—with external obscurations, internal obscurations, or specific obscurations—you suffer the constant deprivation of intense hunger and thirst.[58] And if born as an animal, you suffer from stupidity, from being exploited by humans, or from the constant fear of being killed by another animal. Beings in the three lower realms do not have the leisure to think of anything beyond their basic survival. As such, they have no freedom to engage with the sacred Dharma.

Long-lived gods are so absorbed in the endless sensory pleasures of the heavenly realms that their minds do not turn to the sacred Dharma for even a moment. They might live for an entire eon, but their lives are wasted on distraction, on mere gratification of the senses.

A barbarian refers to someone following a mistaken path—for instance, people who perform blood sacrifices in the guise of spiritual practice or who believe that harming others is a virtuous path. Such people confuse nonvirtue with virtue and so misdirect their spiritual aspirations.

To have wrong view is to lack trust in the Three Jewels and to deny karma, cause and effect. An example of someone with wrong view would be a Maoist. Blinkered by wrong view, the gateway to the Dharma is firmly closed. If you are born in a dark age, a period when there is no buddha, it is impossible to engage in the Dharma for the Dharma is absent.

The last unfree state, being deaf and mute, is slightly contextual. Until recently, it was very difficult for someone deaf and mute to engage in any kind of formal learning and so being deaf or mute was a serious impediment to the study, reflection, and meditation of the Dharma. Fortunately, over the last century or so this has changed significantly. There are now various types of sign language, Braille, and so on. Essentially, "deaf and mute" refers to someone who is limited in their ability to use and understand language, so this also includes mental disabilities that impede one's ability to understand. If born in any of these eight states, you simply do not have the opportunity to engage in the sacred Dharma. This is why they are called the eight unfree states.

In addition to these eight, Omniscient Longchenpa identified eight intrusive circumstances and eight incompatible propensities that leave no freedom to practice the Dharma, making a total of twenty-four circumstances we need to be free from in order to practice the Dharma genuinely. You can learn about these in *The Words of My Perfect Teacher* by Patrul Rinpoche, in *The Wish-Fulfilling Treasury* by Longchenpa, and other precious texts.

The Ten Advantages

The ten advantages are composed of five intrinsic advantages and five extrinsic advantages. We could also call them the ten riches; they are a form of wealth that grant one the resources to accomplish the Dharma.

The Five Intrinsic Advantages

As Nagarjuna taught, the five intrinsic advantages are as follows:

> Born a human, in a central place, with all faculties intact,
> Without a conflicting lifestyle, and with faith in the
> Dharma.

First, in order to practice the Dharma, you really need to be born as a human. If you are born as another type of being, you are not fully able to practice the Dharma.

In addition, you need to be born in a central place. The scriptures distinguish two types of central place: a geographically central place and a place that is central in terms of the Dharma. The geographically central place is the central region of ancient India, which encompasses Bodh Gaya, Sarnath, and the other places Buddha Shakyamuni traveled and taught. In contrast, a central place in terms of the Dharma is any place where the Buddhadharma and spiritual guides are present and accessible.

Tibet is not a geographically central place. Buddha Shakyamuni did not visit Tibet, and he did not teach there. However, due to the kindness of Abbot Shantarakshita, Guru Rinpoche, and the Dharma king Trisong Deutsen, the Buddhadharma was established in Tibet and flourished far and wide. In this way, it became a central place in terms of the Dharma. When the Indian master Lord Atisha visited Tibet, he remarked that in no other country, not even in the Noble Land of India, had the Buddha's teachings of both sutra and tantra spread and flourished to the same extent. Think of the multitude of accomplished and learned masters, real buddhas in person, who have graced Tibet with their presence over the centuries: Dromtonpa Gyalwe Jungne and the great Kadampa masters, the twenty-five heart disciples of Guru Rinpoche, the five supreme Sakya forefathers, Marpa, Mila, and Gampopa, Omniscient Longchenpa and Rongzom Mahapandita, to name but a few.

Similarly, many Western countries can now be considered central places. Indeed, there are some areas in the West where Dharma seems to be flourishing even more than in Tibet. Just think of the easy access people in the West have had to inconceivably sublime masters like His Holiness the Dalai Lama, the late Kyabje Dudjom Rinpoche, Kyabje Dilgo Khyentse Rinpoche, and so on.

Third, we need to have all our faculties intact. It is not enough to just be born human; we need to be a healthy human with fully functioning sense faculties so we can study, reflect, and meditate on the Dharma without impediment.

The fourth advantage is to be without a conflicting lifestyle. This means, primarily, to be born to Buddhist parents who have faith in the Three Jewels. If you are born into a Buddhist family or environment, you will encounter the Three Jewels from a young age and you will be introduced to the Dharma as you grow up. This provides very conducive conditioning. Of course, there are those who are not born to Buddhist parents but encounter Buddha's teachings later in life and develop faith in the Three Jewels from their own side. This is the effect of positive imprints from past lives and a sign of one's inner disposition awakening—and this is excellent, but at the same time it can be very challenging.

When you are born to Buddhist parents, in many ways your parents become your first teachers. In traditional Tibetan Buddhist families, one of the first things a newborn will hear is the *mani* mantra, not from a lama but from their mother who will chant this throughout the day. There was a saying in Tibet that babies learn to say *ama* (mother) and the mani mantra, OM MANI PEME HUNG, at the same time. Later on, their parents will teach them about karma, not formally but in the course of their daily lives. If the child unwittingly kills a bug, for instance, their mother will explain that it is negative karma to hurt other beings, that we should have love and compassion for all. Likewise, parents will teach their children to prostrate to teachers and the Three Jewels and sow within them the seed of faith. It seems to me that in Buddhist families, at least 30 percent of Dharma is taught to children by their parents. The kindness of our parents is difficult to contemplate.

The fifth intrinsic advantage is to have faith in the correct place—namely, the Three Jewels. This applies whether this faith is cultivated from a young age due to one's upbringing or whether one develops faith later on in life. As Buddha taught in *The Sutra on the Ten Dharmas*,

> In those who lack faith
> Nothing positive will grow,
> Just as from a burned seed
> No green shoot will ever sprout.[59]

The Five Extrinsic Advantages

> A buddha has appeared and has taught the Dharma,
> Their teachings still exist and they are followed,
> There are those who are kindhearted toward others.[60]

The first extrinsic advantage is that a buddha has appeared, meaning a buddha has come to our world. If our teacher Buddha Shakyamuni had not appeared in this world, we would be living in a dark age and would not hear a single word of Dharma. That said, in some eons and world systems, buddhas appear but do not teach. Therefore, the second extrinsic advantage is that a buddha has not only appeared but has also taught the Dharma. After conquering the four maras and attaining buddhahood beneath the bodhi tree in Bodh Gaya, Buddha exclaimed,

> Profound, peaceful, stainless, lucid, and unconditioned—
> Such is the nectar-like truth I have realized.
> Were I to teach it, no one would understand,
> So I will silently remain in the forest.[61]

It seems Buddha felt that even if he were to share the profound truth he had discovered, no one would understand it, and so he remained in meditation in the forest. The Great Vehicle sutras state that Buddha remained silent for seven days after attaining buddhahood, whereas the vinaya scriptures of the Lesser Vehicle state that Buddha remained silent for forty-nine days. This latter assertion certainly fits with the Tibetan Buddhist calendar, which celebrates Buddha's awakening on the fifteenth day of the fourth lunar month and his first teaching on the fourth day of the sixth month, exactly forty-nine days later. In any case, after some time, the gods Brahma, Indra, and others came before Buddha and, offering an eight-spoked golden wheel and a clockwise-spiraling white conch, they entreated Buddha to teach. They said, "For three countless eons, you endured hardships on the path, purifying obscurations and gathering vast stores of merit to attain buddhahood for the benefit of all beings. Now your aspiration has been fulfilled. So, we beseech you to turn the Wheel of Dharma for all beings' sake!" Buddha acquiesced, saying, "Now I will open the gateway to this ambrosial Dharma!" He then traveled to Deer Park in Sarnath, and there, to his fortunate first five disciples, he turned the first Dharma Wheel of the four truths.

Whatever teachings we receive, whether they be the words of Guru Rinpoche, of Noble Nagarjuna, of Khandro Yeshe Tsogyal, and so on, they are all rooted in the words of Buddha Shakyamuni. It was Buddha Shakyamuni who lit the lamp of Dharma in our world. All subsequent teachers have appeared in Buddha's wake, due to Buddha's kindness. As Mipham Rinpoche states in *Treasury of Blessings*,

> Whatever pure appearances of the Triple Gems we have
> in this land and in this time
> Only come from your activity.[62]

The third extrinsic advantage is that the teachings Buddha gave are still present in the world. If they had flourished in the past but later disappeared, they would be of no benefit to us now. Buddha foretold that the Buddhadharma would pass through four periods: the period of realization, the period of accomplishment, the period of transmission, and the period when only symbols are maintained. In the scriptures of the Great Vehicle and Lesser Vehicle, we find slightly different presentations of how long these periods will be. However, Omniscient Longchenpa explained, following the intent of the Great Vehicle, that the Buddhadharma will remain in this world for a total of five thousand years: the first three periods of realization, accomplishment, and transmission will be one thousand five hundred years each, and finally there will be a five-hundred-year period when only symbols of the teachings are maintained. According to this schema, we are nearing the end of the period of accomplishment, so the Buddhadharma is still very much alive. We are inconceivably fortunate to be alive at this point in time.

The fourth advantage is that the teachings are followed, meaning that we enter them and engage ourselves in them. If Buddha has appeared, he has taught, and the teachings remain, but we do not follow these teachings, the extraordinary potential of this situation will be utterly lost on us. We enter the teachings by taking refuge, and traditionally this is confirmed in a refuge-vow ceremony. As part of the ritual, the preceptor cuts a small piece of our hair, symbolizing the offering of our body, speech, and mind to the Three Jewels. The preceptor then gives us a Dharma name, signifying that from now on we will revere Buddha's teachings above all else, we will shun unvirtuous deeds, and turn our minds to the Dharma. I remember my root guru Khenpo Dazer Rinpoche explaining this to us.

If you have not yet taken refuge but you are interested in the Dharma and learning about it, in a sense you have already entered the Dharma. It is excellent to confirm this by taking refuge formally. However, as taught in *The Treasury of Abhidharma*, if you feel faith in the Three Jewels from the depths of your heart, essentially you have already taken refuge.

The fifth extrinsic advantage is to meet and be accepted by a spiritual guide, one who is kindhearted toward others. You might possess all the other advantages and have the fervent wish to practice Dharma, but without a qualified teacher's guidance it is simply not possible. We cannot proceed on the path on our own—not genuinely, at least. And simply meeting a qualified teacher is not enough; the teacher needs to accept you as a student, to take you under their wing. For instance, in my case, I was accepted by my root gurus Khenpo Dazer Rinpoche and Khenpo Chokhyab Rinpoche. For ten or eleven years, I stayed with them, receiving constant teachings and guidance. I did not leave their side for a single day during those years. And they would teach every day, often for four hours without break. In addition, I spent many months with my other root gurus, Kyabje Dodrupchen Rinpoche, Dudjom Rinpoche, Dilgo Khyentse Rinpoche, Khenpo Petse, Yangtang Rinpoche, and so on, receiving empowerments, transmissions, and teachings. If those teachers had not accepted me as a disciple, it would have been a different story.

During the years I spent with Khenpo Dazer Rinpoche, I followed him wherever he went—to Bhutan, Kham, and throughout India and Nepal. These days, students often invite teachers to their countries. They have the means to do that, and it seems they prefer to do that than visit their teachers in situ, so to speak. I suppose this is also okay. The point is that the teacher needs to accept one as a disciple. The teacher-disciple relationship needs to be established. Then the fifth extrinsic advantage is fulfilled.

We need to examine our circumstances and check for ourselves whether we possess all eight freedoms and ten advantages. If we find that we do, we should rejoice, and if we find that some of these factors are lacking, then we should work on acquiring them.

A human birth endowed with the eight freedoms and ten advantages is called a precious human birth. Buddha saw that such a rebirth is extremely difficult to obtain. In *The Words of*

My Perfect Teacher, *Finding Rest in the Nature of the Mind*, and other texts, this is explained in detail by means of analogies, causes, and numerical comparisons.

In this regard, Omniscient Longchenpa identifies three different types of human birth—mere, superior, and precious:[63]

1. A mere human birth refers to someone who thinks only of this life and spares no thought for future lives or spiritual goals.
2. A superior human birth refers to someone who dedicates a portion of their time and energy to Dharma, perhaps 5 percent, 10 percent, or 50 percent, but in reality it is usually 10 to 20 percent, at best. Most practitioners fall into this category. They are still tied up, physically and emotionally, with the concerns of this life. As the saying goes, in one hand you hold a *mala*[64] and in the other you hold a stick to beat dogs.

   People lead very busy lives these days. Of course, we all need to support ourselves, and if you have a family, you need to provide for them. But how much do we really need? We need enough food to keep us healthy, clothing to keep ourselves warm, and a safe place to live. In reality, that is what we need. Yet we are not satisfied with that, and so we busy ourselves with work and other projects, telling ourselves we need this and that, that what we are doing is somehow meaningful. From the perspective of the buddhas and bodhisattvas, though, we are no more than little children absorbed in a meaningless game.
3. A most precious human birth refers to someone who devotes their entire being to the Dharma, without cease: like the great yogi Milarepa or Omniscient Longchenpa, who accomplished the state of Vajradhara within a single lifetime through their ceaseless devotion and diligence. Such practitioners do not involve themselves in worldly concerns for even a second.

A true precious human birth is very rare indeed, wherever we look. Even if we possess the eight freedoms and ten advantages, whether our situation becomes truly precious depends on how we put it to use.

I presume those reading this book are endowed with the freedoms and advantages. This is an incredibly great fortune. That said, if you do not make use of these freedoms to practice the genuine Dharma, you cannot really call yourself free. There are many so-called practitioners these days, including lamas and monastics, who busy themselves with worldly activities. They are constantly speeding about on their motorcycles, in a flurry of maroon robes, rushing from one appointment to the next, or they are hunched over their expensive mobile phones. If you remain beguiled by the pursuit of sensory pleasures, by the futile aims of this life, you will sabotage this rare chance to free yourself. As Omniscient Jigme Lingpa said, you set your mind on Dharma, but your feet chase after harmful deeds.

An example of someone who has recognized the value and rarity of a human birth endowed with the eighteen freedoms and advantages is Geshe Chengawa, the Kadampa practitioner that Patrul Rinpoche writes about in *The Words of My Perfect Teacher*. Geshe Chengawa was constantly practicing, day and night. One day his teacher Geshe Tonpa said, "My son, you should take some rest, or you'll make yourself sick." To this, Geshe Chengawa replied, "When I think of how difficult it is to attain these freedoms and advantages, I cannot find the time to rest." He practiced so incessantly that he completed nine hundred million recitations of Miyowa's mantra. It usually takes a practitioner about ten years to accumulate one hundred million mantras, even when on retreat. It is said that he was so diligent he never even slept.

The twentieth-century master Golok Serta Rinpoche[65] once traveled to Ngari on pilgrimage. His plan was to pay homage to Mount Kailash, make several circumambulations, and then return to Serta, his homeland. He was not planning to meet

Degyal Rinpoche, but when he arrived in Ngari, he could not help but hear of Degyal Rinpoche's[66] fame. Serta Rinpoche thought, *Well, Degyal Rinpoche is such a celebrated teacher. Maybe I should go and meet him after all and request a Dharma connection.*[67] *Then I'll continue on my way.* He was not planning to stay long in the area. After all, he already had several root gurus from whom he had received a wealth of instruction.

Degyal Rinpoche's residence was near Mount Kailash at a site called Namkha Khyung Dzong. This remote area was filled with his disciples—many hundreds of devoted practitioners living in small caves and huts, filling the mountain air with the sound of the damaru and bell. This made a profound impression on Serta Rinpoche. *This is what it means to be a practitioner*, he thought.

The next morning Serta Rinpoche went to meet Degyal Rinpoche, and Degyal Rinpoche asked him where he was from. Serta Rinpoche did not know what to say. The truth was that he was from Serta, which is where Degyal Rinpoche himself was from. But he had heard that Degyal Rinpoche did not like meeting people from his homeland. The reason being that so many people had been posing as his relatives and exploiting the people of Ngari in this way. The people of Ngari, being so devoted to Degyal Rinpoche, would immediately offer their support—their money, resources, and also their faith—to anyone they thought was related to him. They had so much faith in Degyal Rinpoche that they would revere anyone who claimed to be from Serta, their teacher's homeland, even if they weren't a relative. Serta Rinpoche did not know what to do. Of course he could not lie, but if he told the truth, Degyal Rinpoche might be displeased. When he replied that he was from Serta, Degyal Rinpoche said nothing in response.

In any case, Degyal Rinpoche was not one to make small talk and rarely asked about one's background, family, and so on. He would just get to the point, teach the Dharma that needed to be taught, and discuss the student's practice as necessary. If students started talking about unimportant, mundane things, he would immediately recite the vajra-guru mantra out loud, bringing the conversation to an end. Everyone would then join in, and all further discussion would cease. People did not dare talk much in his presence. You could not sit around and chat with him about this and that over a cup of tea.

Also, if Degyal Rinpoche was asked to perform divinations for people facing difficulties in their livelihood, health, and so on, he would tell people to have the Kangyur (the Collected Words of the Buddha) recited or to make many feast offerings. No matter what the issue was, this is what he would advise.

Serta Rinpoche then said, "Rinpoche, I have come here to pay homage to Mount Kailash and will soon be heading back to my homeland. I would like to request a Dharma connection."

Degyal Rinpoche replied, "I do not give Dharma connections like that. The Dharma I give is not just sweet talk. It's Dharma that, if put into practice, can lead one to buddhahood in this very body and life. All this talk these days about Dharma connections—I do not go in for that. So, you won't receive any Dharma from me. You should set off tomorrow without looking back."

Upon hearing this, Serta Rinpoche thought, *Well, it seems I won't be able to receive a Dharma connection after all*, and so he prepared to leave, as he had previously planned. Nevertheless, he now felt great faith in Degyal Rinpoche. He was inspired by his surroundings—this great gathering of devoted students all practicing so ardently. And he was inspired by the lama himself.

There were no temples or buildings at Namkha Khyung Dzong. Degyal Rinpoche told his students there was no need to build. Instead, they had an enormous tent where a thousand or more people could fit. It was here that teachings and gatherings would take place. Early the next morning, the conch was blown to announce that the teachings would soon begin. Degyal Rinpoche was escorted from his residence down to the teaching tent by the community's disciplinarian, holding incense and a kata.

Serta Rinpoche was in a meadow further down the hillside. He watched Degyal Rinpoche walking down the path toward the teaching tent. As his faith welled up inside him, he started making prostrations to Degyal Rinpoche from afar. Disciples were flocking to the teaching, a great throng of red as they filed into the tent. These disciples were not just lay men and women but retreatants who had devoted their entire lives to practice.

Degyal Rinpoche was holding a staff, and when he was halfway down to the teaching tent he seemed to notice Serta Rinpoche prostrating in the meadow below. He lifted his staff and swung it up and around toward himself, as if gesturing him to come. There was clearly a karmic connection because Serta Rinpoche immediately understood that Degyal Rinpoche was calling him, and he rushed through the meadow and up the hill.

Degyal Rinpoche said, "Today I'm teaching the four mind changings. These are the common preliminaries so you can attend the teaching and make a Dharma connection in this way. But tomorrow you should leave without looking back! Don't linger here, okay?!" It seems he was testing Serta Rinpoche.

Serta Rinpoche was overjoyed to be given this opportunity. Listening to Degyal Rinpoche's teaching, he was flooded with faith. He thought, *To come across a teacher such as this—what a miracle! I must make the most of this opportunity! Come what may, from this moment onward I will stay by his side and learn from him. I will practice under his guidance and attain buddhahood in this very body and life. In this way, I will make meaningful this precious human rebirth, endowed with the freedoms and advantages that are so difficult to attain.*

And this is exactly what he did. From that day on, Serta Rinpoche stayed by Degyal Rinpoche's side. From him, he received teachings on the entire path, from the common and uncommon preliminaries up to the Great Perfection practices of trekcho and togal,[68] and then he put them into practice accordingly. He gained complete accomplishment and became known as Serta Rinpoche (the lama from Serta). He was famous for his miraculous ability to open freshwater springs, and was revered throughout Humla, Mugum, Karmarong, and surrounding areas. He was the supreme disciple of Degyal Rinpoche. All of this stemmed from his meeting Degyal Rinpoche and resolving to make his precious human birth truly meaningful.

This human birth endowed with the eighteen freedoms and advantages is likened to a great ship. If we want to sail across the ocean, we need a sturdy, well-equipped ship. If we try to swim across, we will drown. Likewise, to traverse the ocean of samsara, we need the support of a well-favored human birth that is like a sturdy ship. With this ship, we can ferry ourselves and others across the turbulent ocean of samsara to the dry shore of liberation and perfect buddhahood.

Having attained this rare and well-favored human birth, we need to put it to good use. Bodhisattvas do this by applying themselves to the study, reflection, and meditation of the Dharma and, most specifically, bodhichitta.

This is the practice of bodhisattvas, and the practice of buddhas as well. The Tibetan word *gyalse* can simply mean "bodhisattva," as it is translated in this and the following verses. However, it should also be understood in a wider sense to be referring to both the victorious ones (*gyal*), the buddhas, and their heirs (*se*), the bodhisattvas. Although the buddhas have completed the two stores of merit and wisdom and thereby attained perfect awakening, their emanation forms, or *nirmanakayas*, continue to enact the bodhisattva practices to guide others on the path.[69] Therefore, these thirty-seven practices are to be applied not only by the bodhisattvas but by the perfect buddhas as well.

Bodhisattvas study the Great Vehicle sutras and treatises and receive teachings from qualified spiritual guides. In this way, they learn about bodhichitta; its essence, characteristics, and benefits; and the precepts a bodhisattva needs to observe. Through reflection, they gain confidence in what they have learned. Then, erecting the victory banner of accomplishment in a solitary place, they bring the teachings into their own experience through meditation.

They do not do this sporadically or in between other deeds. Rather, they apply themselves tirelessly, without procrastination, without distraction, throughout day and night, over the course of many years. They do not tell themselves, "Well, now it's the evening, so I need to rest" or "Now it's the daytime, so I need to focus on my work." The bodhisattva always prioritizes the Dharma, the pursuit of awakening, over mundane pursuits.

CHAPTER 6

Abandoning Your Native Land, Source of the Three Poisons

> 2. Attachment to family and friends overpowers like a surging river.
> Aversion for enemies rages within like a blazing fire,
> While ignorance of what to adopt and reject thickens like the dark of night.
> To abandon your native land is the practice of bodhisattvas.

We might have attained a human birth endowed with the eighteen freedoms and advantages and we might have given rise to bodhichitta, but if we fail to abandon our native land, our bodhisattva practice will be compromised by attachment to loved ones, aversion to enemies, and the obscuring ignorance those afflictions create.

When you remain in your home surrounded by friends and family, your attachment to them overpowers you. You find yourself thinking, *But if I go off to practice, how will my family members support themselves? How will they—and how will I—bear the separation? How will they survive?!* Our attachment carries us away like the currents of a raging river. Think of the Amazon River, the Karnali River in Nepal, or the Ganges in summertime. There is no way you can withstand their power once you are caught in their flow.

Hand in hand with attachment to loved ones comes aversion toward enemies—that is, anyone who we believe harms or threatens us or those we love. When we feel we have been wronged, we become consumed by hatred and the wish to take revenge. We might try to insult our enemy, to obstruct their plans, to sue them, or to hurt them by hurting someone or something they love.

You see this happen all the time. When someone is wronged, they become so embroiled in hatred and indignation that they cannot think of anything else. Ignoring their better conscience, they start plotting their revenge. Hatred burns them up like a fire consuming a forest, like the wildfires that are all too common these days, devastating entire landscapes and communities. In the same way, hatred devastates lives.

Overwhelmed by the attachment and aversion festering in our homes, we become blind to the consequences of our actions. Shrouded by the darkness of ignorance, we forget the basic principles of virtue and nonvirtue, what to adopt and reject. For instance, when someone is consumed by anger, there is no reasoning with them—all they care about is getting their revenge. You can remind them of the consequences of their actions, that if they harm their enemy, they could be imprisoned for life or (depending on the country) even be sentenced to death. Of course, they already know this, but the intensity of their emotion overrides their reason; all perspective is lost. They are unable to acknowledge the consequences of their actions, neither for themselves nor others, neither for this life nor the next.

Forgetting what to adopt and reject—what is helpful and what is harmful—is ignorance. This is the darkened state we fall into if we remain in our native land, mired in attachment to loved ones and aversion to enemies.

On the other hand, if we leave our native land behind, we will be able to practice the Dharma authentically. Freed from the triggers of attachment and aversion, we will gain clarity about what we should adopt and reject. For the bodhisattva practitioner, one's native land is an adverse condition; it is counterproductive to the cultivation of bodhichitta. For this reason, it is the practice of bodhisattvas to leave their native land behind.

Prince Siddhartha was born into a life of luxury, wealth, and security. And yet, for the sake of attaining awakening for his own and others' benefit, he relinquished his palace, his kingdom, his caring parents, and his beloved wife and son. He knew that if he remained in his city of gold, he would not have the freedom, physical or mental, to pursue buddhahood, so he cast it aside without a second thought, like flicking away a piece of snot. Escaping from the palace under the cover of nightfall, he cut his hair, changed his clothes, and set out in search of the truth. On the banks of the Niranjana River, he practiced asceticism for six years. When his body was on the verge of collapse, he accepted a bowl of milk and honey from a young shepherdess. He realized then that the path of austerity would not lead to liberation. At Vajra Seat (Bodh Gaya), he sat down at the foot of the bodhi tree. He entered meditation and over the course of the night he conquered the four maras, transforming their torrent of weapons into a rain of flowers and attaining perfect buddhahood.

Guru Rinpoche was no different. As a young child, he was taken in by King Indrabhuti and treated as his only son and heir. When he came of age, he ruled the kingdom in accord with the Dharma, ushering in a time of happiness and peace. However, he saw that if he remained king, he would be unable to accomplish the Dharma and benefit beings on a vast scale, so he relinquished his kingdom, his queen, and his father, and ventured alone to Shitavana and other charnel grounds. There, he received empowerments from *dakinis* and practiced yogic disciplines, before traveling to Maratika, where, with his consort Princess Mandarava, he attained the state of Immortal Vidyadhara.

We can also look at more recent practitioners as examples of those who left their homeland, such as the first Degyal Rinpoche. Degyal Rinpoche was one of Traktung Dudjom Lingpa's thirteen rainbow-body disciples[70] and founder of the Namkha Khyung Dzong tradition.

One night, Degyal Rinpoche dreamed of an immaculate crystal stupa. Inside was a statue of Buddha Shakyamuni surrounded by many birds, deer, and other animals of various sizes, their fur and feathers gleaming in all the colors of the rainbow. Through meadows of grass and wide-open plains there flowed winding rivers. The ground was carpeted with all manner of flowers.

When he asked his precious guru what this dream might mean, Dudjom Lingpa said, "The meaning of your dream is thus: The crystal stupa is Mount Kailash. The Buddha inside it is you. The small and large birds, the deer and other animals are a sign that you will gather many students. The grass valleys filled with flowers are your sponsors and your realm of spiritual influence. Now you must go to Mount Kailash to benefit beings!"

Mount Kailash is in Ngari, the far western side of Tibet, more than a year's walk from Serta, where Dudjom Lingpa and Degyal Rinpoche were. Nevertheless, Degyal Rinpoche had such deep-seated faith in his guru that he did not hesitate for a moment. He planned to leave for Mount Kailash immediately, but his mother would not let him go. "Until I die, you cannot leave me. I won't allow it," she said. This put Degyal Rinpoche in a difficult bind!

One day, Degyal Rinpoche approached his mother and said, "Mum, I am going to present you with two choices: The first is to think merely about this present life. If you choose to do that, then sure, I will willingly stay by your side and look after you for the rest of your days. The second option is to think of our future lifetimes, to regard them as more important than this present, fleeting life. If you choose this perspective, you won't prevent me from following the guru's command, and I will go off and dedicate myself from the core of my heart to practicing the Dharma authentically. Then I will be able to bring real, lasting benefit to you and others in both this and future lives. I will be able to help you take rebirth in Sukhavati, Buddha Amitabha's pure land, after you die."[71]

In the eastern Tibetan region of Kham, where Degyal Rinpoche and his mother lived, the people have tremendous faith in the Dharma. So, when Degyal Rinpoche put it like this, his mother of course chose the latter option. However, she made him agree to one condition—that when it came time for her to die, he would return and help her through the dying process. This was no small ask. Back then, you could not just get on a plane and be anywhere in the world within a day or two. It was at least a year's journey between Mount Kailash and his mother's home. She took his hand and made him promise to be with her when she took her last breath. Only then did she let him go.

At long last, Degyal Rinpoche set off for Mount Kailash. He encountered many hardships on the way. When he finally arrived, he found Langchen Puk (Elephant Cave) on the western side of Mount Kailash and he practiced there in solitude for three years. He then made his way to the site that he would later name Pal Drakmar Namkha Khyung Dzong (Sky-Garuda Fortress of the Glorious Red Rock) and that would become the main seat of the Namkha Khyung Dzong tradition. He lived there for around seventeen years. Each year for the three months of winter and spring, a total of six months every year, he stayed in strict solitary retreat. During the remaining six months of the year, he would teach. He had many visions of deities and gurus. Most especially, he had visions of Omniscient Longchen Rabjam and of Dudjom Lingpa, whereby his wisdom-realization burst forth, causing mind treasures such as the *Tantra of the Self-Liberation of Dualistic Delusion* to arise within him.

Degyal Rinpoche became renowned and revered far and wide, as far as the reach of the wind. As a result, there gathered around him more than a thousand students from all the surrounding regions: the three provinces of Ngari, the regions of Ladakh, Khunu, Spiti, Humla, Mugum, Karmarong, and Lomontang, as well as from Kham, Amdo, and the four ranges of Central Tibet, and from other regions as well.

When Degyal Rinpoche's mother heard of her son's accomplishments, she was overjoyed. She lived to a ripe old age, well into her eighties I believe, but of course she eventually fell sick. When she knew that death was near, she kept telling people, "Dekyi is coming. Dekyi will be here soon." Dekyi was the affectionate nickname his family used for him. Her relatives kept telling her she was mistaken. They said, "We've heard nothing from him, and besides he's a renowned teacher now. He'll be busy in Ngari with his students and his Dharma activities." As the weeks rolled by, her health declined. She seemed to be on the very brink of death, and yet, day after day, she surprised everyone by remaining alive. Her relatives tried to console her, to reason with her, to encourage her to let go. But she was holding out for Degyal Rinpoche's return.

"Dekyi will be here, just as he promised," she would say again and again. And indeed, one day as she looked out at the valley from her bed in their nomad tent, she saw Degyal Rinpoche appear through the mouth of the valley and felt such joy and relief.

"There he is! Dekyi has come back, true to his word," she said. She died peacefully later that day, with her son by her side. (Degyal Rinpoche never physically returned to Kham. Nevertheless, his mother had this vision of him on her deathbed, and as such she was able to die peacefully.)

Imagine how difficult it must have been for Degyal Rinpoche to leave his mother in the first place, not to mention his five sisters, three brothers, and all his other relatives and friends. He was leaving his entire family, as well as the security of their considerable wealth, for a distant unknown land, an area so isolated and unpeopled that no one would possibly know if he fell sick or needed help. However, he embraced this difficulty for the sake of the Dharma. And by practicing wholeheartedly by Mount Kailash, in accord with his guru's command, he actualized the awakened state, thereby bringing indescribable benefit to the Dharma and countless beings.

Think too of Degyal Rinpoche's mother. How painful it must have been to let her son leave her, knowing she would not see him again for many years. However, she too found the courage to let him go for the sake of the Dharma. This is the way of bodhisattvas, the way of genuine practitioners. For the sake of attaining awakening for themselves and all other beings, they leave their homes behind, travel to unfamiliar places, and make do with the bare necessities.

What a stark contrast this strikes with people like us—people who are unable to make any real sacrifice for the Dharma, unwilling to accept a loss in income for example, to compromise our material comfort and our emotional security. We are so committed to our attachments—attachment to our homes, our status, security, and wealth—it is as if we want nothing more than to remain in samsara! There is no way we will ever attain liberation if we continue in this way.

When we look at the deeds of Buddha Shakyamuni, Guru Rinpoche, Degyal Rinpoche, and others, we might feel overwhelmed. It is understandable that this degree of abandonment might seem impossible for us. However, we should not let this discourage us, nor should we use it as an excuse. We need to start where we are and do what we can to move in the right direction—the direction of the buddhas and bodhisattvas.

This means actively reducing our attachment to our loved ones, reducing our aversion to so-called enemies, reflecting on the shortcomings of attachment and aversion and the futility of the deluded mindset that categorizes people into enemies and friends.

We should also spend time in retreat each year—at least a week, if not a month or more—in a solitary location away from our home environment, with no contact with family and friends. Practice is much more effective when we are removed from the objects of our attachment. With this physical and emotional distance, we can reflect on the transitory nature of so-called enemies and friends. Someone might be an enemy now but become a friend in the future. Your best friend might end up becoming your worst enemy. By reflecting in this and other ways, we can temper our attachment and aversion. If we want to attain buddhahood, and if in the short-term we want more happiness and peace, there are steps we can take to get us there. We need to start where we are. No step, however small, is insignificant. On the other hand, if we just succumb to discouragement and do not make any effort, we will never get anywhere.

If you do find the courage to leave your native land behind, be careful that you do not make a new native land of your new dwelling place with a new set of enemies and friends. As Minyak Kunso says in his commentary, many practitioners give up their native land but then they go and buy another one by transferring their attachments to their new dwelling place. The point of leaving one's native land behind is to abandon attachment. We should aspire to be like the great yogis Milarepa, Shabkar, and so on, who walked out of their homes with renunciation and bodhichitta and never once looked back.

CHAPTER 7

Adhering to Solitude, Source of Good Qualities

> 3. When negative places are abandoned, the afflictions gradually subside.
> In the absence of distraction, virtuous activity naturally gains strength.
> As awareness becomes clearer, certainty in the Dharma deepens.
> Therefore, to rely on solitude is the practice of bodhisattvas.

Having cast aside their native land, a bodhisattva travels far away and adheres to solitude. "Solitude" refers to solitary places such as charnel grounds, snow mountains, hermitages, and so on—the sorts of places Khandro Yeshe Tsogyal speaks of in her famous aspiration prayer:

> In charnel grounds, hermitages, retreats amid the snows,
> And other secluded places with all perfect qualities,
> Let the quintessence of deep meditation
> Be my constant practice.[72]

Since we are strongly influenced by our surroundings, we should adhere to places that are solitary but also beautiful and quiet—open landscapes adorned with gently flowing rivers and large lakes, or perhaps a peaceful forest filled with wildflowers and fruit trees, where sweet birdsong fills the air. We should not keep to solitary places that are hostile, such as jungles so dense the sunlight barely filters through the trees, mountainsides where the air is filled with the thundering sound of waterfalls or fearful animal calls. The bodhisattva keeps to solitary places as a support for their practice, so it is important to find a location that is spacious, pleasing, and inspiring. In short, a place that is free of the "thorns of meditation," meaning free of adverse factors that disturb the mind.

Such places are the opposite of the negative places that are our native lands. Here there are no objects of attachment and aversion, no triggers such as enemies and friends, so merely by virtue of being there our afflictions gradually subside.

I have not spent long stretches of time in total solitude, but I have done shorter retreats in such places, "places free of humans and dogs," as they say, where you are unlikely to see or hear another person for months at a time. The benefit is palpable and immediate. Since there are no external triggers or familiar reference points, the mind is not stirred to anger, pride, or desire; the mind gradually settles into a state of lucid calm.

Of course, the afflictions are not uprooted simply by living in solitude. If that were the case, the deer, bears, and bees in the wild would all be buddhas—but they are not. We still need to practice, and solitude is the best support for that. For in solitude there are no distractions. There is really nothing to busy yourself with up in the mountains or in a hermitage, and you can't just lie around all day. So, naturally, in the absence of distractions, you will apply yourself to virtuous activity. By virtue of the conducive location, your spiritual practice will naturally gain strength. On the other hand, if we go off to the mountains but do not apply ourselves to practice, all we are doing is sullying the mountain slopes with our excrement.

We need to bear this in mind! Living in a remote location is not a virtuous activity in and of itself.

"Virtuous activity" refers to the practices of the buddhas and bodhisattvas, to the various Dharma activities prescribed by Buddha, which are often condensed into the following ten: transcribing the teachings, paying homage, practicing generosity, listening to the teachings, memorizing, reading, instructing others, reciting, contemplating, and meditating. With nothing else to occupy you, you will naturally find yourself engaging in these virtuous activities, and as a result the wonderful qualities of spiritual practice will arise. Faith in the Three Jewels, renunciation toward samsara, awareness of the Buddha's extraordinary qualities and the guru's great kindness, confidence in karmic cause and effect, and so on—these and many other qualities will develop, and in turn your enthusiasm for practice will increase.

Smartphones and internet access pose a real threat for practitioners these days. A practitioner might go off to a solitary place, but then they bring their smartphone with them and so have access to the internet. Perhaps you tell yourself you won't use the internet, even though it is there, but your habits get the better of you, and instead of focusing on practice, you end up whiling away much of your time on social media or looking things up on Google, convincing yourself that you need to know these things right now. Your solitude is sabotaged by the internet and you never experience solitude's benefits.

Admittedly, for many people these days, it might be difficult to be entirely out of touch for a significant period. Nevertheless, when practitioners go on retreat, they should limit their contact with others as much as possible. Ideally they will communicate only with the person helping them with supplies and so on.

By virtue of staying in solitude, awareness naturally becomes clearer. The mind becomes brighter, calmer, more lucid.

These are the natural qualities of the mind. In the absence of disturbing emotions, the mind's natural clarity can manifest.

The Kagyu and Nyingma teachings are forever telling us to relax the mind, to let it be. This might seem simplistic at first, even a little foolish, but the reason this is emphasized so much in the Kagyu and Nyingma teachings, in the teachings of the Great Seal and the Great Perfection, is because when the mind is relaxed, its inherent qualities can manifest. The mind is naturally endowed with all the qualities of awakening—faith, compassion, insight, and so on. When you relax the mind, or awareness, and let it return to its natural state, these qualities will manifest.

In this way, as awareness becomes clearer, you will gain certainty in the teachings. Certainty means conviction, or confidence: confidence in the truth of profound emptiness, in the wondrous qualities of bodhichitta, in the undeceiving nature of the Three Jewels, and so on.

Without adhering to solitude and applying yourself to contemplation and meditation, there is no way to gain such certainty. Dry learning alone will not help. This is why Buddha Shakyamuni and all the great masters who have followed in his wake have emphasized the importance of solitude. As Buddha himself said,

> First focus on study, then hold fast to solitude.

Likewise, in the "Teachings on Meditation" chapter of *Entering the Way of the Bodhisattva*, Shantideva extols the benefits of solitude at length:

> With solitude of body and mind,
> Distraction won't occur.
> So you should thus forsake the world
> And also give up discursive thoughts.[73]

He also says,

> Thus I'll remain in solitude,
> In the delightful atmosphere
> Of joyful forests with few hardships,
> Where all distractions are quieted.[74]

First, we need to study the Dharma. We do this by receiving teachings and guidance from a qualified spiritual guide. Then we need to practice—and we need to practice in solitude, not amid hustle and bustle, preoccupied by worldly concerns.

Adhering to solitude was the practice of all the buddhas and bodhisattvas of the past, it is the practice of all buddhas and bodhisattvas of the present, and it will be the practice of all buddhas and bodhisattvas of the future. All the buddhas of the three times have relied on solitude, including great tantric adepts such as Guru Rinpoche, Khandro Yeshe Tsogyal, and so on. It is true that there are a handful of masters, like King Indrabhuti of the eighty-four *mahasiddhas*,[75] who attained buddhahood while living seemingly ordinary lives in cities and busy places. But these are very rare exceptions: 99.9 percent of buddhas and mahasiddhas attained accomplishment by remaining in solitude.

My root guru Khenpo Dazer Rinpoche (1922–1990) spent a large part of his life in retreat. He left his home, Tsangtang, and his home monastery, Rahor, to devote himself to practice. After receiving teachings from his precious gurus, he stayed in retreat for nine years at Tarpa Ling, the sacred site of Longchenpa in Bhutan. He then stayed in retreat for six years in Manali and for shorter periods in various other places, before spending his remaining years in a hermitage near Dzogchen. This is the way of all the buddhas of the past, present, and future, such as Khenpo Dazer Rinpoche. We do not need to look as far back as Omniscient Longchenpa and the great yogi Milarepa. We can look to the examples of our own root gurus.

By contrast, in these degenerate times, most practitioners and lamas, myself included, adore busy places. We are enthralled by the spectacles of cities and modernity. However, this is not the way of bodhisattvas. This is not the route to accomplishment. We need to adhere to solitude, where the afflictions gradually subside, where virtuous activity naturally gains strength, and where certainty in the sublime Dharma deepens. This is the practice of all the buddhas and bodhisattvas of all the three times.

The points covered in these first three verses describe the physical supports conducive for cultivating bodhichitta. The following four verses describe the conducive mental supports. Although both of these are necessary, the mental supports are the most important because mind is the driving factor; the body is governed by the mind. It is for this reason that the mind is the focus of the bodhisattva's training, as the term *mind training*[76] suggests.

The purpose of mind training is, in short, to inspire our minds with weariness toward samsara and delight in liberation and buddhahood. From among all the many methods of mind training, the very best and most widely taught are the four mind changings, also known as the four thoughts that transform the mind. These are the reflections on the difficulty of attaining the freedoms and advantages, impermanence and death, the defects of samsara, and karmic cause and effect. They are often presented as the four common preliminaries in the five sets of one hundred thousand preliminary practices. These reflections are common to all vehicles of Buddhadharma, from the vehicle of the shravakas up to the vehicle of Ati yoga.[77] Whether we are practicing the vehicle of characteristics or the Great Perfection, we cannot become genuine practitioners without taking these four thoughts to heart.

The five hundred thousand preliminary practices are the basis, or foundation, for Great Perfection practice. They are composed of the outer and inner preliminaries. The outer, common preliminaries are the four mind changings. These reflections are common, and indispensable, to all vehicles—the three vehicles of shravakas, pratyekabuddhas, and bodhisattvas, all the way up to the vehicle of the Great Perfection. Without taking these four mind changings to heart, there is no way into the Great Perfection. There is simply no way to proceed.

The inner preliminaries begin with taking refuge and generating bodhichitta. Taking refuge is a fundamental preliminary for all vehicles (though it has further inner divisions, such as the refuge of shravakas and pratyekabuddhas, of bodhisattvas, of Secret Mantra, and so on). Generating bodhichitta is the indispensable preliminary for the Great Vehicle. The meditation and recitation of Vajrasattva is the preliminary for the generation-stage practices of Secret Mantra. The mandala offering, through which the store of merit is gathered—and in the case of the Longchen Nyingtik preliminaries, the *kusali*[78] offering as well—is an important preliminary for both stages of Secret Mantra practice and is indispensable for the practice of all vehicles. Finally, guru yoga is the preliminary practice of the Great Perfection, the practices of trekcho and togal. We can talk about the Great Perfection all we like, but without practicing the outer and inner preliminaries, there is no way to proceed. If we consider the full title of the famous instruction manual, *The Words of My Perfect Teacher: A Guide to the Preliminaries for the Heart-Essence of the Great Expanse (Longchen Nyingtik) from the Great Perfection*, we see that it is essentially a book about the preliminary practices of the Great Perfection. Half of the text is dedicated to the four mind changings, the common preliminaries, precisely because they are indispensable to the practice of the Great Perfection.

Among these four mind changings, the reflection on the difficulty of attaining the freedoms and advantages was covered in verse 1, and the third and fourth reflections will be taught later on. The most crucial and the most potent is the reflection on impermanence and death. This is the topic of the next verse.

CHAPTER 8

Reflecting on Impermanence and Thereby Renouncing the Concerns of This Life

> 4. Friends and kin, long acquainted, will go their separate ways,
> Wealth and possessions, so hard-earned, will be left behind,
> Consciousness, a guest in the body's hotel, will in time depart.
> To give up this life's concerns is the practice of bodhisattvas.

If you fail to take impermanence and death to heart, it is really not possible to become a genuine practitioner. As Padampa Sangye said,

> At first, to be fully convinced of impermanence makes you take up the Dharma; in the middle, it whips up your diligence; and in the end, it brings you to the radiant dharmakaya.[79]

Remembering impermanence is crucial at all stages of the path.

As Khenpo Kunpal Rinpoche states in *The Nectar of Manjushri's Speech*, bodhichitta is the highway of all buddhas of past, present, and future. It is the one and only route to awakening. Therefore, we need to generate bodhichitta, and to that end we need to take impermanence to heart. Otherwise, this precious human birth that we have attained, this priceless support for bodhichitta, will go to waste.

We all have friends and relatives whom we cherish and love, whom we have spent many years with and are so dear to our hearts. Nevertheless, sooner or later we will be separated from them. It is unavoidable. At best you might spend forty or fifty happy years with your spouse, or with your closest friends, but in the end death will be sure to pry you apart. These days, it is more likely for people to be separated by personal differences or some unseen circumstance, long before the Lord of Death arrives. Life is so volatile these days. In any case, no matter how much we love one another, no matter how much we want to stay together, at death we have no choice but to part.

It is the same with wealth and possessions. No matter how much money you might have saved up, no matter what wealth and assets you might have acquired, you cannot take any of them with you. Regardless of the effort you spent acquiring them, when the Lord of Death arrives, you will have to leave them all behind.

Whether it be your wealth and possessions, your relatives and friends, your status and accomplishments, or something else, if you fail to let go at the time of death, you risk being reborn as a hungry ghost. No matter how much practice you might do—reciting millions of mantras, making hundreds of thousands of feast offerings, doing many hundreds of hours of meditation—if you do not reduce your attachment, you will continue to take rebirth in samsara. As Tangtong Gyalpo prays in his Avalokiteshvara sadhana, *Far-Reaching Benefit of Beings, Extensive as the Sky*,

> Through the force of negative karma, accumulated
> throughout beginningless time,
> Beings who are overcome with miserliness take birth in
> the preta realm,

> Where they suffer the torments of intense hunger and
> thirst:
> May they all be reborn in your supreme Potala pure land!

You might think you have shunned unvirtuous deeds because you have not killed or stolen, told any grave lies, or been particularly unkind, and therefore you will not be reborn in samsara. But as Nagarjuna said,

> Desire, hatred, ignorance, and
> The actions they generate are unvirtuous.
> Nondesire, nonhatred, nonignorance,
> And the actions they generate are virtuous.

If you want to liberate yourself from the ocean of suffering that is the three realms of samsara, you need to identify its cause. The cause of samsara is attachment. Harboring attachment is an unvirtuous deed. So, if you want to find freedom, you need to uproot your attachment. You need to actively reduce your attachment in whatever way you can. This does not necessitate giving up your belongings. You do not have to sell your house, give away your savings, and become a mendicant. Objects themselves do no harm. It is our attachment that does the harm—attachment to wealth, loved ones, possessions, status, our body, as well as the seemingly virtuous attachment to the Buddhadharma, the path, our practice, and so on. As the mahasiddha Tilopa taught his disciple Naropa,

> It is not what you perceive that binds you,
> It is your clinging to it that binds you.
> Cut through your clinging, Naropa![80]

We need to practice the Dharma, but more importantly we need to know the Dharma's vital points. This means knowing how to practice the Dharma effectively so that the teaching we apply in any given situation remedies our afflictions. It is similar to taking medicine: For instance, we should not take blood-pressure medicine when our problem is diabetes. Otherwise, we will never recover. We could even make ourselves worse.

From beginningless time until now, not a single person has been able to take their friends and possessions with them into the next life. We need to face this truth: When death arrives, we will be parted from everything and everyone. We cannot take anything with us, so we must make meaningful use of what we have; we must use our wealth to stay healthy, to accumulate merit, to benefit others, and to prepare ourselves for the day when we will have to leave it all behind.

Our physical bodies are our most cherished possessions; there is nothing we value more. Yet in the end, we have to part from them as well. Our bodies are like a hotel in which our consciousness is residing as a guest. Our mind is only lodging here temporarily. Sooner or later, the mind will depart.

At death, mind and body will part ways. The body will be discarded, and the mind will continue into the intermediate state and the next life. This cherished body will become a lifeless corpse. It will stiffen and start to rot. If the body is cremated, it will be reduced to a pile of smoldering ash and bone fragments within a matter of minutes or hours. In a Tibetan sky burial, the body is hacked into pieces and offered to the birds who will devour the flesh, leaving nothing but naked bones. If buried, the corpse will be slowly consumed by bacteria, fungi, and worms. This is going to happen to all of us, sooner or later, no matter how much we pamper ourselves.

Renouncing this life's concerns does not mean giving up on life itself. It means relinquishing meaningless worldly concerns such as longing for fame, wealth, and status; getting caught up in protecting loved ones and defending enemies; and so on. In short, worldly concerns are summed up as the eight worldly concerns of gain and loss, pleasure and sorrow, fame and disgrace, and praise and slander. Noble beings see that these mundane concerns are utterly futile.[81] Therefore, it is the practice of buddhas and bodhisattvas to renounce this life's concerns and give rise to immaculate bodhichitta.

Even if you are a renowned teacher, a seasoned practitioner, a monastic, a scholar, or the like, if you remain attached to the concerns of this life, you are not a genuine practitioner, no matter how accomplished you might appear.

It is true that it is difficult to let go of attachment. After all, it is only on the first bodhisattva bhumi of Perfect Joy that attachment is truly uprooted and the eight worldly concerns are relinquished once and for all. Nevertheless, until we reach that point, we need to be doing whatever we can to reduce our attachment. We need to wear it away bit by bit. We must not be defeatist or lazy. Otherwise, we will never get anywhere.

Lord Gampopa, also known as Dakpo Lhaje (the Great Doctor of Dakpo), is one of the three great pillars of the Kagyu tradition, together with Marpa Lotsawa and the great yogi Milarepa.[82] Dakpo Lhaje was born in 1079 in Central Tibet into a wealthy family. His father was a physician called Nyepa Gyalpo, and his mother was Shonu Za. He was given a fine education, and he excelled in the study of medicine. As was the custom at the time, his marriage was arranged from an early age, and as a young adult he was wedded to a beautiful young woman named Dharma O. They soon gave birth to a son and then a daughter, and for a time they lived a happy and enviable life. But then a pandemic befell the region and their son fell sick. Dakpo Lhaje, the most skilled doctor in the area, tried every treatment and cure but it was all in vain. His beautiful son died. Then his daughter fell sick. Within a few days, she too was dead, leaving Dakpo Lhaje overcome with grief. A few days later, his beloved wife Dharma O fell sick. He applied every medical treatment he knew and performed countless pujas and prayers, but again it was all in vain. Her condition worsened, and she was in constant pain. Dakpo Lhaje stayed by her side and nursed her day after day. He washed and dressed her, helped her to the bathroom, and cleaned away her urine and excrement when she was too weak to rise from her bed.

Things had started out so well for Dakpo Lhaje and his wife. They were a beautiful, successful couple with two charming children, but overnight their life was turned upside down. Dakpo Lhaje soon grew weary of his householder life. There was no end to his duties and chores, and they brought no benefit, no relief. The futility of it all was like a sharp thorn digging into his heart. As the days rolled by, he watched helplessly as his wife's condition degenerated until she was barely conscious much of the time. But still she hung on, clinging desperately to this life.

Dakpo Lhaje could not bear to see his wife struggling like this, so one day he sat down by her side. He took her hand and said, "My love, it seems you won't recover from this illness, that the time of your death is near. I want you to know that after you die, I will not remarry. I have resolved to renounce worldly life and to become a monk. I will devote the rest of my life to the Dharma. And my love, even if you make a miraculous recovery, it would be best that you do the same."

When she heard these words, the frail Dharma O breathed a sigh of relief. She had been afraid that her husband would remarry and forget her. Now that she knew that would not happen, she could let go. Soon afterward, she passed away, finally at peace. After performing her funeral and making many offerings and prayers on her behalf, Dakpo Lhaje left his householder life behind. He sought out a Kadampa geshe, took full ordination, and immersed himself in the practice of the Kadampas.

One night, he dreamed he was blessed by a yogi with green skin and clad in threadbare robes. Shortly afterward, when he was walking outside one day, he passed a group of beggars and overheard them talking about a yogi named Milarepa. He was enraptured by the mere sound of Milarepa's name. Enlisting the help of one of the beggars, he set out immediately in search of him.[83]

Dakpo Lhaje came face-to-face with death and impermanence through the loss of his son, daughter, and wife. Seeing the futility of worldly life, that you cannot take anything or anyone with you when you die, he renounced his family wealth, his social status, and his medical expertise. He devoted himself to the path, and through his efforts he attained awakening as a Vidyadhara of the Great Seal[84] in that very body and life.

CHAPTER 9

Avoiding the Adverse Condition That Is Bad Company

> 5. In bad company, the three poisons increase,
> Study, reflection, and meditation decline,
> And loving-kindness and compassion vanish.
> To avoid bad company is the practice of bodhisattvas.

There is a saying that "when the Dharma is profound, obstacles are profound." Keeping bad company is an obstacle. It can cause terrible destruction—of people, prospects, and the path. Bad company refers to destructive friends, anyone who has a negative influence on a bodhisattva practitioner and their development of bodhichitta.

We are very impressionable. If we spend time with someone who drinks and smokes, to use a coarse example, we are likely to end up drinking and smoking ourselves. If we hang out with someone rude and disrespectful, their attitude will slowly rub off on us. In this way, we are just like children. Children learn by example and copy what others do.

The three poisons are attachment, aversion, and ignorance. They are called poisons because of their function: Just as poisonous substances destroy our physical life force, these mental poisons destroy the life force of liberation. They kill our chances of attaining the state of freedom and omniscience. If we spend time with someone very emotional and flawed—for instance, someone very prejudiced and close-minded, whose mindset is in discord with the Dharma—this will have a detrimental effect on us and hinder our bodhisattva practice.

Bodhisattva Gyalse Tokme is not saying that bodhisattvas should not help destructive people. Bodhisattvas must help them, of course, but first they need to develop the ability to do so. As Longchenpa said,

> To be the guide and teacher of others,
> Not having yourself reached liberation's shore,
> Is as contradictory as giving your hand to someone
> drowning
> While you yourself are being swept away by the flood.[85]

When you want to save someone from drowning, first you need to save yourself. Otherwise, you will not be able to save them and both of you will drown. It is like what they say during the safety demonstrations on airplanes: In an emergency, you should put your own oxygen mask on first before helping others to put on theirs. This is a very important point. In order to help others, first of all you need to be stable yourself. Once you gain real certainty and stability in the Dharma, then you can befriend destructive people. Then you can influence them, instead of the other way around. However, until you reach that point, keeping bad company is self-destructive. It harms you, and it harms your efforts to benefit others in the long run.

In *Treasury of Precious Qualities*, Omniscient Jigme Lingpa says,

> Like a log of common timber
> Lying in Malaya's forest groves
> Absorbs the fragrance of the moistened sandal leaves—
> You will take after those whom you frequent.[86]

If we spend time with negative people, our own negative qualities will increase; and as a result, our study, reflection, and meditation will decline. The focus of a bodhisattva practitioner's study, reflection, and meditation is bodhichitta. Destructive friends will not value bodhichitta and the bodhisattva path. They will question the value of our practice and try to discourage us. They could even sow seeds of needless confusion and doubt.

"Study" means to receive teachings and study the scriptures, while "reflection" refers to contemplating the meaning of what one has learned, thereby dispelling confusion and doubt. Meditation means to internalize what we have ascertained through study and reflection by familiarizing ourselves with it. For the bodhisattva practitioner there is nothing more important than studying, reflecting, and meditating on bodhichitta. Simply speaking, keeping bad company prevents the bodhisattva from doing this, thereby causing loving-kindness and compassion, the roots of bodhichitta, to fade away until they are no more. Therefore, if we are not careful, we will be sullied by the adverse condition of bad company just like a white cloth that gets stained by red dye.

During Buddha's time, there was a man who came to be known as Angulimala (Finger Garland). He had murdered 999 people and, in order to keep count, he had taken a thumb from each of his victims and strung them onto a garland. Angulimala was born into a wealthy family and was well educated in the arts, sciences, and sports. He was handsome and talented—an eligible bachelor—but he was not interested in getting married. His interests lay in the spiritual path. He went to study at the feet of a brahmin who was a celebrated spiritual guide. This teacher took Angulimala under his wing and, over the course of many years, gave him much excellent guidance in study, reflection, and meditation.

Angulimala was very handsome, and soon the brahmin's wife fell in love with him. Intoxicated by her desire, she did all she could to seduce him, but Angulimala just ignored her. She grew increasingly desperate, increasingly flirtatious, but Angulimala continued to turn a blind eye.

One day, the brahmin was called away for a few days. He told Angulimala to stay at his residence and perform the daily rituals in his absence. Seizing this window of opportunity, the brahmin's wife upped her antics. Lust can make us do crazy, deceitful things. She flirted with Angulimala at every opportunity, but he remained steadfast.

"You are my teacher's wife," he said. "How could I even think about getting involved with you? It would be a terrible form of adultery. Please, just leave me alone."

However, she would not be reasoned with. She was blinded by desire. Growing increasingly desperate, she started to threaten him. "You must come to bed with me! You must! I give you no choice," she said. When he withstood even her threats, she became enraged, but anxious too. What if Angulimala were to tell her husband what she had done in his absence? What if she was exposed? Unable to bear the thought of this, she decided to lay a trap. On the day of the brahmin's return, she messed up her hair, scratched her face with her nails, tore and sullied her clothes. As the brahmin was approaching the house, she ran outside, calling out to him in distress. "What on earth has happened, my wife? Who did this to you?" he said. "It was Angulimala. You don't know what he is really like. He tried to rape me while you were gone," she said. Then she broke down in a flood of tears.

The brahmin was beyond furious. His student could not have wronged him more gravely in his eyes: *After all I have given him, all the time I have spent guiding him, this is how he behaves?!* The brahmin was determined to take revenge. But, he knew that Angulimala, being young and fit, would beat him in a fight. He considered banishing him from the area, but he did not think that would be true revenge. He pondered for some time and finally struck upon an idea.

The brahmin acted as if nothing had happened, as if his wife had said nothing to him. Then, one day, he sat Angulimala down and told him the time had come for him to receive some very special instructions. "There is in fact great virtue to be found in negative actions," he said, "most especially the act of killing. If you kill in offering to Goddess Kali and the wrathful deities, you can generate tremendous virtue." Thus, he encouraged Angulimala to generate anger, pride, and jealousy and to embrace heinous actions, all in the name of the virtuous spiritual path.

After some time, the brahmin appraised Angulimala and told him, "Son, you are doing very well. Now, if you really want to attain liberation in this life, you must murder one thousand people. If you can do this, liberation will be guaranteed." The gullible, eager Angulimala had such unerring faith in his teacher that he did not question a single word he said. He had no idea that his teacher was pushing him onto a path of evil in revenge for supposedly raping his wife. He eagerly began his killing spree, and to keep count of his victims, he cut a thumb from each one and strung them together into a garland. He eventually reached 999 and was just one murder away from attaining liberation, his longed-for goal.

Angulimala's mother was due to visit him, so he decided she would be his final victim. It was at this point that Buddha Shakyamuni saw that the time was now ripe for him to tame Angulimala. In order for the buddhas and bodhisattvas to connect with beings, the time, and hence a person's karma, needs to be "ripe." This ripeness creates a receptiveness, a window of opportunity.

Before Angulimala's mother arrived, Buddha himself appeared before him, walking slowly along a path. Angulimala thought, *Well, I was planning to kill my mother, but here comes a monk. How excellent! I can avoid killing my mother and fulfill my mission at the same time.* And so, Angulimala set off after Buddha, armed with his razor-sharp knife. But however fast he walked, he could not reach him. Buddha was walking slowly and serenely, but even when Angulimala ran after him at full speed he could not catch up.

Once Angulimala was sweating and exhausted, Buddha stopped walking and turned around. Looking Angulimala in the eye, he explained the four noble truths: the truths of suffering, the origin, cessation, and the path. Buddha explained to him in detail how samsara is the nature of suffering, how this suffering arises from attachment, aversion, and ignorance, and how the cessation of suffering can be attained by uprooting its origin through training on the path.

Angulimala was receptive to this teaching. He was delighted to hear these words of truth, and he immediately realized he had been following a heinous, mistaken path. He saw that by killing 999 people, he had only perpetuated the root of samsara. He was overcome with remorse. The correct view swiftly took birth in his mind, he confessed his wrongdoings to Buddha, and despite the evil deeds he had performed, he quickly attained the state of an *arhat* through his diligent practice.[87] As Nagarjuna teaches in *Letter to a Friend*,

> Those who formerly were careless
> But then took heed are beautiful and fair,
> As is the moon emerging from the clouds,
> Like Nanda, Angulimala, Darshaka, Udayana.[88]

If we keep company with destructive companions, our good qualities will decline, our study, reflection, and meditation will degenerate, and, like Angulimala, we could even be led onto perverted paths.

CHAPTER 10

Relying on the Conducive Condition That Is the Spiritual Friend

> 6. By following a spiritual friend, your faults will fade.
> Good qualities will grow like the waxing moon.
> Therefore, to consider your teachers even more precious
> Than your own cherished body is the practice of
> bodhisattvas.

In addition to shunning bad company, we need to rely on the conducive condition of genuine spiritual friends. "Spiritual friend" refers to the best type of friend—to the buddhas and bodhisattvas, one's precious root gurus and spiritual guides.

To begin with, before taking someone as our spiritual friend, we need to examine them well. The importance of this cannot be stressed enough. It is said that if a teacher fails to examine the student, it is like drinking poison, and if a student fails to examine the teacher, it is like jumping into an abyss. Furthermore, as Omniscient Jigme Lingpa taught,

> At first, be skillful in examining a teacher.
> Then be skilled in knowing how to follow him.

> At last, be skilled in training in his view and action.
> Acting thus, you'll tread a perfect path.[89]

Thus, at the beginning we need to be skilled in examining the teacher, in the middle we need to be skilled in following them, and in the end, we need to be skilled in emulating them.

The word *follow* implies remaining in the company of our spiritual friend for a prolonged period. We should spend at least a decade by their side. When it comes to the teacher-disciple relationship, there needs to be a mutual sense of connection and care. The teacher needs to accept the student, to take the student under their wing, and the student needs to follow the teacher closely for many years. Khenpo Chokhyab Rinpoche stayed with his root guru Botrul Rinpoche for seventeen years, living by his side, receiving teachings from him daily, and practicing under his constant guidance. Similarly, Khenpo Dazer Rinpoche spent seven years with Botrul Rinpoche. Their living conditions were incredibly poor at that time. They lived in flimsy huts made from stacked tussocks of grass and made do with the poorest and scantiest of food. But these hardships did not deter them.

Khenpo Dazer Rinpoche and Khenpo Chokhyab Rinpoche both walked for several months to meet their teacher. They left home and set out for an unfamiliar place where they had no acquaintances or contacts, no one to offer them shelter or food. When studying with Botrul Rinpoche, each summer the student would have ten or fifteen days to go out and gather donations of barley flour (*tsampa*) and tea to sustain them through the coming months. When Khenpo Dazer Rinpoche was receiving *The Treasury of Abhidharma*, his barley flour began to run out. If he were to go out to gather more, he would miss a day or more of teachings, so rather than compromise his studies, he rationed the little barley flour he had and made do with one tiny bowl a day until the teachings came to an end.

Their only shoes at the time were traditional handsewn leather boots. At some point, the soles of Khen Rinpoche's shoes wore through, so during the long harsh winters he had to walk through the snow barefoot, following the tracks of others where the snow had been packed down. Prior to this, when Khen Rinpoche was studying at Shechen, he lived in a makeshift grass hut. The hut did not have a proper roof, so in the evenings he would drape his woolen shawl over the top of the hut to protect himself from the snowfall. In the morning, he would shake the snow off, put the shawl on, and head off to class. These are just a few examples of the hardships they embraced for the sake of the Dharma. Hearing these stories strengthens our own determination and shows us what qualities we lack.

The great masters who are the objects of our prayers became the great beings that they are by following their root gurus, by spending time with them. That is how they developed their qualities of knowledge and realization. That is how they became worthy objects of refuge and supplication, sources of genuine benefit for the Dharma and all beings throughout all time. Such is the importance and benefit of relying on spiritual friends. In *The King of Aspiration Prayers: Samantabhadra's "Aspiration to Good Actions,"* we pray,

> May I always meet spiritual friends
> Who long to be of true help to me
> And who teach me the Good Actions;[90]
> Never will I disappoint them![91]

In the seventeenth-century master Lochen Dharmashri's[92] commentary on this prayer, he explains that spiritual friends, the buddhas and bodhisattvas, are the best kind of friend.

Among all gurus, or spiritual friends, here we are talking specifically about the guru who teaches you about bodhichitta. There is no greater kindness than this. Lord Atisha had many precious gurus, but he revered Guru Serlingpa above them all. Likewise, His Holiness the Dalai Lama often says that his most important teacher was Khunu Lama, because it was from Khunu Lama that he received teachings on bodhichitta. You may have many teachers from whom you receive many different teachings, but know that among all of them, the teacher who grants you the bodhisattva vow and teaches you the oceanic conduct of the bodhisattvas is the greatest—the kindest—of all.

These days we might not have the merit to perceive our teachers as buddhas and bodhisattvas. However, that does not mean that they are not buddhas and bodhisattvas. As Buddha Shakyamuni told Ananda when he was about to pass into parinirvana,[93]

> Don't feel sad, Ananda.
> Don't lament, Ananda.
> In future times, I will
> Take the form of spiritual teachers
> To help you and others.

Such is the compassion of the buddhas and bodhisattvas. For the benefit of us obscured beings, they appear in this degenerate age in the form of human beings. The spiritual teachers of the degenerate age are said to be equal to Buddha in terms of their qualities but even greater than the Buddha in terms of their kindness.

By following a spiritual friend, your faults and flaws will gradually fade and disappear. When you take the words, thoughts, and deeds of a bodhisattva as your example and seek to emulate them, your afflictions will naturally reduce, and at the same time, all virtues, or good qualities, will naturally expand, like the waxing moon.

In the past, my root guru Khenpo Dazer Rinpoche instructed me to go and meet Khenpo Chokhyab Rinpoche. He said,

"He is an incredible master. You needn't request any formal teachings from him. Just observe him from head to toe. That will be a teaching in itself." I did not know what to make of this, but I went to meet him as instructed. Khenpo Chokhyab Rinpoche's mere presence—his comportment and every aspect of his conduct, the way he lived, ate, walked, and spoke—made the deepest impression on me. I felt as if I was in the presence of Milarepa incarnate, and I wished more than anything to emulate him. I have not been able to do that, not in the slightest, but I gave rise to the heartfelt aspiration to do so.

An authentic spiritual friend will influence us through their very being. Even if they grant us no formal teachings, the way they walk and talk, the way they lead their lives and conduct themselves will serve as profound instructions showing us what the genuine Dharma is and what it means to be a genuine practitioner.

These days most so-called lamas and practitioners, including myself, are engrossed by the eight worldly concerns. There are people who have completed multiple three-year retreats but are still tangled up in attachment to family and friends, still caught up in worldly aims. This is a clear sign that one has not been practicing effectively, that you have not merged the Dharma with your mind. In contrast, genuine spiritual friends, like Khenpo Dazer Rinpoche and Khenpo Chokhyab Rinpoche, are totally free of worldly concerns. These two masters were pure renunciates, perfect teachers endowed with the nine attributes of the wise: they were learned, righteous, and kind; rich in study, reflection, and meditation; and adept in exposition, disputation, and composition. *Wise* means to be wise in the ultimate meaning—to have realized bodhichitta, the unity of compassion and emptiness. As taught in *The Chronicles of the Lotus-Born*,[94]

> Those learned in the words are not wise;
> Those learned in the meaning are wise.

I have had the amazing good fortune to meet and train with great beings like them. It is shameful, really, to have trained at the feet of such extraordinary masters and yet remain so ordinary myself. When you spend time with these kinds of spiritual friends, these kinds of pure bodhisattvas, your worldly concerns and attachments, your petty emotions, and so on will all be worn away, and in their place bodhichitta will arise, increase, and expand.

We value nothing more highly than our body, no matter who we are. Think of all the care and attention, the money and effort we expend on this body—and what benefit does it bring us? At best, it keeps us alive for seventy, eighty, or maybe ninety years. That is no more than the blink of an eye. Then the body dies, and consciousness moves on.

However, if we make good use of this precious human body, it can become an invaluable ship that helps us sail across the ocean of samsara and reach liberation's dry shore. To make that happen, though, we need the guidance of a spiritual friend. It is simply not possible to instruct ourselves. This is why it is the practice of bodhisattvas to consider the sacred spiritual friend even more precious than their own body, even more precious than their own lives.

This is exemplified by the lives of all the great masters of the past. Think of how Milarepa followed Marpa Lotsawa, how Naropa followed Tilopa, and how Longchenpa followed Kumaraza: They disregarded all physical hardship, risking their lives to receive guidance on the path.

The ability to value one's gurus in this way—to recognize their true value—stems from an understanding of bodhichitta, which itself stems from the guru's kindness.

CHAPTER 11

Taking Refuge, the Gateway to the Buddhist Teachings

> 7. Bound themselves in samsara's prison,
> Whom can the worldly gods protect?
> Therefore, to take refuge in the unfailing
> Three Jewels is the practice of bodhisattvas.

Taking refuge in the unfailing, undeceiving Three Jewels is the gateway to all three vehicles of Buddhadharma—the Lesser Vehicle of the shravakas and pratyekabuddhas; the Great Vehicle of the bodhisattvas; and, within that, the Vajra Vehicle of Secret Mantra. Refuge is also the foundation and prerequisite for taking the bodhisattva vow, and likewise for receiving Vajra Vehicle empowerment. As Chandrakirti explains in *Seventy Stanzas on Taking Refuge*,

> All may have the vows,
> Excepting those who have not taken refuge.[95]

Worldly gods—such as Brahma, Indra, and Vishnu of the Vedic traditions; Allah of the Islamic tradition; and the Almighty God of the Christian tradition—are all praiseworthy in many ways. Compared to other sentient beings, they are indeed very special. But in comparison to the buddhas they are not. They possess certain degrees of power stemming from merit, aspirations, and samadhi cultivated in the past, and they can grant mundane boons and protection, such as rebirth in the heavenly realms. However, they cannot grant the ultimate, lasting happiness of buddhahood, and they cannot free you from samsara. Why not? Because they themselves are not yet free. They have not severed the root of samsara within themselves; they have not uprooted the conception of a personal self, which obstructs liberation, nor the conception of a self of phenomena, which obstructs omniscient buddhahood.[96] Such gods can serve as temporary protectors, and indeed, many gods, such as Lord Shiva, act as protectors of the Dharma. However, they are not ultimate protectors. We need to be aware of this.

As followers of Buddha and seekers of liberation and awakening, we will reap no benefit from taking refuge in such gods. As Omniscient Longchenpa said, to take refuge in someone who has not yet attained liberation is like asking someone who is drowning in a river to pull another drowning person out. Only someone standing firmly on the dry shore of liberation and omniscience can save those drowning in the ocean of samsara.

The Three Jewels of Buddha, Dharma, and Sangha are the genuine objects of refuge for those seeking liberation and awakening. Buddha is our guide on the path, the Dharma is the path itself, and the Sangha are our companions on the path. Since they themselves are free from samsara, if we place our trust in them and follow them, we can gain freedom ourselves. As *Seventy Stanzas on Taking Refuge* states,

> The Buddha, Dharma, and Sangha
> Are the refuge for those seeking liberation.

We need to take refuge in the Three Jewels with three types of faith: inspired faith, longing faith, and irreversible faith.

Inspired faith refers to the joy and attraction you feel when seeing an image of the Buddha or hearing the life stories of the Buddha and his followers, for example.

Longing faith arises once you have some understanding of the exceptional qualities of Buddha, Dharma, and Sangha. You then develop the longing to be free from samsara and attain buddhahood—to develop the qualities of the Three Jewels within yourself.

Irreversible faith is a trust so firm and unchanging that you would sooner give up your own life than forsake the Three Jewels. No matter what ups and downs you encounter in life, you entrust yourself resolutely to the Three Jewels.

When you take refuge in the Three Jewels with irreversible faith, you become a genuine Buddhist. On the other hand, if you go through the motions of taking refuge but you lack irreversible faith—you lack certainty in the Three Jewels—you certainly do not qualify as a genuine bodhisattva practitioner. You cannot even be called a genuine Buddhist.

There are two ways to enter and follow the Dharma: the approach of discipline and the approach of the view.

Some people naturally feel faith in Buddha and his teachings, even without studying or examining. Inspired by this faith, they take refuge in the Three Jewels, and then they take one of the seven types of personal liberation vows.[97] This is the approach of discipline. It is also called the approach of faith.

Others approach the Dharma by means of the view, or wisdom. This is the approach taken by Udbhatasiddhasvamin and his brother (whose story is told below) and by Ashvaghosha, the ancient non-Buddhist Indian *pandita* who famously lost a debate with the Buddhist master Aryadeva and subsequently converted to Buddhism. In this approach, one must begin by scrutinizing the teachings, like a goldsmith analyzing gold. As Buddha taught,

> O monks and wise ones,
> Just as a goldsmith would test his gold by burning,
> cutting, and rubbing it,
> So must you examine my words and only then accept them,
> Not merely out of reverence for me.

Then, having gained certainty in the value and validity of Buddha's teachings, one enters the gateway of Dharma and takes refuge in the Three Jewels.

Most Tibetan and Himalayan people have a natural faith in the Dharma, and they are guided well by this faith. The Buddhadharma has been analyzed in minute detail for many centuries in Tibet, and of course many centuries previously in India,[98] by supreme scholars, such as Sakya Pandita, Je Tsongkhapa, and Longchenpa—the three famed emanations of the bodhisattva of wisdom, Manjushri. The validity and inestimable worth of the Buddha's teachings has been established and demonstrated again and again by these erudite Buddhists, so it is easy for people who are immersed in Buddhist cultures to feel faith. In a sense, there is little need for those Buddhists to analyze the teachings in detail themselves, since this has already been done by such esteemed masters. On the other hand, most Westerners and modern people do not have this kind of instinctual faith. Instead, they are guided by their wisdom, or insight. They begin by studying the teachings, and as they come to see their unique qualities, they gradually develop faith.

Regardless of whether you analyze it or not, the Dharma is the Dharma, just as pure gold is pure gold. It is not improved by analysis. If you have faith in the Dharma without analyzing it, that is excellent. And if you do not have faith initially, you can examine the Dharma, and as you come to recognize its value, faith will be sure to grow.

In the past in India, there lived two brothers, Udbhatasiddhasvamin and Samkarasvamin.[99] They were brahmins by birth and were exceptionally well versed in the four Vedas. However, they had encountered Buddha Shakyamuni's teachings and were very drawn to them. They felt conflicted about this and for some time they were not sure what to do. Eventually, they decided to go to Mount Kailash and ask their deity, Lord Shiva, for advice.

It is said that ordinary people cannot see Lord Shiva, so these two brothers must not have been ordinary. Perhaps they had mastered the meditative states taught in the Vedas. The written accounts of their story don't discuss this, but I wonder if that was the case. They embarked on the long journey from their home in India to Mount Kailash in Tibet. When they finally arrived, they found themselves in a heavenly landscape of luscious forests and meadows, not the rather barren landscape seen by Buddhists and Hindus who would travel there on pilgrimage. Perhaps the landscape was part of a meditative experience. Amid this exquisite setting, they saw their deity, Lord Shiva, surrounded by many thousands of disciples and an abundance of divine food, drink, flowers, and other luxuries. Lord Shiva's sublime consort Umadevi was presenting him with offerings of flowers and fruits, much to his delight.

At lunchtime, a billowing mass of arhats and bodhisattvas wearing saffron robes appeared above them, soaring through the sky like a shining rainbow. They flew down and landed before Lord Shiva, who proceeded to offer them a meal of the finest quality, accompanied by performances of music and dance, and offerings of sweet incense, flowers, and other heavenly delights. The two brothers were astonished to see Lord Shiva worshipping Buddha's disciples.

Not knowing what to make of it, they asked Lord Shiva directly what was going on. Lord Shiva told them that he made such offerings to Buddha Shakyamuni and his disciples every day. "Buddha is more worthy of homage than me; Buddha is the ultimate refuge," he said. The brothers were delighted to receive this confirmation of their own kindling faith. If Buddha was Lord Shiva's object of refuge, there was no doubt that Buddha should be their object of refuge too.

Later on, Udbhatasiddhasvamin composed a praise to the Buddha titled *In Praise of the Unique Qualities of the Bhagavan.*[100] The opening verse states,

> Having abandoned other teachers,
> I take refuge in you, Bhagavan,
> Because you, Bhagavan, are
> Free of faults and rich with qualities.

"Bhagavan" is one of the many epithets for Buddha. The Tibetan equivalent of this Sanskrit term is Chomdende, meaning "Transcendent, Endowed Conqueror." Buddha has conquered (*chom*) the four maras, is endowed (*den*) with the six excellent qualities, and has transcended (*de*) mistaken states of mind. Since Buddha himself is flawless, his teachings too are flawless—free of confusion, and free of all selfish, distorted aims. For those seeking liberation and awakening, only Buddha, who expounds the path of the four noble truths that leads to perfect buddhahood, is a valid teacher, no one else.

The focus of the bodhisattva is the generation of bodhichitta, and the foundation of bodhichitta is taking refuge. Trying to generate bodhichitta without having first taken refuge is like trying to draw a picture without a canvas. Therefore, to take refuge in the unfailing Three Jewels is the practice of bodhisattvas.[101]

The Main Part

The Paths of the Three Types of Beings

CHAPTER 12

The Path of Lesser Beings

Avoiding Sinful Actions in Fear of the Suffering of the Lower Realms

> 8. The sufferings of the lower realms, so difficult to bear,
> Are the fruit of sinful actions, so the Sage declared.
> Therefore, to never commit sinful actions,
> Even at the cost of your life, is the practice of bodhisattvas.

When the scriptures speak of lesser, middling, and supreme beings, they are describing beings' capacity for training on the path. Lesser beings are those who feel overwhelmed at the thought of pursuing perfect buddhahood, or the liberation of the shravakas and pratyekabuddhas, and focus instead on avoiding rebirth in the three lower realms and attaining rebirth in the higher realms of humans and gods. To this end, they engage in the ten virtuous actions, shun the ten unvirtuous deeds, and place their trust in the Three Jewels.

The lower realms are the realms of hell beings, hungry ghosts, and animals. These states are filled with intense, unimaginable suffering. In the hot, cold, and ephemeral hells, beings are tormented by inconceivable heat, cold, and terrible violence. The hungry ghosts are tortured by intense hunger and thirst. Likewise, animals, whether living in water, in the air, or on the earth, whether domesticated or wild, are afflicted by countless miseries—stupidity, slavery, being slaughtered, or the constant fear of being preyed upon. In comparison, life in the human or god realms is certainly preferable.

We struggle to endure minor hardships, such as missing a meal, losing a night's sleep, or encountering a heat wave or a cold spell. The next time you are really hungry, ask yourself what it would be like if you were reborn as a hungry ghost, who is constantly famished, year after year. When you are feeling too hot or too cold, think of the hell beings who are engulfed by indescribable heat and cold for eons at a time. Likewise, when you feel vulnerable, threatened, or powerless, reflect on the sufferings of animals. In this way, take a sobering look at life in the lower realms.

I once visited a hot spring with Khenpo Dazer Rinpoche and a small group of his students. While Khen Rinpoche bathed in the spring, the rest of us sat around him on the grass. After a while, Khen Rinpoche told me to join him. At first, I refused—how could I bathe in the hot spring at the same time as my teacher? But Khen Rinpoche insisted, so eventually I undressed and got in. The water was so hot that I had to lower myself in slowly, letting my body acclimatize. Soon the heat was too much for me, so I stepped out. I splashed some water on my arms and legs, then slowly lowered myself back in. As I was going through all these motions, Khen Rinpoche, who was sitting comfortably in the steaming spring, said, "This water is not very hot, you know? It's only the heat of the human realm. Think of the heat of the hell realms and all those suffering there right now." Likewise, in the depths of winter, when the entire valley was frozen solid and the wind was so cold it could lacerate your skin, Khen Rinpoche would say, "This is only the cold of the human realm. Think of the cold of the hell realms and all those suffering there right now." Teachers like Khenpo Dazer Rinpoche are in a constant state of bodhichitta, a constant state of great compassion. His words helped me so much. Now, whenever I feel too hot or cold, I immediately remember his instruction.

Our teacher, the omniscient Buddha Shakyamuni, saw that suffering is the ripening of harmful deeds. Suffering is not random; it does not come about without a karmic cause. Rebirth in the lower realms is the fruit of one's own sinful actions, primarily the ten unvirtuous deeds. As Nagarjuna explains,

> Desire, hatred, ignorance, and
> The actions they generate are unvirtuous.
> Nondesire, nonhatred, nonignorance,
> And the actions they generate are virtuous.

The worst possible thing that could happen to us is to be killed, is it not? Our life is our most cherished possession; the thought of losing it is our greatest fear. Nevertheless, it is the practice of bodhisattvas to avoid all sinful actions—all actions that cause harm—even at the cost of their lives. Why? Because they are vividly aware of the karmic repercussions of such sin—repercussions that are much graver and long-lasting than the loss of this fleeting life.

With skillful means and great compassion, Buddha is adept at taming beings according to their needs. In this way, Buddha tamed Ananda who was lustful, Angulimala who was aggressive, and Chudapanthaka who was ignorant. Ananda is now revered as one of Buddha Shakyamuni's supreme disciples. He was Buddha's cousin and, later on, his attendant. However, Ananda was not always devoted to the Dharma. It was due to Buddha's compassion and skillful means that he renounced worldly life and entered the path.

To begin with, Ananda was married to the ravishingly beautiful Pundarika. Buddha encouraged him to renounce the life of a householder and become a monk many times. Buddha would tell Ananda of the great merit of taking monastic ordination.

He would say, "The life of a householder is like living in a cauldron, whereas the life of a renunciant is like living in a cool and comfortable house." But Ananda was deaf to Buddha's entreaties. He was far too attached to his gorgeous wife to be remotely interested.

One day, seeing that the time was ripe, Buddha set out on his alms round and headed to Ananda's house. When Pundarika saw Buddha and his disciples approaching, she offered to give alms on her husband's behalf. She knew Buddha had been talking to Ananda about becoming a monk, so she was keen to limit their interactions. However, Ananda insisted on going himself as a gesture of respect.

Ananda took Buddha's alms bowl from him and filled it with the finest portions of the food they had prepared, but when he offered the bowl back to Buddha, Buddha simply turned and walked away. Ananda could scarcely let Buddha walk off without his alms bowl, so he followed after him. Buddha strode on, all the while extolling the virtues of renunciation and the monastic life and talking in detail about the flaws of samsara and the shortcomings of householder life. But still, Ananda remained unmoved. He followed Buddha all the way back to his hermitage, still holding his alms bowl.

By now, dusk was approaching and Ananda was growing restless. He told Buddha he would take leave and return home. The thought of spending a night away from his beloved wife was unbearable! However, Buddha told him to spend the night at the hermitage. "You can return home in the morning," he said, much to Ananda's distress. Ananda had such a restless night. Time seemed to stretch to eternity. He was missing Pundarika with every cell of his being, and he was so tempted to go against Buddha's word and flee home in the dark of the night. (Buddha of course knew he would be tempted, so he had instructed some of his monks to keep watch over him and not let him leave.)

As soon as the sun rose, Ananda leaped to his feet and rushed to Buddha's hut. He greeted Buddha and told him he would now be heading home, at which point Buddha asked Ananda if he would like to visit the god realms with him. Well, this stopped Ananda in his tracks. *I am longing to get home*, he thought, *but the god realms—well, that's where we aspire to be reborn. How wonderful it would be to see them. They must be pure paradise!*

So, Ananda followed Buddha to the peak of a mountain. As they were standing there, Buddha gestured to an old woman nearby. Her face was covered with wrinkles, her hair was lank and gray, and her toothless mouth was caved in.

"Tell me, Ananda. Who is more beautiful? That woman or Pundarika?" Buddha asked. "Pundarika, of course!" Ananda scoffed. "Even the sole of Pundarika's foot is more beautiful than that old hag."

"Indeed, indeed. Now, take hold of the corner of my robe," Buddha said, and with that they flew up to the god realms.

They landed near an exquisite celestial mansion surrounded by beautiful ponds and flower gardens, where hosts of gods and goddesses were reveling in unimaginable luxuries. Buddha sent Ananda off to explore.

"Have a good look around, take it all in," he said.

Ananda wandered through the heavenly palaces and gardens in bliss. Then he arrived at a palace that made him curious. Like all the others, it was brimming with luxuries and goddesses, but in its center there was no god. Winding his way through the mass of food and flowers and performances of live music and dance, he approached one of the goddesses and asked her, "Why is this palace lacking a god?" The goddess replied, "We are awaiting his arrival. Down in the human realm, Buddha Shakyamuni's cousin Ananda is observing monastic discipline. Through the merit of doing so, he will immediately be reborn here when he dies."

Ananda could scarcely believe his ears. He was overjoyed. When he arrived back at their meeting spot, Buddha asked him, "Ananda, now tell me, who is more beautiful? Your beloved wife Pundarika or these goddesses you see before you?"

"These goddesses are more beautiful by far. I'm ashamed to admit it, but by comparison my Pundarika is like that haggard old woman we saw." Buddha had Ananda take hold of the corner of his robe once more, and they flew back to the human realm.

As soon as they touched down, Ananda told Buddha that he wished to become a monk.

"Are you sure, Ananda? What about Pundarika? You must consider this carefully," Buddha said. But Ananda was insistent, and so Buddha ordained him.

The discipline of observing vows can be colored by a variety of motivations. In this vein, the scriptures talk about three types of discipline:

1. *Discipline seeking protection from fear* refers to observing one's vows out of fear of suffering. For instance, in Buddha's time, monastics were exempt from many punishments, including the death penalty. One day a man had been caught stealing, and as he was fleeing his persecutors, he met Buddha on the road. He begged for his protection, and so Buddha, out of compassion, ordained him right then and there. The man thus gained immunity. These days, in Tibet and other places, parents will sometimes offer their children to a monastery because they cannot afford to raise them. That is another example of maintaining discipline in search of protection from fear.
2. *Discipline aspiring for goodness* refers to observing one's vows in order to gain rebirth in the higher realms.

3. *Discipline of renunciation* is genuine discipline. It refers to observing one's vows in order to attain liberation and awakening.

The motivation for observing discipline differs, but in all three cases, one observes the same precepts, such as, in the case of a fully ordained monk, the four root vows, the thirteen remainders, the thirty abandoning downfalls, and so on.

Buddha told Maudgalyayana and his other disciples that Ananda had become a monk merely to ensure rebirth in the god realms. Since Ananda's motivation was not genuine and he did not share the same discipline as them, Buddha told them not to associate with him. Ananda was Buddha's cousin, and even before his ordination he had been friends with many of Buddha's disciples. But now that he had finally joined the *sangha*, his friends and brethren would stand up and walk away whenever he appeared. At first Ananda was perplexed, then he became lonely and depressed. When he couldn't stand it a moment longer, he asked Buddha's disciple Maudgalyayana directly, "Maudgalyayana, what on earth is going on? Before we were friends, but now that I'm a monk, you won't even look at me!" When Maudgalyayana told Ananda that Buddha had instructed them to shun him because of his lack of renunciation, Ananda was so hurt. Nevertheless, he was determined to be reborn in the god realms, to savor the divine goddesses and luxuries he had witnessed there, so he endured their cold treatment and continued to observe his vows meticulously.

One day, Buddha asked Ananda if he would like to visit the hell realms. Ananda thought, *Well, this is an opportunity not to be missed!* And so, Buddha transported him there with his miraculous powers, and just as when they visited the god realms, Buddha told him to have a good look around. Ananda wandered through the eight hot hells, the eight cold hells, and the ephemeral hells, viewing their unthinkable sufferings. He watched Yama's fearful henchmen, bearing the heads of birds and beasts and brandishing gruesome weapons, hacking hell beings to pieces, beating them to a pulp, and boiling them alive in giant cauldrons. These horrific sights filled him with fear of the karmic consequences of sinful deeds.

In one area, there was a huge cauldron bubbling away. It was surrounded by henchmen with the heads of tigers and leopards. They had bulging muscles, like wrestlers, and were holding giant hammers and tridents in their hands. When Ananda asked them why this cauldron was empty, they replied, "Buddha's cousin Ananda is observing the monastic precepts in order to be reborn in the god realms. When he dies, he will take rebirth there, but after five hundred years of perfect luxury, his merit will be exhausted. Then he will fall into this cauldron and be boiled alive for five hundred years."

Ananda was distraught. *What good will it do?* he thought. *Even if I keep observing my vows and am reborn in heaven, if it ends in this unthinkable suffering, what is the point?!*

When he returned to their meeting point, he declared before Buddha that henceforth he would observe his precepts with renunciation, the wish to be free from samsara's three realms. "What has changed?" Buddha asked. "It's just as you said, after all. Karma is undeceiving. Now that I have seen both heaven and hell, finally I can see the truth of that. From this point onward, I will shun all misdeeds!"

There are two types of misdeeds: natural misdeeds and proscribed misdeeds. Natural misdeeds are actions such as the ten nonvirtues that are harmful by nature. Proscribed misdeeds, such as transgressing monastic precepts, were prohibited by Buddha for certain types of practitioners and in certain contexts. If you avoid proscribed misdeeds, you will automatically avoid natural misdeeds.

Even in our human realm, we witness the horrendous suffering of war, famine, poverty, and plagues. Even in the wealthiest of countries, such as Canada and the USA, you find homeless people living in squalor and despair. They go unwashed for many months at a time, and have to make do without shelter, without regular food, drink, or care. And of course, in poorer countries like Somalia, tens of millions of people are suffering terribly. All this suffering is the ripening, or result, of negative karma—of sinful deeds—accumulated in this or previous lives.

Dodrubchen Jigme Trinle Ozer[102] was the heart son of Jigme Lingpa. He became an incredible master, like Guru Rinpoche in the flesh. And yet he began his life as a gangster! He thieved, robbed, and hunted throughout his youth. He got up to all manner of mischief. One day he went out hunting, and soon he spotted a deer. He aimed his gun, pulled the trigger, but the bullet missed. He pursued the deer and shot at it again, and again, and again. He was usually a good shot, but much to his ire, this deer was managing to evade every shot he fired.

Eventually, the deer fled onto the spur of a hill and stood with its hindquarters facing him. As he aimed his gun, his gaze was drawn into the deer's genitals where, to his amazement, the three lower realms appeared as vividly as a scene on a movie screen. When he looked up, the deer was now standing with its torso facing him, and within its torso appeared the higher realms of humans and gods, brim full of suffering. Right there and then he saw directly with his very own eyes that no matter where you are born in samsara, in the higher or lower realms, there is not a drop of real happiness to be found. This experience was a turning point in his life. It inspired him to give up his errant ways and devote himself to the Dharma. To this end, he set out for Tsering Jong in Central

Tibet where he met Omniscient Jigme Lingpa. He became one of Jigme Lingpa's greatest disciples, an object of refuge for all beings. (Dodrupchen Rinpoche, Tubten Trinle Pal Zangpo,[103] who recently passed away was his fourth incarnation.) Seeing that the unbearable sufferings of samsara are the ripening of negative karma, bodhisattvas shun all sinful deeds. They guard against negative karma as vigilantly as one guards one's own eyes.

This verse concerns the path of lesser beings, who are concerned primarily with avoiding the lower realms and attaining rebirth in the higher realms. Needless to say, this is not the motivation of bodhisattvas. However, the bodhisattva still needs a healthy fear of the lower realms and the sinful actions that propel one there. If rebirth in the higher realms cannot be attained without shunning the ten unvirtuous actions, there is certainly no hope of attaining liberation and awakening while still engaging in unvirtuous deeds. And if they are trapped in the lower realms, the bodhisattva cannot fulfill their pledge to establish all beings in perfect buddhahood. That would be like someone whose knees are so bad that they can barely stand up suddenly announcing that they are going to leap to their feet and sprint.

CHAPTER 13

The Path of Middling Beings

Detaching Yourself from Samsaric Pleasures and Redirecting Your Efforts Toward Liberation

> 9. The happiness of the three realms is like dew
> on grass.
> It evaporates in an instant. Therefore,
> To strive for the supreme state of liberation,
> Everlasting, is the practice of bodhisattvas.

The path of middling beings is that of the shravakas and pratyekabuddhas. Practitioners of middling capacity seek liberation from the three realms of samsara.[104] They are not content to continue circling in samsara, not even in the higher realms.

The three realms are the desire realm, form realm, and formless realm. They make up the whole of samsara, from its most degraded to its most elevated states. The three realms are an ocean of suffering; there is no genuine happiness to be found there. As Buddha Shakyamuni taught,

> On the needle tip of samsara,
> There is not a moment of happiness.

And as Guru Rinpoche, the Great Master of Oddiyana, also stated,

> It is said that in this samsara there is not as much
> As a pinpoint's worth of happiness to be found.[105]

And,

> In samsara there is no happiness,
> Just as there is no sweet scent to excrement.

In the human realm, no matter how admirable someone's situation might seem, they are still subject to suffering. Dissatisfaction, restlessness, and mental angst continue to plague them, not to mention the inescapable sufferings of aging, sickness, and death. You might go to a five-star restaurant, or even a six-star restaurant, and enjoy a buffet brimming with the finest food from all corners of the world, and then you might go home and tell all your friends how amazing it was. I have done this myself. But think about someone who is even better off than you are, such as the owner of this restaurant, or the owner of a chain of five-star hotels. They can have this kind of food every day of the year. But despite their wealth and privilege, they continue to suffer in so many ways.

In my role as a teacher, I meet many different people. Sometimes I will meet a wealthy businessperson who seems perfectly content. *How wonderful*, I'll think to myself. But then I will meet them a second time, and maybe a third, and inevitably they will start revealing their discontent. They will tell me they are unhappy in their marriage, or they are worried about their children, or their investments are not doing as well as they would like, or perhaps they are simply troubled by a lingering sense that despite all they have achieved in life, something is missing. As Gendun Chopel wrote,[106]

> When looked at, the marvels of the world seem pleasing.
> When attained, each has its own suffering.[107]

Once I was flying in business class, thanks to the kindness of some friends. Behind me I heard a croaky voice. Turning around, I saw an elderly gentleman who was partly paralyzed and barely able to speak. He was clearly very wealthy—he was well-dressed and had two personal assistants attending to his needs—but he was suffering terribly. The loneliness etched on his gaunt face, his frail body propped up in the luxurious business-class seat—the mere sight of him filled me with compassion and dread.

The so-called happiness of the mundane world is not genuine happiness. The things we aspire to—wealth, status, worldly companionship—are not worthy aims because they do not deliver the fulfillment we long for. These supposed pleasures do not last. They are as transient as drops of dew on blades of grass; the dew quickly evaporates in the morning sun. The only lasting happiness to be found is in the Dharma, in the true nature of things. As the Great Tropu Lotsawa said,[108]

> When you take to heart a single Dharma,
> All suffering is happiness,
> All samsara is nirvana,
> All thoughts are dharmakaya,
> All afflictions are primal wisdom.

Forget about the lofty teachings of the Great Seal and the Great Perfection. If you really gain confidence in the truth of a single point of Dharma, such as the principle of karma or the difficulty of attaining a well-favored human birth, then you will be happy. You will be content and at ease. If you fall sick, you will know that it is the ripening of your negative karma, so you will be able to accept your situation and work with it. Your body might be suffering, but your mind will be at ease. Similarly, if you find yourself struggling financially, despite being frugal and working hard, you will recognize that it is the result of stinginess and a lack of merit from past lives. And, as Khenpo Chokhyab Rinpoche would say, if you have taken impermanence to heart, even if you are suffering today, you will not be disheartened for you know that everything is subject to change. Likewise, when things are going well for you, you will not swell with pride because, who knows, tomorrow things might change. Such is the power of taking just one of the four mind changings to heart.

As the saying goes, the Buddhadharma lifts you up when you are down and keeps you grounded when you are high. You might react to misfortune with anger or by falling into depression or low self-esteem. Or you might react to mundane success with pride and euphoria. Regardless, the remedy for all these painful reactions is the same: Whether it be profound emptiness or impermanence, or karmic cause and effect, when you take a single point of Dharma sincerely to heart, your suffering will ease.

These days, much of our physical suffering has been eradicated by modern medicine. In the past, think of the suffering a single tooth cavity would cause! Now you can take painkillers to numb the pain until your dentist appointment, then the dentist can fill your cavity and the problem is solved. However, modern medicine and material improvements cannot solve mental suffering—as is made painfully clear by the mental-health crisis plaguing the materially developed world. As Mipham Rinpoche said,

> Worse than the suffering of an empty stomach
> Is the mental suffering of being overlooked.

The cure for mental suffering is the Dharma—the pure Dharma. *Pure* means unsullied by worldly concerns, by the concerns of this life. When we practice, we really need to check our motivation and discard all attachment to the things of this life.

Otherwise, no matter how much seeming Dharma practice we engage in, it will not bring us happiness. We will be like someone holding tight onto a burning coal and screaming out in pain. Only when we drop our attachment to the three realms of samsara and engender confidence in karmic cause and effect will we begin to discover genuine happiness. As Omniscient Longchenpa said,

> When you see the truth of awakening, you will become the victors' heir.
> When realization dawns within you, you will be eternally at ease.

Once you have realized the Dharma, the true nature of all things, even if you are thrown into the lower realms, you will not suffer—you will be "eternally at ease." These lines remind me of the late Dilgo Khyentse Rinpoche. He seemed to embody freedom from thought. He was so stable, so at ease. He was as vast and open as the sky. It was a joy just to be in his presence. Due to the strength of their realization, masters like Dilgo Khyentse Rinpoche are "eternally at ease." Until we attain such realization for ourselves, we will never be truly at ease, no matter what samsaric "pleasures" we might attain.

You might think that, even if human life is laced with suffering, the gods in the form and formless realms must have some happiness, with their heavenly sense pleasures and refined mental states. However, the so-called happiness of the gods is limited and impermanent, because it is the conditioned result of positive karma. As this karma ripens, it is exhausted, and the gods then fall to lower and lower states. Eventually, they fall from the god realms altogether, perhaps to the human realm, if they are lucky. But if their time in the god realms has exhausted all their positive karma, they will fall straight into hell.

In the god realm, their death is foreshadowed by five signs: the brilliant effulgence of the god's body begins to dim; they begin to tire of their throne for the first time; their flower garlands, which until then had been perpetually fresh, begin to wilt; their clothes, which had always been clean and fragrant, begin to smell; and their body, which had never perspired before, begins to sweat. When these five signs appear, their friends and consorts abandon them, and they suddenly realize that death is imminent. With their clairvoyance, they can see where they will be reborn, which is almost always the lower realms, and seeing this causes untold anguish—an anguish that lasts seven days. You might think, *That doesn't sound too bad. After all, it's just seven days.* But these seven days are said to be the equivalent of several hundred human years. Time is not a fixed phenomenon. We can see this for ourselves. When life is going well, entire months fly by in what feels like a few seconds, but when we are unhappy or in physical pain, a single night can feel like eternity. Pain and pleasure are mental perceptions, or mental projections, and their duration is too.

My uncle once heard a story from another lama that illustrates this point. In the past, there was a lama living in a hermitage in the mountains of Tibet. One of his students was struggling to understand the teaching that an eon can transform into an instant and an instant into an eon.

"Is that really possible?" he asked.

"It is indeed possible," the lama said.

"But, how? I mean, can you transform time like that?"

"Yes, I can," the lama said.

When he heard this, the student was stunned. He was silent for a moment. Then he said, "Can you show me?"

"Sure," the lama said.

The lama then told his student that he was going to begin a three-year retreat in several days. "Go down to the village and inform everyone," he said. The student did exactly that, and the next day many villagers and local students came up to the hermitage to pay their respects. They presented offerings and katas, requested prayers, and extended their best wishes for his retreat.

That evening the lama sealed the boundary and began his three-year retreat. Then, the following morning, the lama told his student he would be wrapping up his practice for his retreat had come to an end. "What do you mean? You said you'd be on retreat for three years. Only one night has passed," he said. The lama, however, was insistent. He dismantled the boundary and announced that he had concluded his three-year retreat. The student thought his teacher had lost his mind.

"Now, go down and tell everyone that I've finished my retreat," the lama said.

Hearing this, the student cringed and thought to himself, *What will everyone think, when our teacher leaves his three-year retreat after a mere twenty-four hours?* Nevertheless, heeding his teacher's word, he went down to the nearby village and informed everyone that their teacher was now out of retreat.

With great delight, the villagers hurried up the mountainside to see him. One after the other, they asked the lama how his health was faring, how he had been these last few years. Some remarked that he had put on weight, others that he had lost it. They all shared the perception of three years having passed, whereas in the student's perception it had been just a single day. This lama, through the strength of his realization, had transformed the experience of a day into the experience of three years, and vice versa. Such things are difficult for us to understand.

Time, like all things, is neither permanent nor real. It is dreamlike and illusory. Time is a mental perception, a product of delusion, and so too are pleasure and pain. This is why a supposedly short period can stretch into eons when we are in pain and why entire years can feel like mere days when we are happy. Therefore, we should not belittle the suffering of the god realms. A god's final seven days of suffering are unbearably long, each moment filled with incredible pain.

In short, the three realms of samsara are an ocean of suffering. As Guru Rinpoche and Buddha Shakyamuni both said,

> On the needle tip of samsara,
> There is not a moment of happiness.

And,

> In samsara there is no happiness,
> Just as there is no sweet scent to excrement.

Could you bear to live in a filthy latrine, amid piles of reeking excrement and pools of putrid urine? Likewise, how can we bear to remain in samsara, where all seeming happiness is the nature of suffering and unease?

Knowing this, practitioners of middling capacity strive for liberation from samsara, the cessation of suffering. This is a state of partial awakening, or semi-buddhahood, attained by shravaka and pratyekabuddha arhats. This state should not be belittled. Here, one is freed from taking rebirth in samsara ever again, and one abides for many eons in a state of deep meditative absorption. By comparison, how futile and fleeting our mundane pursuits are shown to be.

As Chandrakirti taught in *Introduction to the Middle Way*,

> Beings think "I" at first and cling to self;
> They think of "mine" and are attached to things.
> They thus turn helplessly as buckets on a waterwheel—
> To compassion for such beings I bow down![109]

It is our belief in the existence of a self that traps us in samsara. We perceive a truly existent self in the five aggregates, and so we develop a sense of "I." For instance, I believe I am Pema Rigtsal, that I exist as an independent, whole, substantial person, like a neatly rolled long-life pill.[110] With reference to "me" comes the notion of "mine," which triggers attachment, aversion, and a stream of other afflictions. These afflictions generate karma, which keeps the wheel of samsara spinning around and around. Liberation is achieved by realizing the nonexistence of "I," the personal self, while perfect buddhahood is achieved by realizing, in addition, that all phenomena lack reality.[111]

In short, to attain liberation, we need to uproot our self-clinging, our conception of self. To do this, we need to apply ourselves to the Dharma, from shunning the ten unvirtuous actions up to training in profound emptiness through the teachings of the Great Middle Way, the Great Perfection, and the Great Seal. Even if we are unable to attain liberation in this life, by reducing our self-clinging, we will ensure a positive rebirth for ourselves and be able to continue training on the path. We will gradually traverse the lesser, middling, and greater stages of the path of accumulation, and then the stages of warmth, summit, acceptance, and supreme attribute on the path of joining.[112] And as taught in *The Ornament of Clear Realization*, when you reach the stage of acceptance on the path of joining, you will never again be reborn in samsara; you are sure to attain liberation in this life.

To reiterate, whatever practice we do, it should erode our self-clinging. That is the real sign of progress, not the number of mantras we have accumulated or the number of years we have spent in retreat. The attainment of mundane accomplishments, or *siddhis*, such as higher perceptions or powers, is also not a genuine sign of progress. Such accomplishments are defiled, limited phenomena—nothing to brag about.

Devoting oneself to practice in solitude is the indisputable method for transforming our minds. However, there is a potential pitfall here. There are people who have spent many years in retreat, who have recited millions of mantras and meditated for thousands of hours, but they are still writhing with attachment, still arguing with their neighbors and bickering with their families. Failing to merge the Dharma with their minds, they have become immune to its power, like a patient who has become resistant to antibiotics. Khenpo Chokhyab Rinpoche would say, "When you see someone like this, rouse compassion." When you see a practitioner with these kinds of faults, even if they are a lama, just feel compassion for them. Think, *Poor them! They still haven't eliminated their self-clinging, they still haven't turned their minds to Dharma.* This is a totally unmistaken response. This was one of Khen Rinpoche's pith instructions, and we should take this to heart. Because we will encounter all sorts of people in life, people going through all sorts of ups and downs.

Khenpo Chokhyab Rinpoche would say, "In self-clinging, there is nothing but the stench of shit!" Whether the self-clinging is yours or another's, it makes no difference. It stinks of shit, simple as that. He would say, "Even if you prostrate your way from Kham to the precious Jowo in Lhasa,[113] even if you stay on a strict three-year retreat, even if you circumambulate the most precious stupas thousands of times, if self-clinging is still trailing behind you, there's nothing to brag about. There's nothing special going on." There is no greater instruction than this.

We need to relinquish our attachment to the things of this world. When we do so, it is such a relief. It is like putting down a heavy backpack after a long, arduous journey. Finally, you are released from that burdensome weight.

It is the practice of bodhisattvas to strive for the supreme state of liberation, the state of shravaka- and pratyekabuddha-arhat. This is not to say that a bodhisattva pursues this goal for themselves, just as a bodhisattva does not seek rebirth in the higher realms. A bodhisattva does not follow the paths of lesser or middling beings. However, since they have pledged to benefit all beings, and since beings have various inclinations and capacities, it is the duty of the bodhisattva to have knowledge of all paths that can help beings, even in temporary ways.

It would be wonderful if every being could be set on the path to perfect buddhahood immediately, but that is not always possible. Some beings are more interested in attaining rebirth in the higher realms, while others are more interested in pursuing mere liberation from samsara instead of perfect buddhahood. While these states are not the complete fulfillment of our potential, they are still worthwhile goals, and they are significant steps toward perfect buddhahood. As Regent Maitreya teaches in *The Ornament of the Mahayana Sutras*,

> Without being diligent in the five sciences,
> Even the highest of noble beings will not attain
> omniscience.
> Therefore, in order to subjugate others, to care for them,
> And to know all things themselves, they are diligent in
> these.[114]

Thus, the bodhisattva must equip themselves with knowledge of all five major sciences in order to benefit beings. The five major sciences are the secular sciences of craftsmanship, medicine, logic, and linguistics, and the inner science of Buddhadharma. The bodhisattva should be skilled in linguistics and logic so they can communicate skillfully with others and dispel their doubts. They should be skilled in the arts of medicine and craftsmanship so they can care for beings and attract students. And of course, they should be skilled in the inner science of the Buddhadharma so they can lead beings to liberation and awakening. In short, there is nothing a bodhisattva should not learn for the benefit of beings.

CHAPTER 14

The Path of Greater Beings

Generating the Motivation of Supreme Bodhichitta[115]

> 10. When all mother-beings, who have loved you through the ages,
> Are still suffering, what use is your own happiness?
> To generate bodhichitta, so as to free all beings
> Beyond count, is the practice of bodhisattvas.

With this verse we begin studying the path of greater beings. This is the actual path of bodhisattvas, those who arouse supreme bodhichitta, the mind set on perfect buddhahood that transcends the extremes of existence (*samsara*) and peace (*nirvana*). Those following the shravaka and pratyekabuddha paths can attain personal liberation from the extreme of existence, but they cannot attain the state of perfect buddhahood that is free also from the extreme of peace.[116]

One's intention determines one's destination. For example, if your aim is to reach the neighboring village, you are not going to get any further than that. Shravaka and pratyekabuddha practitioners aim for personal liberation alone. They do not aim for the state of perfect buddhahood that is endowed with the awakened powers, aspirations, paramitas, and so on that can benefit beings on a vast scale, and so they do not accomplish that. However, the bodhisattva has pledged to lead all beings to awakening, so it is insufficient for them to attain liberation for themselves alone. They must attain perfect, complete buddhahood, and to do that, they must arouse the vast and courageous mind of bodhichitta, the unity of emptiness and compassion. To benefit beings on a vast scale, one needs a vast mindset. The bodhisattva who generates bodhichitta and strives for others' benefit will automatically attain buddhahood themselves along the way.

We defined bodhichitta earlier, but to reiterate, bodhichitta is a mind that is focused on beings with compassion and focused on perfect awakening with wisdom. As *The Ornament of Clear Realization* states,

> The generation of bodhichitta is, for the welfare of others,
> The desire for completely perfect enlightenment.[117]

And *The Ornament of the Mahayana Sutras* teaches,

> The bodhisattva's intention
> Is the mental factor associated with two aims.[118]

The first two lines of the root verse, "When all mother-beings, who have loved you through the ages / Are still suffering, what use is your own happiness?" encapsulate the compassion aspect of bodhichitta, while the third and fourth lines, "so as to free all beings / Beyond count," encapsulate the wisdom aspect. In short, bodhichitta is the wish to free all beings from the suffering of samsara and establish them in the lasting happiness of perfect buddhahood. Bodhichitta is focused on achieving lasting, ultimate happiness for all beings, not the temporary, limited happiness of good health, prosperity, security, and so on.

Furthermore, bodhichitta can be classified according to the three degrees of courage, the bodhisattva levels, and in many other ways.[119] When classifying bodhichitta in terms of its nature, we can speak of relative bodhichitta and ultimate bodhichitta. Relative bodhichitta has two aspects: aspiration bodhichitta and application bodhichitta.

Aspiration bodhichitta is the thought, *How wonderful it would be if all beings were awakened!* To act on that wish and train in the six paramitas to that end is application, or engaged, bodhichitta. As Shantideva explains in *Entering the Way of the Bodhisattva*,

> Just as they know the difference
> Between the wish to go and going,
> The wise should understand the contrast
> Between these two, respectively.[120]

Aspiration bodhichitta is like wishing to go somewhere. Application bodhichitta is like setting out on the journey.

Relative and ultimate bodhichitta are both minds set on attaining perfect buddhahood for the benefit of all others, free of selfish aims. Both are endowed with compassion focused on beings and with wisdom focused on buddhahood. However, in terms of their reference points, they are slightly different. Relative bodhichitta, with its aspects of aspiration and application, arises with reference to the way things appear. Through this subjective lens, one sees the apparent suffering of beings and so resolves to establish them in the lasting happiness of buddhahood. Ultimate bodhichitta, which is essentially the realization of the ultimate nature, emptiness with a natural core of compassion, is focused on *dharmadhatu*.[121] Its reference point is the true nature of things, not the way things appear. Seeing that all phenomena, the world and all beings, lack true existence, that they are like illusions and dreams, great nonreferential compassion arises, and with that, ultimate bodhichitta is born.

The buddhas, with their unimpeded wisdom, see that all beings are related as mother and child. Every being, without a single exception, has, at some point in our countless past lives, been our mother and showed us tremendous kindness and love. As Nagarjuna states in *Letter to a Friend*,

> A heap of all the bones each being has left
> Would reach to Meru's top or even higher.
> To count one's mother's lineage with pills
> The size of berries, the earth would not suffice.[122]

In the sutras, we can read the many stories Buddha Shakyamuni told to illustrate the kindness of our mothers. One such story tells of a mother bird nursing her three chicks in their nest when a fire broke out in the forest. The fire quickly gained in strength, and soon the entire forest was encircled by flames. At first the mother bird tried to lift her chicks up with her beak and fly them to safety, but they were too heavy and too big. As the flames began to engulf the surrounding trees, as smoke filled the air, she realized that since she could not fly her chicks to safety, the only way to save them was to extinguish the fire. She flew through the billowing smoke to a nearby lake and dove down into the water. With her feathers dripping, she flew back to her chicks. She sprinkled the water from her wings on the encroaching flames, then turned around and flew straight back to the lake. Her heart was pounding in her chest. Her eyes and throat were stinging with the smoke. Still, she carried on, soaking her wings and then flying back into the blazing forest to extinguish the flames, again and again.

It goes without saying that the chicks were killed in the fire, and the mother bird too. There was never any chance that she could extinguish the fire by herself, but her love for her chicks compelled her to try anything and everything to save them, even if it meant sacrificing her own life. Such is the strength of a mother's love for her child, even in the animal realm.

Around 1979, a group of nomads were camping in Nakchuka in Tibet. These nomads kept large flocks of sheep, and the sheep were being preyed upon by a local wolf. Sick of losing their livestock, the nomads decided to kill the wolf. One day, a group of forty or fifty men headed up into the mountains in search of the wolf's lair. They did not find the adult wolf; instead, they found three cubs. Some of the men suggested stoning the cubs to death right then and there. They reasoned that once her cubs were gone, the mother wolf would surely leave. The others were not so sure. They suggested catching the cubs and taking them down to the plains. Then the mother wolf would be sure to come looking for them, and they could kill them all together, like killing two birds with one stone. So, they took the three wolf cubs down to the plains, planted a stake in the ground, and tied all three cubs to the stake. They surrounded them with a ring of foliage and wood and doused it with oil.

As dusk was approaching, they set up watch, armed with guns, sticks, and stones, and then they set the ring of foliage and wood alight. As the flames rose up around them, the cubs, in their terror, began to howl, and sure enough their mother soon appeared. She came racing down the mountainside. Without a moment's hesitation, she ran past the men and leaped through the flames to her cubs. She picked each one up by the scruff of the neck, but they were tied to the stake and no matter how hard she pulled she could not free them. When the men began firing at her and her cubs with bullets, pelting them with stones and sticks, she dropped her cubs and turned on the men, leaping at them with bared fangs. But then she heard her cubs howling in fear, calling to her, so she turned back. She leaped back through the fire and tried once more to free them. Then, when the men started aiming stones at the cubs, she jumped back through the flames and launched herself at them. She kept on like this until the nomads had shot, stoned, and beaten her and her three cubs to death. Such is the love that mothers have for their children, even in the animal realm.

All beings have been our kind mothers in the past, and right now they are suffering in so many ways. If they are currently in the lower realms, they are being tortured by unbearable heat, cold, hunger, and other unthinkable pains. Even if they are currently in the higher realms, there is no reprieve for them. They are afflicted by the suffering of suffering, the suffering of change, the all-pervasive suffering of conditioning, and by the inescapable eight sufferings of birth, aging, sickness, and death, being parted from the things they love, having to encounter the things they dislike, having to live with unfulfilled longings, and being burdened by these defiled five aggregates—and so the list goes on.[123]

When our loving mothers are suffering like this, how could we even think to seek out happiness for ourselves alone? That would be like eating in a Michelin-star restaurant while our mothers are sitting outside on the pavement, hungry and alone.

There is no true happiness to be found in samsara's three realms. True happiness, and true freedom, can only be found in perfect buddhahood, and there is no way to reach buddhahood without bodhichitta. This is the case whether you are following the path of the Great Vehicle or the path of the Vajra Vehicle. It is simply not possible to reach buddhahood without bodhichitta. Knowing this, the bodhisattva generates bodhichitta, the compassionate resolve to establish all beings in perfect buddhahood.

What is the object of bodhichitta, or the object with reference to which bodhichitta is generated? It is sentient beings who have all been our mothers in past lives and who are as limitless in number as the infinite reaches of space. When these beings were our mother, they showed us great kindness and selfless love. Every one of them longs for happiness and wants to avoid suffering. And yet, unaware that virtuous actions are the cause of happiness and unvirtuous actions are the cause of suffering, they engage in constant self-sabotage. Performing unvirtuous deeds in their search of happiness, they unwittingly destroy their chances of happiness with their own hands. Moved by the sight of their suffering, the bodhisattva thinks, *Now that I have attained this well-favored human birth, now that I have met with the sublime Dharma and a genuine spiritual friend, for the benefit of all mother-beings, I will practice the Dharma purely, free of all worldly concerns*. This is the mind of bodhichitta.

In books such as *The Words of My Perfect Teacher* and *Entering the Way of the Bodhisattva*, it is explained very clearly that to generate bodhichitta we first need to realize that all beings have been our mothers in past lives. Second, we need to recognize the kindness they showed us. Third, we need to wish to repay their kindness. If we take these three points to heart, bodhichitta can dawn.

In a similar vein, Lord Atisha elaborates on these three points with a seven-point causal sequence for generating bodhichitta. All of these points were first taught by Buddha Shakyamuni himself, but later on the great masters organized them into pith instructions for our benefit. The seven points are as follows:

1. realizing that all beings have been one's mother,
2. remembering their kindness,
3. wishing to repay that kindness,
4. generating loving-kindness,
5. generating great compassion,
6. generating pure intention, and
7. generating bodhichitta.

All of us came from our parents, no matter how old we might be. Without our parents, especially our mother, we would not be here. Think—really think—about the care and attention a mother shows her child in its early years. If a baby or young child is left unattended for a few seconds, they can injure themselves beyond repair. The very fact that we are here, alive and well with our limbs and sense organs intact, is a testament to our mother's care. If you were not raised by your biological mother but by your father, aunt, or someone else, recall their kindness. Even if you do not know your biological mother, nevertheless recall the kindness she showed you by carrying you in her womb for nine months and birthing you into this world.

About fifteen years ago, a gentleman I knew was unable to pay his son's school fees one year. With much regret, he had to pull him out of school. One day the father and son came to see me. When I asked about his son's education, the father told me what had happened. "How much are the fees?" I asked.

"Thirty-six thousand Nepali rupees," he said.

I thought about it for a second, then offered to pay the boy's school fees for that year, or a few years, until they could find a sponsor or find the money themselves. My younger brother, who was with me at the time, then turned to the young boy and said, "Did you hear that? Rinpoche is showing you even more kindness than your own father. Do you see what he just did?" He actually said this to the young boy, in front of his father as well. His words pierced my heart, and for a moment I was reduced to tears. Then I gave my brother a real scolding. I told him that while I had offered to pay the boy's school fees, that did not mean I loved the boy more than his father or that I was doing more for him. His father would not hesitate to sacrifice his own life for his son. If his son needed a blood transfusion, a kidney, or another organ, he would offer his own body without a second thought. We cannot put a price on love. To equate love with money—to think a parent's love for their child is as large or little as the money they spend on them—is utterly stupid. To think that way is not human; it is animal.

Even in the lower realms, mothers have tremendous love for their children. There is a story about the Indian master Jetari meeting a hungry ghost. This hungry ghost was the mother of five hundred children. In spite of her own overwhelming suffering, her only concern was their hunger and pain.[124] Not only do we need to recognize the kindness of all mother-beings, we need to wish to repay their kindness as well. Buddha Shakyamuni went all the way to heaven to repay his mother's kindness directly. His mother Mayadevi died seven days after giving birth to him and was reborn in Tushita Heaven. Years later, once he had grown up, renounced his kingdom, and attained buddhahood under the bodhi tree, he traveled to Tushita Heaven to repay his mother's kindness by sharing with her the nectar-like truth he had realized. Buddha stayed in Tushita Heaven for forty-nine days, teaching Mayadevi continuously until she was ripened and freed. Only then did he return to the human world. His return is now celebrated annually as one of the four major Buddhist festivals.

Likewise, the Tibetan warrior Gesar of Ling, who was an emanation of Guru Rinpoche, traveled to the hell realms on his magical horse to free his mother, who had been reborn there. The epic of Gesar tells the heart-wrenching story of how he battled the henchmen of hell to free his mother from suffering. As Patrul Rinpoche explains, even if you were to serve your parents by carrying them around the three-thousand-fold universe on your shoulders—your father on your right shoulder, your mother on your left—it would still not repay their kindness.[125] The only way to repay their kindness is to introduce them to the Dharma and cultivate virtuous deeds.

In the Western world, and in other corners of the world, modern mentalities seem to be eroding the precious bond between parents and children. These days, many children give little thought to their parents' kindness, and many parents regard their children with a troubling attitude. They regard parenting as an obligation and often think of it in financial terms. They feel they are obliged to pay for their children until they graduate from school or maybe from university. Of course, such parents love their children, but they view their parental role as a duty that at some point will come to an end, much to their relief.

As human beings, our minds are sharp and creative. This means that our mentality is quite changeable, and so our cultures and beliefs can change, for better or worse, very fast. In the United States and other developed countries, I have heard people say that they struggle to find inspiring examples of a mother's love. If that is the case, you can always look to the animal world, and to more traditional countries such as Nepal and India where the bond between parents and children is still very strong.

Our relationship with our parents is not always straightforward. But at the very least, our parents gave us our body, and it is thanks to this body that we are here, that we can be sitting here reading this book, that we can practice the sacred Dharma and enjoy life. As Buddha said,

> At best, this body is the support for your liberation.
> At worst, it is an anchor dragging you to the lower realms.

Everything rests on this body, and this body was given to us by our parents, most especially by our mother. This alone is an extraordinary gift that can never be repaid.

Followers of Buddha need to love and care for their parents. The way we show our love and care might differ according to the customs of our culture, country, and family, but no amount of cultural difference can negate the importance of loving and caring for one's parents. If we fail in this, we have failed as a practitioner. The Buddha himself stated this very clearly: You cannot be a genuine practitioner, a genuine Buddhist follower, if you fail to care for your parents. This he stated without any doubt.

Without recognizing the kindness of your parents—recognizing this deep in your heart—bodhichitta cannot dawn. And without bodhichitta, you cannot attain buddhahood. Bodhichitta is rooted in compassion, compassion is rooted in the awareness that all beings have been one's parents, and this begins with recognizing the kindness of our parents in this present life. To neglect one's parents and yet attempt to generate bodhichitta is nothing but a joke.

CHAPTER 15

The Application

Cultivating the Two Types of Bodhichitta

Cultivating Relative Bodhichitta

In Meditative Equipoise, Training in the Exchange of Self and Other

> 11. All suffering comes from seeking happiness for yourself.
> Perfect buddhahood is born from the wish for others' good.
> Therefore, to make a genuine exchange of your own happiness
> For others' suffering is the practice of bodhisattvas.

The previous verse taught that we enter the bodhisattva path by generating bodhichitta. That is the crucial first step. However, the job is not over yet. We need to nurture our bodhichitta—to strengthen it and ensure that it does not wane. As a famous bodhichitta prayer aspires,

> May the precious mind of bodhichitta
> Arise in those in whom it has not yet arisen,
> And where it has arisen, may it never wane
> But increase forever more!

For example, a couple might long for a baby, and then finally they get pregnant. But their child being born is not the end of the story. The baby needs to be looked after, to be fed, washed, and nurtured, day and night, for many years. Only then can it grow into a healthy child and into a capable adult. Similarly, once the bodhisattva has generated bodhichitta, they must nurture and develop their bodhichitta by training diligently in the bodhisattva practices.

Meditative Equipoise and Post-Equipoise

The cultivation of relative bodhichitta involves training in meditative equipoise and training in post-equipoise. All the various practices of the path can be condensed into meditative equipoise and post-equipoise. Simply speaking, meditative equipoise refers to an undistracted state of mind sustained in formal sessions of meditation, while post-equipoise, or post-meditation, refers to maintaining the continuity of one's practice during the ordinary activities of eating, traveling, sleeping, and so on.

In meditative equipoise, the bodhisattva trains in the exchange of self and other, which pertains to aspiration bodhichitta.[126] In *The Words of My Perfect Teacher*, the "Teachings on Meditation" chapter of *Entering the Way of the Bodhisattva*, and other more detailed books, training in aspiration bodhichitta is taught to involve three stages: learning to see others as equal to oneself, then learning to exchange oneself with others, and finally learning to consider others more important than oneself. Here, these three stages are condensed into one: exchanging self and others.

All our suffering comes from self-grasping, the erroneous belief in a true self. It is as simple as that. The root of samsara and its suffering is self-grasping, or self-cherishing. We conceive of a self, an "I," with reference to the five aggregates, and from this sense of self comes attachment, aversion, stupidity, pride, jealousy, and so on. These emotions are suffering in and of themselves, but they also create karma, which then ripens as further suffering. The root of all our suffering is self-cherishing, yet this cherished self does not exist. As Shantideva says,

> All the violence in the world
> And all the fear and suffering
> Arise from clinging to a self.
> What does that ogre do for me?[127]

The bodhisattva's practice of exchanging self and other is a profound method for reversing our clinging to this sense of self. As Shantideva says,

> All the happiness in the world is born
> Of wishing others happiness.
> All suffering in the world is born
> Of wanting happiness for yourself.
>
> What need is there to explain at length?
> The childish act for their own ends;
> The sages act for others' sake.
> Look at the difference between them.[128]

There really is not much more to say than this: Sentient beings pursue their own happiness. The result is suffering in samsara and the lower realms. Buddhas pursue the benefit of others. The result is the lasting happiness of awakening for others and for themselves. If you want to keep on suffering, continue just as you are. If you want to be freed from suffering, to attain liberation and buddhahood, you need to learn to exchange yourself with others and cherish others more than yourself. For as Shantideva says,

> If you do not exchange your pleasures
> For other beings' miseries,
> You will not achieve buddhahood
> Or have any happiness in samsara.[129]

As taught in *A Cornucopia to Fulfill All Wishes, a Commentary on the Three Sets of Vows*, the root of the personal liberation vows is renunciation of samsara, the root of the bodhisattva vow is altruism, and the root of the Secret Mantra *samayas*[130] is pure perception. Altruism is put into practice by exchanging one's happiness for other's suffering. One's happiness includes one's merit, wealth, health, status, and security. The bodhisattva gives this all away to others, and in return they take on all of others' physical and mental suffering, their misfortune, ill health, poor reputation, angst, and poverty.

There was once a teacher named Dharmarakshita, a pandita of the Shravaka Vaibhashika tradition in India. He had never heard the Great Vehicle teachings, but he was naturally very compassionate.

A man living nearby was afflicted by a severe illness. The doctors told him that the only thing that could possibly heal him was the flesh of a living human. The poor man fell into despair, wondering who on earth would give him their own flesh.

One day, Dharmarakshita happened to pass this man on the street. He could feel the man's distress, so he walked over to him and asked him what was wrong. When the man told him of his quandary, Dharmarakshita immediately offered to donate his own flesh. The man could not believe his ears. He was hesitant to accept, but Dharmarakshita immediately cut a chunk of flesh from his thigh and offered it to him.

Once you have realized emptiness, you no longer suffer or experience pain. As the Indian master Dharmakirti teaches in his *Commentary on Valid Cognition*,[131] for those who have directly realized profound emptiness, all sensations are of an equal taste. There is no difference between the feeling of being lovingly massaged with sandalwood oil and having one's limbs hacked off by someone filled with rage. However, Dharmarakshita had not yet realized emptiness, so he suffered terribly from this wound. For several days, he could not sleep. The pain was relentless, all-consuming. After a few days, when the pain had ebbed a little, he forced himself up and went to visit the sick man.

"I have recovered very well, thanks to your sacrifice. But look at the suffering I've caused you," the man said.

"Oh, you needn't worry about me. I have no regrets! I would happily give up my life if it could help you," Dharmarakshita said.

That night when Dharmarakshita lay down to sleep, he was filled with joy at the man's recovery, and despite the pain, he managed to drift off to sleep. In the early hours of the morning, he dreamed that a man with a radiant white complexion said to him, "O Great Being, those who wish to attain buddhahood must embrace hardships like this! Your actions are wonderful indeed!" He then spat on Dharmarakshita's wound and rubbed it gently with his hand, and the wound immediately healed.

When Dharmarakshita awoke, the dream was still vivid in his mind. He noticed that he was free of pain, and when he looked down at his thigh he saw, to his astonishment, that the wound had healed overnight. The man in his dream was an emanation of Avalokiteshvara, the bodhisattva of great compassion. Through the blessings of this encounter, the realization of emptiness soon dawned within Dharmarakshita, and a collection of seminal Indian texts on the topic of emptiness,

Nagarjuna's *Collections of Reasoning*, arose spontaneously in his mind. He had never heard of these treatises previously nor seen copies of them, but from then on he could recite them all by heart. This realization came from exchanging his happiness with others' suffering.

Exchanging one's happiness with the suffering of others is the vital practice of bodhisattvas. Nevertheless, to do so authentically is only possible once we have reached the first bhumi, Perfect Joy, and directly realized emptiness. Until then, the bodhisattva must train in a semblance of this profound practice. This is likewise the case with the six paramitas, meditation on emptiness, and so on. As ordinary beings in this degenerate age, where emotions run wild and debased views dominate, this practice is very difficult, but this does not mean it is impossible.

You can start with basic empathy—sympathizing with others when they are suffering and rejoicing when they are happy. You can start with small gestures, like taking the thinner cushion for yourself and letting someone else have the better cushion, instead of squabbling over seats in the teaching hall. In this and other ways, you can train in the mind-training maxim, *Profit and victory to others; loss and defeat to myself.*[132] When you are feeling unwell, train in thinking, "May others never suffer like this! May my sickness free them from their pain!" When you are enjoying a nice meal in good company, train in wishing that others might enjoy the same. Do not belittle the significance of these small acts. They are all valuable stepping stones.

If we do not start where we are, there is no way we will ever get somewhere else. If we train, gradually and consistently, in accord with our ability, we are sure to make progress. Then we will traverse the paths of accumulation and joining, and then reach the path of seeing, becoming a noble bodhisattva on the first bhumi, Perfect Joy.[133] This is how the path works: We traverse it step-by-step. On the other hand, if you have a defeatist attitude and do not even try, you will never get anywhere. A defeatist attitude closes the doorway to buddhahood and locks it firmly from outside.

Some people say bodhichitta feels like a burden and thinking about others' suffering makes them depressed. This a symptom of small-mindedness, of lacking the courageous bodhisattva mindset, and it is a symptom of not having understood that phenomena are no more real than illusions and dreams.

How does one practice exchanging one's happiness with others' suffering in meditative equipoise? What is the actual method to apply? Sit down in the meditation posture and imagine that lying in front of you is someone utterly destitute. They are terminally sick and in terrible pain. Alternatively, imagine a hell being or hungry ghost. Look at their suffering, feel compassion for them, and as you breathe out, visualize sending them all your health and happiness, security and strength, and your merit and practice of the Dharma in the form of clear white light. As the light dissolves into them, they receive all your health, happiness, and so on. Then, as you breathe in, imagine you are drawing in their ill health and poverty, their vulnerability and angst in the form of black light. Visualize it dissolving into you and really think that all their misfortune and suffering has exited them and entered you. Continue practicing like this, taking in their suffering and giving away your happiness, with a calm and concentrated mind. In Tibetan, this meditation technique is called *tonglen*: giving (*tong*) and taking (*len*).

If you continue to practice like this in formal meditation sessions, your jealousy will be replaced with joy and your depression with compassion and care. When you see others enjoying good fortune, you will not feel envious. Instead, your heart will be filled with delight. You will even come to feel fond of your enemies. When you encounter misfortune, you will think, *Through this suffering of mine, may I take on the suffering of countless beings! May they enjoy all my good fortune, my joy and wealth!* Thus, you will no longer be intimidated by personal suffering. Instead, it will become a valuable source of compassion by turning your mind to the sufferings of all other beings and fueling your wish to alleviate them. At the same time, others' happiness will become a source of joy, so you will always be happy yourself.

During Post-Equipoise, Using Adverse Circumstances on the Path

When the bodhisattva rises from the meditative equipoise of exchanging self and other, they enter post-equipoise, and here they encounter all sorts of circumstances. If the bodhisattva is not well prepared, these circumstances can become obstacles. The following post-equipoise practices equip the bodhisattva to make skillful use of all circumstances, thereby transforming them into supports for accumulation and purification, for progressing on the path. In this way, every possible situation can become an aid for enhancing bodhichitta, like fuel being poured on fire. And by extension, the bodhisattva's own suffering can be transformed into happiness. If we follow the way of bodhisattvas, we will not really suffer, no matter what we go through in life.

CHAPTER 16

How to Use Loss on the Path

> 12. If someone, in the grips of great desire,
> Steals all your wealth, or incites others to do so,
> To dedicate to them your body, possessions, and virtue
> Of past, present, and future is the practice of bodhisattvas.

You might lose your property to thieves, or your wealth might be taken from you by force. You could lose your wealth to relatives or close friends, even your spouse. Or perhaps someone in a position of authority uses their power to strip you of your property and status. Whether they steal from you themselves, "or incite others to do so," they act in the grips of great desire—an overpowering lust for wealth and property, or perhaps for status and power.

Worldly people would react with indignation. They would fight to get their property back, and they would try to take revenge on those who stole from them. However, a bodhisattva does not act like a worldly person. When a bodhisattva encounters loss, they respond not with outrage but with bodhichitta. They use the opportunity in the same way they use every other opportunity: to enhance their bodhichitta.

Bodhisattvas know that all beings, without exception, have been their loving parents in the past. They have trained in the profound practice of exchanging self and other. They understand that there is in fact no real self to be harmed by loss, and they are vividly aware of the faults and flaws of self-grasping. They also reflect on the workings of karma, and so they know it is likely that the person who stole from them was a karmic creditor from whom they themselves have stolen in past lives. In any case, they recognize that this person has been their mother in the past and has given them the priceless gift of love and life.

The word translated here as *dedicate* has two layers of meaning. The original Sanskrit term, in which the Tibetan is rooted, is *parinata*. The literal meaning of *parinata* is to transform. Its essential meaning is *dana*, to give. In this instance, the translation "dedicate" holds both meanings. By dedicating your merit as a cause for the awakening of all beings, you are giving it away to others and transforming it into such a cause.

Thus, when encountering loss, it is the practice of bodhisattvas to dedicate their body, possessions, and merit of past, present, and future to those who have taken from them and to pray that through this they may attain buddhahood.

My root guru Khenpo Dazer Rinpoche told us a story of a lama in Kham who was the head of a large, reputable monastery. Back then, all the best ritual items and supports of awakened body, speech, and mind (statues, scriptures, stupas, and so on) came from Lhasa. It seems this lama was quite wealthy in his own right. He saved up money and assets for many years, planning to acquire top-quality statues, instruments, and all the rest for his monastery. Then he set off for Lhasa with a traveling party of sixty or more officials and monks. There were no roads or cars at the time. They were traveling all the way on horseback and foot. Halfway through their journey, they were ambushed by an infamous gang of bandits called Golok Lojak, numbering in the hundreds and notorious for their yearlong pillaging sprees. They were perhaps the Tibetan version of India's feared armed robber Gabbar Singh. The lama and his caravan suddenly found themselves surrounded by this army of bandits, all armed with swords, knives, and guns. There was no way they could defend themselves, and nowhere they could run. The bandits closed in on them and robbed them dry. They took their livestock, their personal possessions, and all the money the lama had saved up over the course of many years. When the bandits were finished with them, the lama and his entourage were left with nothing but the clothes on their backs and the wooden bowls tucked inside their *chuba* folds.[134]

Many of the monks were dispirited and felt they should head back home. After all, even if they managed to reach Lhasa, they had no money to buy the statues and ritual objects they were traveling there for. The lama, however, urged them to continue.

"We may have been stripped of our wealth, but we are already halfway there. Let us continue as pilgrims and pay homage to the Jowo and the other sacred sites in the area," he said.

And so, they kept walking, in severely reduced circumstances, and a month or two later they arrived at Lhasa, the famed City of Gods. They spent several months there, practicing before the Jowo and at other holy sites. Eventually, though, the monks felt the urge to return to their monastery. When they suggested this to their lama, he surprised them by saying he would not be going anywhere.

"I didn't accomplish what I was hoping for, so I have no statues and the like to take back. Personally, I see no need to return. You can all go back if you like, but I'm staying here," he said.

His monks were distraught and said, "How can we even think of going back without you? Not only would we be returning empty-handed but without our precious lama too! Please come back with us, we beg you."

They wept, prostrated, and supplicated, but the lama was unmoved. He insisted that they return to their monastery and continue to practice and serve the Dharma there to the best of their ability. But he told them again, in no uncertain terms, that he would not be taking a single step in the monastery's direction. Rather, he was going to Samye Chimpu to practice. When they entreated him to at least let one of them stay with him as his servant, he said, "What need do I have for servants when I own no more than a single bowl?" His monks then set off back home with heavy hearts.

The lama practiced one-pointedly at Samye Chimpu for several years. He practiced so intently that he soon gained accomplishment. As the years passed, he became renowned for his realization. His fame even spread all the way to his monastery in Kham. Whenever he would teach, he would first pay homage to the bandits, Golok Lojak, with his palms joined at his crown: "My realization is due to the kindness of Golok Lojak. If they hadn't pillaged me, I would still be caught in the samsara of monastery management, entangled in the net of attachment and aversion. Thanks to Golok Lojak, those entanglements were torn away and I was given the chance to practice the Dharma authentically." Each time he paid homage to Golok Lojak, tears would fill his eyes.

This gang of bandits showed him greater kindness than his own root gurus and were the catalyst for his realization. Is it not true that enemies often show us greater kindness than friends? This lama's life story is a true example of turning adversity into a friend. Buddha taught that we should not flee from adversity. We will never escape it like that. We need to embrace adversity, to face it head on. This is the practice of bodhisattvas. When you encounter loss, infamy, illness, attachment, anger, or pride, take that very adversity as the path.

Whatever practice we are focused on, or if we are focused on scriptural study and debate, the same principle applies. We must make use of all circumstances: They must be brought onto the bodhisattva path. Otherwise, our study and practice are no more than a child's game.

CHAPTER 17

How to Use Suffering on the Path

> 13. If someone should seek to cut off your head,
> Though you've done them not the slightest wrong,
> To take upon yourself, with compassion,
> All the sins they've amassed is the practice of bodhisattvas.

The worst thing someone could do to you is cut off your head! If they cut your arms or legs off, there is still a chance you will survive, but if someone beheads you, it's "game over"—you're dead. If you hurt, steal, or disparage someone, it is understandable, in a worldly sense, that they would want to hurt you in return. Generally speaking, if you slap someone, they will slap you back. If you insult someone, they will insult you back. But imagine someone hurting you even though you have done them not the slightest wrong. People do all manner of monstrous things to each other, like siblings assaulting one another, children murdering their parents, parents killing their own children, and so on. Think of the Nepalese crown prince who murdered his siblings and parents in cold blood. Horrors that would once have been unthinkable are now happening daily throughout the world.

Even when faced with such unprovoked violence, it is the practice of bodhisattvas to take their aggressor's negative karma upon themselves. They know the infinite benefits of bodhichitta, as taught to them by their spiritual guides. So rather than reacting with anger, the bodhisattva responds with compassion and uses their suffering to strengthen their bodhichitta. They think, *This poor person is possessed by destructive emotions. They know nothing of the sacred Dharma, of what to adopt and what to reject. I, on the other hand, have attained a well-favored human birth. I have met the sacred Dharma, met genuine teachers, and learned how to distinguish virtuous from unvirtuous deeds. This person, who has been my loving parent in the past, is blinded by ignorance. In the future, they will have to experience the karmic ripening of killing—the unbearable torment of the hot and cold hells.* In this way, the bodhisattva gives rise to tremendous compassion, and without hesitation, they aspire to take on the harm doer's negative karma, including the karma of having killed.

In ancient India, there lived a Buddhist monk named Ravati.[135] He had attained the state of arhat and had mastery over miraculous powers. One day, he was in the forest with some fellow monks dying cloth for his robes. As he was busy dying his cloth, a man appeared. He explained that he had lost his calf and had been searching for it everywhere.

"You haven't seen him, by chance?" he asked.

"No, I'm sorry," Ravati replied.

Nearby, the monks had lit a fire on top of which they were heating a large pot of dye. Out of curiosity, the man looked into the pot, and to his horror he saw his calf's butchered head, hooves, flanks, and shoulders boiling away.

"You've killed my calf! How dare you?" the man cried out.

The monks protested, but before they could stop him, he seized Ravati, dragged him out of the forest, and took him before the king.

"Your Majesty, this monk not only stole my calf, but he slaughtered it for his own consumption! He poses as a follower of Buddha, but look at how he behaves! I entreat you to punish him for his wicked ways!"

The king turned to Ravati and asked if these accusations were true. Ravati replied that he had been falsely accused, and he had done nothing of the sort.

In order to settle the matter, the king ventured into the forest to examine things for himself. When he looked into the cooking pot, he saw, just as the calf's owner had, the butchered pieces of the calf's body boiling away.

"Shame on you!" the king said, and he promptly had Ravati thrown into an underground dungeon that was sealed from above so that not a single ray of sunlight could get in.

Several days later, much to his surprise, the man found his calf. He immediately went to see the king and apologized for falsely accusing the monk: "Your Majesty, I made a mistake. Please forgive me, and please release the monk at once."

The king agreed to do so but then got caught up with other affairs and completely forgot. Bhikshu Ravati languished underground for another six months.

Ravati's disciples, like their teacher, had miraculous powers. When Ravati failed to return after so long, they used their powers to find out where he was. They went to the king and, attesting to the monk Ravati's noble character, requested an appeal.

"Our teacher is a noble being," they said. "He would never kill or steal!"

This jolted the king's memory, and he rushed to the underground dungeon to have the innocent Ravati released. When they pulled him out of the dungeon, Ravati was little more than skin and bones. The king was mortified by his oversight, and when Ravati's students displayed their powers by soaring through the sky, it only deepened his remorse.

Turning to Ravati, the king said, "Monk, if your students are this accomplished, you, their teacher, must have similar, if not superior, powers. Why then did you let yourself be imprisoned for so long? Surely you could have freed yourself?"

"Your Majesty, my miraculous powers were suppressed by my negative karma. In a past life, I stole someone's calf and then framed a pratyekabuddha for the crime. The ripening of this negative karma made me unable to exercise my powers. That is also why the calf's owner saw a slaughtered calf in the cooking pot even though the pot was actually full of dye."

When the king, so ashamed of what had happened, announced that he would punish the calf's owner for his false accusation, Ravati requested to let him be.

"It was not his fault, Your Majesty. He perceived a slaughtered calf in that pot due to my past karma. It's my karma that was at fault, not him."

Both the king and the calf's owner confessed their wrongdoings before Ravati, even though he assured them that there was no wrongdoing to absolve. Following the way of bodhisattvas, out of compassion, Ravati took others' misdeeds upon himself. He bore no grudges and felt no anger. He understood that he had suffered because of his own negative karma created in past lives.

CHAPTER 18

How to Use Disgrace on the Path

> 14. If someone should declare before the world
> All manner of unpleasant things about you,
> To speak only of their qualities in return,
> With a loving heart, is the practice of bodhisattvas.

The abhidharma teachings tell of an infinite number of worlds. Each world, or world system, has at its center a Mount Meru surrounded by seven oceans with seven rings of golden mountains separating them. Encircling Mount Meru are the four continents and eight subcontinents. Humans live on the southern continent known as Jambudvipa. All of this is surrounded by a ring of iron mountains, and all together this makes up one world. One thousand such worlds constitute a thousandfold world system. A thousand of these makes up a second-order thousandfold world system. Then, when multiplied a thousand times further, this makes a third-order thousandfold world system, a universe of a billion worlds.

Imagine that someone sets up loudspeakers in every valley in every country in every continent in every single one of these billion worlds. Through these loudspeakers, all set to the highest volume, they blast insults and personal criticisms. Maybe they are accusing you of being a liar and thief, of being useless, immoral, passive-aggressive, abusive, or manipulative. They are saying terrible things about you, and not a single one is true. Not just one or two people but every single person in the billion worlds hears what is being said. Today, social media is probably a better example than a loudspeaker. Imagine someone spreading fake news about you online, resulting in you getting vilified and canceled, not just in this world but throughout all billion worlds. An ordinary person would react with anger and rage, or maybe they would become paranoid and depressed. However, the bodhisattva practitioner simply responds with patience and love.

An ordinary person would find this very difficult to do. They would probably struggle to even make sense of this response. Many years ago in the United States, Dungse Thinley Norbu Rinpoche gave an army general, who was a student of my late brother Shiva Rinpoche, a copy of his book *White Sail*.[136] Thinley Norbu Rinpoche told him, "Read this book and let me know what you think." When the general returned a few days later, he shook his head and said, "Rinpoche, your book is very beautifully written, but your message is just too extreme. There's simply no way an ordinary person can think the way you suggest."

Upon hearing this, Rinpoche burst out laughing. Then he said, "Well, you're certainly very honest! In a sense, what you say is true. It may well be near impossible for an ordinary person to adopt this mindset. After all, since time without beginning, we have been wandering blindly in samsara, and we are so habituated to the deluded state. However, you still need to try. You need to start moving in that direction. Otherwise, you will never reach buddhahood; you'll just keep circling through samsara with no end in sight."

Even though it is challenging, it is imperative that the bodhisattva practices like this. If you want to attain buddhahood, you need to train like this. To "train" does not necessarily mean you will succeed straight away; it means you apply yourself to the practice. You commit to moving in a certain direction and try your best.

I heard the following story about the Vidyadhara Jigme Lingpa from Tsewang Rinpoche. This story is not found in his written hagiographies but has been passed down through the oral tradition. This story illustrates how disgrace can inspire us to virtue, how a painful circumstance can be a great support for the path.

Jigme Lingpa's father was a *ngakpa*, a tantric lay practitioner, and he was adept in the esoteric practices that allow one to manipulate the weather and protect areas from hail. This was incredibly important, for hail was common in these areas. A single hailstorm could destroy an entire season's crop, resulting in severe food shortages and loss of livelihood. Jigme Lingpa had been trained in these esoteric practices by his father, and one day he was employed to protect a specific area of crops against hail. But that day, try as he might, he failed, and all the crops in the area were destroyed. The local people were furious, not to mention distraught. They bombarded him with insults, calling him a failure, a good-for-nothing, an embarrassment to his father, powerless, and inept. Jigme Lingpa was wounded by these insults, but he also thought, *What they are saying is true—I have no power, no realization.* He was disheartened—with himself and with the whole situation—but he did not try to defend himself. Instead, he resolved to leave his homeland and devote himself to practice. By accepting the criticism and facing his faults, this negative circumstance became a transformative support. In a sense, this defamation made him who he became—the peerless Vidyadhara Jigme Lingpa, who is universally revered up to this day.

How does the bodhisattva manage to practice like this, when ordinary beings cannot? First, the bodhisattva's goal—to attain perfect buddhahood for the benefit of all beings—gives them a vast perspective. Second, the bodhisattva has knowledge of emptiness. They understand that the self, this sense of "I," is a delusion and that self-clinging has countless faults. Third, they know that all beings have been their kind mothers, and they long to repay that kindness by leading them to ultimate happiness. They also know that their suffering is the ripening of their negative karma, so they do not try to defend themselves. On the contrary, they accept even baseless insults, and, on top of that, they embrace their critics with love, actively praising them for pointing out their faults.

CHAPTER 19

How to Use Slander on the Path

> 15. Even if someone, amid a great crowd,
> Should expose your hidden faults and deride you,
> To regard them as a spiritual friend
> And bow in respect is the practice of bodhisattvas.

Whereas the previous verse taught us how the bodhisattva should practice when falsely accused, this verse explains how they respond when their actual faults are exposed. "Someone" could refer to your parents, teachers, and the like who point out your faults with good intentions, or it could refer to people who do so out of malice. In any case, as Lord Atisha said,

> The best teacher is one who attacks your hidden faults;
> The best instruction is that aimed squarely at those faults.

Kind and gentle words certainly have their place in the teacher-disciple relationship, but more important than praise is criticism. This is how teachers tame their disciples. This is how they help disciples change. Like a surgeon operating on a patient, they open the student up and expose their inner faults so that those faults can be removed.

This approach might not appeal to modern people, especially those raised in the West. Nevertheless, this is how it is and how it needs to be—the guru's instructions should aim right at the student's faults. This teacher-disciple dynamic is a crucial part of the Buddhist path. If you are sick and you want to get better, sometimes you need to take bitter medicine. These days, it seems the teacher-disciple relationship is often compromised by modern environments and ideas. If a teacher criticizes their student, as is their duty, there is the real danger they will end up being vilified or even sued.

If someone reveals a bodhisattva's hidden faults before many people, the bodhisattva does not react with anger or defensive retorts. Nor do they become depressed or demoralized. Instead, they perceive the person reproaching them as none other than their spiritual friend, and they bow to them with respect. The bodhisattva thinks, *This person's criticism must be the compassionate activity of my root guru. They are exposing my shortcomings for my benefit so that I can begin to transform my negative character. Or maybe they are shaming me to dispel my obstacles*. This is the outlook a student should adopt. Even if they are being falsely accused, they should think this way. In short, they should view all criticism as the guru's helping hand in transforming themselves.

The great twelfth-century Tibetan yogi Milarepa is the best example of this. His guru Marpa Lotsawa treated him so harshly, not just for a month or two but for years on end. Marpa did this out of compassion, to help Milarepa purify his negative karma—the karma of murdering thirty-five people in this life, and all the misdeeds performed in his past lives as well. If Marpa's consort Dakmema had not intervened and shortened Milarepa's suffering, it is said that he would have been spared the hardship he endured when practicing in the mountains later on. No matter how tough things got, Milarepa always responded to Marpa's treatment with humility and respect. Even in his darkest moments, he did not doubt that his teacher's harsh treatment was for his own benefit. The criticism, the snubbing, the physical suffering—he took it all as the path. This is the main lesson of Milarepa's life story.

Once, when the nineteenth-century Tibetan master Patrul Rinpoche was living at Dzachuka, a respected Geluk geshe named Alak Gyawa came from Amdo to see him. By this point, Patrul Rinpoche was revered by all four major traditions of Tibetan Buddhism and universally renowned as an emanation of the great bodhisattva Shantideva. His scholarship was unparalleled, and his discipline was immaculate. He was perfectly learned, righteous, and kind, and he was a pure renunciate. Practitioners and scholars from all traditions flocked from all directions to receive teachings from him. (It is impossible to convey his qualities, but you can read Dodrup Tenpe Nyima's *In Praise of Patrul Orgyen Jigme Chokyi Wangpo*[137] and Patrul Rinpoche's hagiographies to get a taste of who he was.)

Patrul Rinpoche was in his seventies at this point. When Geshe Alak Gyawa, having heard of Patrul Rinpoche's great learning, requested him for teachings on the Prajnaparamita treatise *The Ornament of Clear Realization*, Patrul Rinpoche declined.

"First of all, I am an old man," he said, "so I'm not up to giving such lengthy teachings anymore. Second, you've already studied these teachings for many years, so you don't need to receive them again from me." When the geshe begged him to reconsider, Patrul Rinpoche said, "But you've been studying the Prajnaparamita for more than twenty years! If you haven't understood it in all that time, what use will it be to receive some brief teachings on it from me?" However, the geshe was determined and entreated Patrul Rinpoche once more. Eventually, Patrul Rinpoche said, "Well, if you really insist, then go away and stay away for three years. Stay completely out of my sight. After three years, if you still want to receive these teachings, and if I am still alive, then come back and I will think about it."

Back then, students really respected their teachers and took their instructions very seriously. So, Geshe Alak Gyawa did exactly as Patrul Rinpoche said. He went away for three years and then returned. When he arrived at Dzachuka, he was told that Patrul Rinpoche was presiding over a puja called "Cultivating Amitabha's Pure Realm" in one of the nomad encampments. The geshe made his way there and quietly took a seat at the back of the large crowd. How happy he was to be in Patrul Rinpoche's presence again!

A little while later, when one of the attendants informed Patrul Rinpoche that Geshe Alak Gyawa had returned after three years, Patrul Rinpoche, still seated on his throne at the head of the assembly, began laying into him: "That lousy Alak Gyawa! He's nothing but a dry intellectual, forever chasing after words. He roams around, debating with this and that teacher, and the more he studies the more his arrogance swells! He hasn't internalized a single word of his learning or taken a drop of it to heart." Pointing to a grimy trunk at the far end of the tent—a storage space for dirty shoes and other grubby odds and ends—he said, "Alak Gyawa is like that trunk." Then he pointed to the ornate cabinet behind him that contained fine food and valuables.

"And me? I am like this fine cabinet," Patrul Rinpoche said. "That is the difference between my learning and his!"

And on he went, reproaching Alak Gyawa ruthlessly in front of everyone. As this torrent of criticism rained down, the geshe simply remained in his seat with his head hung low. He spent the evening making prostrations in the direction of Patrul Rinpoche's tent. Eventually, Patrul Rinpoche called him inside.

"You did as I asked and stayed away for three years, and now you're back. That's good," he said. "Nevertheless, if you haven't understood the Prajnaparamita after all your years of study, I don't think an old man like me can teach you anything new. Still, I'll give you a short teaching today. If you understand it, very good, and if not, well, that's that."

Patrul Rinpoche was eating buttered *droma* (a wild sweet potato) and gave Alak Gyawa a handful. Then he began running through the eight topics of the Prajnaparamita treatise, *The Ornament of Clear Realization*—omniscience, knowledge of the paths, knowledge of the basis, and so on. Counting them out on his fingers, he quickly summarized each topic and clarified its difficult points.

When Patrul Rinpoche finished, Alak Gyawa burst into tears. Weeping at his feet like a small child, he said, "Despite studying this treatise for more than twenty years, only now have I understood it with clarity." In the time it takes to drink a cup of tea, in the time it took him to eat the handful of *droma* he had been given, Patrul Rinpoche had clarified the entire meaning of this vast treatise with utmost precision and profundity. Genuine understanding took root in Geshe Alak Gyawa and he saw Patrul Rinpoche as the Buddha in person. From then on, he stayed by Patrul Rinpoche's side and received many more teachings from him. This just shows that when a receptive student meets an authentic teacher, transformation does not take long.

When Patrul Rinpoche laid into Geshe Alak Gyawa in front of hundreds of people, he did not react. Patrul Rinpoche, of course, did this to shatter his pride and conceit, and he accepted the criticism as a valuable teaching. When we are instructed to regard our critics "as a spiritual friend / And bow in respect," this is how to do it.

Furthermore, in Karkung, a village in Humla, there was an old practitioner named Lama Rikdrol.[138] He was not a famous teacher like Patrul Rinpoche, but he was a genuine practitioner who had devoted his life to practice in mountain retreats. One day, Lama Rikdrol was having a drink with some neighbors and friends, as the lamas in the mountains sometimes do. It seems he said something offensive—who knows what—and one of the neighbors flew into a rage and beat him up. News spreads fast in the mountains, so by the time Lama Rikdrol arrived home, his children had heard what had happened. But when they asked him about it, he told them it was just gossip and not to worry themselves. He knew they would retaliate if he told them the truth, and no good would come from that.

The next day, the neighbor, now sober (and quite mortified), came to see Lama Rikdrol and offered him a kata and gift in apology.

"There's no need to apologize," Lama Rikdrol said. "If anything, you should have hit me harder, knocked me around a little more. You did me a favor, my friend. I am a lousy person. I deserve a beating. If only you'd beaten me up more!"

Of course, we see sublime beings such as Patrul Rinpoche demonstrating the way of bodhisattvas, but we see it in sincere practitioners as well. Genuine practitioners, regardless of which vehicle they are following, can get on well with anyone.

CHAPTER 20

Being Wronged in Return for Kindness

How to Use on the Path Being Wronged in Return for Kindness

> 16. Even if someone you've cared for like your own child
> Should turn on you and treat you as an enemy,
> Like a mother tending her ailing child,
> To love them even more is the practice of bodhisattvas.

Imagine you have cared for someone with the enduring love of a mother for her child. You have given this person so much of your attention, resources, and time. You have done nothing but your best for them. And then, all of a sudden, they turn on you and show you ill will and ingratitude. This is a situation that is truly "difficult to bear."

Sadly, this does happen these days. You read about adult children turning against their parents and taking them to court, or cheating them, or just cutting them off. You also see adult children who feel no affection for their parents. They are only interested in getting their inheritance and are just waiting for their parents to die. These are truly unbearable situations.

A mother might have several children, but if one of them falls sick, she will direct more of her attention to that child because they are suffering and in more need of help. If the child lashes out at their mother, pulling her hair and scratching her face, she will think nothing of it. No matter how badly the ailing child behaves, the mother will happily endure it; her sole concern is returning her precious child to a state of health. In the same way, if wronged in return for their kindness, it is the practice of bodhisattvas to generate even more love for the wrongdoer, like a mother for her ailing child.

When I was in my youth, I spent a few days at a hospital in Kathmandu with my late father when he was unwell. There were several psychiatric patients in the same wing. One of them was a young man around twenty years old. I do not know what he was diagnosed with, but it seemed to be a form of psychosis. He was being cared for by his parents, who looked to be in their sixties; they had wrinkled faces and gray hair. The young man was constantly lashing out at his parents, so much so that much of the time his hands had to be handcuffed to the bedposts. He would hurl his food at them, hurl himself at them, shout at them, but no matter how aggressive he was, his parents just continued caring for him with patience and love. In between dodging his kicks and blows, they would give him his medicine, spoon-feed him his meals, dress him, wash him, and try to soothe him with sweet words. One day the son got his hand free and slapped his elderly father across the face so hard that the sound echoed through the hall. The father was sent reeling. But as soon as he got back on his feet, he lovingly attended to his son again, saying "babu babu" (my sweet boy, my sweet boy) in an attempt to calm him down.

Anyone else would have given up on this young man long ago. But his parents did not falter in their love for a moment. They knew he was sick, so they showed him even greater love and care. The kindness of our parents is inconceivable. Only a devoted parent could have such enduring patience in the face of such relentless abuse. The sight of these parents straightening their son's clothes, picking up the hat he had just torn off and gently putting it back on his head, all the while showering him with loving words—it was heart-wrenching. I have never forgotten this.

If a bodhisattva finds that their kindness is returned with harm, they think, *This person has been my loving mother in the past. They are only behaving like this because they themselves are suffering.* They respond with yet greater love and care, and they never hold a grudge.

In one of his lifetimes before Buddha Shakyamuni lived as Sidhartha Gautama, he was a prince in the kingdom of Saketa in India. As a result of merit gathered in past lives, the crown of his head was adorned with a protuberance made of a precious jewel. For this reason, he was named Jewel Crest.[139] When he came of age, he was enthroned as king and ruled his kingdom with great benevolence. He shared the kingdom's wealth with all his subjects and gave whatever was asked of him. The reputation of the king's generosity spread far and wide, and one day a brahmin named Marichi came to see him. He told the king that his spiritual teacher had grown old and he wished to offer him some domestic help. To this end, he asked the king to give him his wife and his son, Lotus Crest. The king was so committed to generosity that he fulfilled the brahmin's request.

One of the neighboring kingdoms was ruled by King Jewel Crest's friend, a king named Hard to Endure. King Jewel Crest had a magnificent elephant called Excellent Mountain. This elephant was unmatched in strength and perfectly trained in warfare. King Hard to Endure had long coveted this elephant, and one day his covetousness got the better of him. He sent a message to his friend demanding that the elephant be given to him. But King Jewel Crest had just given the elephant away to one of his ministers. He told his friend that, sadly, he could not give him Excellent Mountain, but he would happily give him whatever else he wished. When King Hard to Endure received his friend's reply, he was overcome by rage and threatened to wage war.

King Jewel Crest was deeply saddened by this. He knew that if he fought back, he could win, since his kingdom was more powerful than his friend's. But he also knew that many soldiers would be killed in the process, not to mention civilians and animals and not to mention the damage done to the land. With a heavy heart, he decided to surrender his throne and flee. At this point, four pratyekabuddhas appeared before him.

"Your Majesty, it is time for you to go to the forest," they said.

The king then retreated to the forest, where he lived in solitude, foraging for food and passing his time in peaceful meditation.

In the meantime, King Hard to Endure seized the kingdom, and his misguided rule soon brought famine, plague, and unrest upon the land. In their desperation, the people sought out Brahmin Marichi and beseeched him to let the king's son, Prince Lotus Crest, take command of their army so they could retaliate against King Hard to Endure. The brahmin agreed, and Prince Lotus Crest led the kingdom's army to victory. King Hard to Endure retreated and soon the kingdom was restored to peace and harmony.

However, in King Hard to Endure's kingdom, the negative karma of his recent actions began to ripen. Harvests failed and plagues broke out. People were struggling to survive. Having performed their divinations, the brahmins told the king that only one thing could dispel these ills: King Jewel Crest's precious protuberance. This was not what King Hard to Endure wanted to hear. Why would King Jewel Crest, the friend he had turned against, ever consider helping him, after all that he had done? The brahmins consoled him, saying, "King Jewel Crest is a bodhisattva. If you ask him for his crown protuberance, he will not turn you away." King Hard to Endure then sent a messenger to make the request.

As King Jewel Crest was foraging for food in the forest, he happened to wander nearby Brahmin Marichi's house. At the same time, unbeknownst to him, his wife and queen consort, whom he had not seen for many years, was assaulted by a hunter. When the hunter grabbed her, she cried out, "King Jewel Crest, protect me!" Hearing this call in the distance, the king went to investigate, and when the hunter saw him coming, he fled. Seeing his estranged wife in such distress, the king was overcome.

Alas! All conditioned things are impermanent! he thought to himself.

At this point, King Hard to Endure's messenger arrived before King Jewel Crest and told him he had come bearing a request.

"But what could I have to give you? I gave away my power, status, wealth, and family long ago," the king said. The messenger told the king how plague and famine had ravished their kingdom and how the subjects were suffering.

"No amount of medicine, prayer, and ritual will help," he said. "Divinations show that it's only your precious crown protuberance that can dispel these miseries. If we take your protuberance, perform an ablution over it, and the subjects then drink the blessed ablution water, then, and only then, will our miseries come to an end. Your Majesty, it is your precious crown protuberance that we request."

The king saw that the time to give away his own body had come, and without a moment's hesitation, he acquiesced. The messenger, heartless as he was, immediately took a knife from his belt and hacked the precious protuberance off the king's head. A fountain of blood gushed from the wound and ran down the king's face, drenching his entire body. Racked with pain, the king felt a surge of compassion for those suffering in the hot hells. Then, growing weak from the loss of blood, the king passed out.

Prompted by this act of selfless charity, Indra and other gods appeared before the king. "To what end have you made this sacrifice? What is it you desire?" they asked. The king, having regained consciousness, replied, "I gave away my crown protuberance so the miseries afflicting King Hard to Endure's kingdom might come to an end. As for what I desire, I simply wish to establish all beings in liberation from samsara and the perfect happiness of buddhahood."

"King, we rejoice in your noble aspirations and your courageous act. Nevertheless, you seem to be in excruciating pain. Do you really feel no regret?"

"No, I have not a drop of regret! I gave away my crown protuberance with the pure wish to benefit my friend and his kingdom, and to lead all beings to liberation and omniscience. If this be true, with the Three Jewels as my witness, may my body be returned to its former state!"

As the king made this declaration of truth, his wound healed, his pain vanished, and the jewel protuberance reformed on the crown of his head.

Prince Lotus Crest then assumed the throne, and Brahmin Marichi offered the king's wife back to him. His subjects entreated the king to return to the royal palace, but the king refused. At this point, the four pratyekabuddhas appeared once more before the king and said, "Your Majesty, if you go to such lengths to help your enemies, why not help your kingdom and subjects too?"

The king then returned to the royal palace in Saketa and brought peace and prosperity to all corners of the land.

To attain buddhahood for the benefit of all beings, we need to be willing and able to practice like King Jewel Crest. We can also look at the great yogi Milarepa. He was abused by his aunt and uncle throughout his childhood, but he used that suffering to fuel his renunciation and compassion. We need to recognize the kindness and value of harm doers and be willing to use all difficulties on the path. This is the practice of bodhisattvas. They cultivate unwavering patience and love for all beings, most especially for those who show them ingratitude and do them harm.

CHAPTER 21

How to Use Disparagement on the Path

> 17. Even if your peers or inferiors should,
> Out of pride, do all they can to disparage you,
> To revere them like your teachers
> On the crown of your head is the practice of
> bodhisattvas.

If a superior disparages you, you might get annoyed, but you probably would not think to retaliate. After all, they are in a higher position, so even if you tried to get back at them you would be unlikely to succeed. For instance, around 2008 the Maoist party in Nepal began threatening my monastery. It was a very difficult situation, and it went on for several years. We stood firm and tried not to react, but we never considered pushing back because we knew we would lose if we did.

On the other hand, if someone equal or inferior to you—in terms of status, knowledge, accomplishments, and so on—disparages you due to pride, the worldly response is to speak back, to put them in their place, to stand up for yourself. However, the bodhisattva responds not with retaliation but with respect. They honor the person disrespecting them in the same way they would honor their root guru; they hold them in the highest esteem.

This is what is meant by the phrase "to revere them on the crown of your head." This phrase is used to illustrate the way the bodhisattva should respond to disparagement, but given how so many modern people struggle to relate to their teachers with deep reverence, I wonder how well it translates. These days, in Western countries such as the United States, it seems many people are studying and practicing the Buddhadharma and longing, apparently, for the blessings of realization to enter them. And it does seem that many of these Dharma students have become very knowledgeable, but it also seems that many of them are unable to relate to their teachers in an authentic way. If you regard your guru the same way you regard an ordinary, secular teacher, like a university professor, the blessings will never enter you. The way devotion is expressed can be cultural or contextual, but devotion itself is not. The guru-disciple relationship is not cultural; it is an indispensable aspect of the Buddhist path. This is a long-standing spiritual tradition with a history of more than twenty-five hundred years in India, and more than one thousand years in Tibet. If you wish to receive the blessings of this tradition, you need to follow the tradition accordingly.

Several years ago, a Tibetan lama was with some of his students in the United States. While scolding one of them, he pushed them on the shoulder in order to hammer home his point. One of the other students then stood up and said, "Hey, this isn't India or Tibet, you know?! This is the United States of America. You can't treat us like that, not here. If you don't watch out, I'll report you to the authorities." The teacher fell silent. What else could he do? In such an environment, amid such attitudes, how can the blessings ever be received? And how can the precious guru-disciple tradition be maintained? All Buddha's teachings, from the vehicle of characteristics up to the vehicle of Secret Mantra, explain explicitly and repeatedly how a disciple should relate to their teacher, how they should accept their teacher's scoldings with respect and regard them as pith instructions for their personal benefit. When the teacher is a realized being, their scoldings have enormous blessings and transformative power.

The best illustration of this is Marpa Lotsawa and his disciple Milarepa. Following Marpa's command, Milarepa had been building a nine-story tower for Marpa's son with his bare hands. He had been working day after day and was on the verge of physical breakdown. His back was raw and aching, his hands were covered with blisters, and his arms and legs were red with wounds. But still Marpa had not given him any teachings. One day, some disciples were requesting a Hevajra empowerment. Milarepa thought, *Surely my guru will let me join them. After all, I have been working so hard and the tower is almost finished.* When he realized he had nothing to give as an offering, Marpa's consort Dakmema took pity on him and gave him a precious turquoise stone. When the empowerment began, Milarepa followed the other students into the hall, but when he offered the turquoise, Marpa scowled and demanded to know where he had gotten it from. When Milarepa told him, Marpa was furious.

"Whatever belongs to Dakmema also belongs to me! You cannot offer me what is already mine," he said, and with that he kicked Milarepa out of the teaching hall yet again.

Milarepa placed Marpa's commands and reprimands on the crown of his head, time and time again. He endured his harsh treatment with devotion and trust, and as a result, his misdeeds and obscurations, including the murder of thirty-five people, were fully purified, and he was able to attain the state of Vidyadhara of the Great Seal in that very body and in that very life. Such is the power and purpose of a genuine guru's reprimands. Therefore, when encountering disrespect, it is the practice of bodhisattvas to revere those disrespecting them, just as Milarepa revered the reprimands of his guru Marpa Lotsawa.

As it is said, "There is no misdeed like hatred; / No austerity like patience."[140] Knowing the faults of anger and pride, the bodhisattva accepts all disparagement with humility, and they arouse compassion for the person disparaging them—a kind mother-being who is temporarily afflicted by pride.

CHAPTER 22

How to Use Poverty on the Path

> 18. Even when utterly destitute and constantly maligned
>   by others,
> Beset with terrible illness and plagued by evil forces,
> To draw upon yourself the sins and sufferings of all beings
> Without ever losing heart is the practice of bodhisattvas.

A bodhisattva might fall into poverty and find themselves with no money and nothing to eat or drink, like the homeless people living under bridges and underground. The bodhisattva might be scorned by others, the way societies often ridicule the uneducated or poor. On top of that, they might be afflicted with a severe illness, like a new variant of COVID-19, drug-resistant tuberculosis, or a terminal disease. Or they might be plagued by evil spirits who make them violently sick and curse them with bad luck.

A bodhisattva might experience these terrible circumstances as the karmic result of negative deeds they performed in past lives. However, no matter how tough their situation gets, they never part with bodhichitta and never lose heart. Their self-esteem is not affected by these challenges, and they do not become depressed. As ever, they use their circumstances to strengthen their bodhichitta for the benefit of all.

Looking at their own suffering, they rouse compassion. They think, *Through this suffering, I alone will take upon myself all the suffering of all other beings—their poor health, destitution, hardship, and heartache, as well as all the misdeeds and obscurations that are suffering's cause. The heat and cold of the hell beings, the hunger and thirst of the hungry ghosts, the confusion and enslavement of animals, the discontent of humans, the strife of demigods, the gods' suffering of falling to lower states—I take it all upon myself!*

When you have bodhichitta, you have the strength to endure suffering, no matter how intense. These days people struggle to tolerate suffering, especially mental suffering, and as a result, we see more and more people struggling with depression, resorting to self-harm, or even ending their own lives. In contrast, the bodhisattvas, with their vast mindsets and tremendous courage, are immovable as mountains. Suffering cannot shake them. As bodhisattvas, we need to develop this kind of unshakable courage, like the courage of the great yogi Milarepa who endured endless hardships for the sake of benefiting beings and attaining buddhahood.

Many centuries ago, in present-day Kashmir, there lived a beautiful young princess named Palmo (Lakshmi in Sanskrit). She declined to marry and instead became a nun and devoted herself to Buddhist practice. At some point, she contracted leprosy. This was the most feared contagious disease at the time; there was no cure for leprosy back then. Her skin became covered with lesions constantly seeping with puss and blood. Her fingers and toes began to rot and fall off, leaving her crippled and riddled with pain. Fearing contagion, the community exiled her, so she fled to a cave in the wilderness, far away from everyone. Since she had no money or provisions, she had to go begging for food, even though she struggled to walk, even though she struggled to hold her bowl and feed herself.

She was shunned and reviled by everyone. Her situation was truly pitiful.

Despite everything, she never once lost heart. She never forsook her bodhichitta resolve. She knew that her suffering was the result of past karma, and that now this karma was being purified. Day and night, she prayed that through her suffering she might take on the illness of all others and free them from suffering. She made such persistent, heartfelt prayers that early one morning Avalokiteshvara revealed himself to her. Avalokiteshvara flooded her with his blessings and immediately her health was restored. Her fingers and toes grew back, her lesions were healed, and she ended up even more beautiful than before. Later on, Gelongma Palmo founded the profound fasting practice of Thousand-Armed Avalokiteshvara (*nyungne*), a practice that continues to flourish throughout the world today.

Such is the power of bodhichitta. If we were to suffer like Gelongma Palmo, most of us would probably be tempted to take our own lives, to throw ourselves into a river and end it all. At the least, our bodhichitta would falter under the burden of this suffering. But Gelongma Palmo used her suffering to increase her bodhichitta, and as a result, she became a wellspring of benefit for so many beings, in her own lifetime and ever since.

Similarly, many hundreds of lifetimes before Buddha Shakyamuni reached the state of buddhahood, he was reborn in the Reviving Hell due to his sinful deeds. He was chained to a chariot with another hell being, and together they were made to pull this leaden chariot. The henchmen of Yama were whipping them from behind. They would not allow them a second's rest. The chariot was so heavy that it was impossible for them to make any progress. When Buddha looked at his companion, at his bruised and beaten face, he saw how deeply he was suffering.

"Even if the two of us try to pull this thing, we can't move it," he said, "so why should you suffer needlessly? Let me do it myself."

When the henchmen of Yama heard this, they were enraged.

"How dare you suggest such a thing?! Everyone must bear the results of their own karma. You cannot interfere!"

Boiling with rage, they then beat him so hard that he died and was then reborn in the god realms through the merit generated by this act of compassion. Many lifetimes later, this same person sat down under the bodhi tree in Bodh Gaya, attained buddhahood, and became our teacher, Buddha Shakyamuni.

CHAPTER 23

How to Use Prosperity on the Path

> 19. Though you may be famous, and revered by many,
> And as rich as the God of Wealth himself,
> To see that worldly wealth and glory is futile
> And to remain free of arrogance is the practice of
>   bodhisattvas.

In their delusion, ordinary people ascribe great significance to material wealth and status. They will make enemies and hurt others to attain these things, and when they do attain them, they become arrogant. These days, practitioners often fall into the same trap and become arrogant with regards to their learning or practice, or the respect others show them. As the sublime Nagarjuna said,

> Amassing wealth, guarding it, and making it grow will
>   wear you out;
> Understand that riches bring unending ruin and
>   destruction.[141]

Even if a bodhisattva becomes world famous, or if they become as rich as the wealth deity Vaishravana and live in mansions made of diamonds, emeralds, and gold, they do not become arrogant. For they know that fame and wealth are impermanent and insubstantial, just like everything else.

It is taught that "the water of good qualities does not gather on the iron ball of pride." Just as water cannot accumulate on a ball but just runs down its sides, good qualities cannot develop in someone puffed up by pride. Pride creates suffering for oneself, it creates suffering for others. There is nothing to be gained from it.

The practitioner who is free of pride will always be content, regardless of their circumstances. Whether they are given a special seat at a teaching or left to sit on the bare ground, whether they are acknowledged or ignored, it makes no difference to them. In contrast, for the practitioner who is proud, it is as if they are constantly sitting on thorns.

Khenpo Dazer Rinpoche would often mention the three useless things that Patrul Rinpoche taught:

> Patience toward those you dare not confront.
> Loving-kindness for those to whom you are attached.
> Compassion toward objects of stinginess.

There might be people in your life that irritate you or mistreat you, but because they are of a higher standing, you dare not confront them. You tell yourself you're being patient with them, but really you are just scared. You might talk about the burning love you have for your friends and family, and you might tell yourself this is loving-kindness, but in reality it is just self-centered attachment. You might own a horse that is strong, fast, and handsome, but you can never bear to ride the horse or use it for farmwork. You tell yourself it is because you do not want the horse to suffer, but really it is because you do not want your valuable possession to be damaged. You do not have compassion for the horse, just stinginess.

We should avoid these three charades and practice patience, loving-kindness, and compassion genuinely. We all have objects of patience, humility, and so on in our immediate environment. We all have objects of pride and jealousy in our lives, so we have ample opportunities to practice right here and now. We do not need to go off to some special place in search of special circumstances.

Khenpo Chokhyab Rinpoche (1920–1997) was born in Serta, Kham. He was inconceivably learned, but he always remained totally free of pride, and he lived in a very simple, low-key way. As a result, he was not well known while he was alive.

In the latter part of his life, Tulku Nyila, the renowned scholar and grandson of Traktung Dudjom Lingpa, came to meet Khenpo Chokhyab Rinpoche at his hermitage. Tulku Nyila was well learned in the scriptures of the Sarma schools[142] and had previously been to Larung Gar to debate with Khenpo Jigme Phuntsok Rinpoche.[143] In a similar vein, he came to see Khenpo Chokhyab Rinpoche. At this point, Khen Rinpoche was not widely known. He was living in his hermitage with twenty or so students. Tulku Nyila and Khen Rinpoche discussed the Dharma informally over a cup of tea, and Tulku Nyila was quickly impressed by the depth and breadth of Khen Rinpoche's knowledge and his profound renunciation. As a result, he stayed on at the hermitage for a week or so and was captivated by the teachings he received.

When Tulku Nyila was ready to depart, Khenpo Chokhyab Rinpoche took his hand and said to him, "You are an esteemed scholar of the Sarma tradition, and being the grandson of Traktung Dudjom Lingpa, no doubt you are learned in the Great Perfection as well. Nevertheless, I would like to make one request: Promise me you will read Mipham Rinpoche's Collected Works from beginning to end." Tulku Nyila agreed. Later on, he said that before he met Khenpo Chokhyab Rinpoche, he could set forth Je Tsongkhapa's position with confidence and clarity, but after reading Mipham Rinpoche's works he could no longer do this. Such are the special qualities of Mipham Rinpoche's writings. Tulku Nyila was well known throughout Serta and Kham, and when he returned to Serta, he declared that there was no one on earth like Khenpo Chokhyab Rinpoche, who had accomplished the wisdom intent of Jamgon Mipham Rinpoche, Omniscient Longchenpa, and Jigme Lingpa. As a result, Khen Rinpoche's reputation began to spread, and more students—monks, scholars, and accomplished lamas—began journeying to Khen Rinpoche's hermitage and requesting teachings from him.

My root guru, Khenpo Dazer Rinpoche, was quite a stubborn character. He had vast pure perception, of course, but there were very few people he openly praised. Nevertheless, he would often join his palms at his heart and extol Khenpo Chokhyab Rinpoche for his unmatched renunciation and his unparalleled scholarship and realization. In this way, through Tulku Nyila and Khenpo Dazer Rinpoche, Khenpo Chokhyab Rinpoche gained some renown in the latter part of his life, but it was only after his passing that his reputation really began to spread. He is often praised as the second Milarepa and is celebrated by all four traditions of Tibetan Buddhism as an unequaled master of his time.

It was at Khenpo Dazer Rinpoche's instruction that I went to meet Khenpo Chokhyab Rinpoche for the first time. It was two days' walk to get from Khenpo Dazer Rinpoche's hermitage near Dzogchen to Khenpo Chokhyab Rinpoche's hermitage.

"You needn't receive any formal teachings. Just take a good look at him, from head to toe," he said.

I wondered what he meant by that, but as soon as I met Khenpo Chokhyab Rinpoche, I understood. Khen Rinpoche lived in a flimsy hut. It was made from thin wooden planks and covered from the outside with a yak skin to give some protection from the rain and wind. It was barely two meters square. There was just enough room for his bed, which doubled as a seat, a small stove, and a place for an attendant to sit while making tea. The hut had a large window with a thick outdoor curtain that could be used to block the wind and sun. An animal hide on the floor served as Khen Rinpoche's cushion. He had been using the same hide for most of his life, so it was stiff with grime, and it certainly did not look warm. He had one worn and tattered woolen robe, a wooden bowl for his food and tea, a brass kettle for making tea, a small pot for making soup, a small *mani* wheel, and a bag to store his barley flour in. That was it.

This was how he chose to live. It was not due to a lack of offerings or support. Indeed, people would make offerings to Khen Rinpoche all the time, often very valuable offerings of hundreds of yaks and other livestock, but Khen Rinpoche would not accept them. If he had accepted what was offered to him, he would have become a rich man within a year. He was the same with requests for blessings and the like. He might run the sleeve of his chuba over someone's head when they requested a hand empowerment,[144] but he would never place his hand directly on their head. Likewise, he would not accept katas from his students, let alone monetary offerings. It was only at the very end of his life, when his retinue of disciples had grown to a considerable number, that he began to accept offerings for the pujas we would perform on the tenth and twenty-fifth lunar days.

Khen Rinpoche lived so incredibly simply. He would eat the same food everyday—just barley flour and soup. On the rare occasion that someone offered him some dry meat, he would cook the meat in butter until it softened, for his teeth were not very good, and then make a simple meat stew. He wore the same tattered robes year after year and did not even have a full change of clothes. In *The Words of My Perfect Teacher* and

Entering the Way of the Bodhisattva, it is taught that when practicing the Dharma, we should make do with meager provisions. As Patrul Rinpoche said, "Be content with a meager amount of food and just enough clothing to keep out the wind."[145] Khenpo Chokhyab Rinpoche embodied this.

This is how Khenpo Chokhyab Rinpoche lived for more than thirty years. Moreover, he would teach his students every single day, without a break. Never once did he leave the hermitage to perform pujas, or house rituals, in return for which one could expect to receive offerings.

Khenpo Chokhyab Rinpoche's root guru was Omniscient Botrul Rinpoche, Dongak Tenpe Nyima.[146] In the early 1950s, Botrul Rinpoche was preparing to head to Central Tibet and Khenpo Chokhyab Rinpoche wished to accompany him. However, Botrul Rinpoche instructed him to stay put in Kham.

"It's better not to travel too much in these troubled times," he advised him. "You have received from me the teachings in their entirety, so better you stay where you are. In these degenerate times, there are few people interested in the Dharma, so it is unlikely that you will find people to teach. However, if you are requested to teach, then you must teach! You must teach!"

Honoring his guru's command, from that point onward Khen Rinpoche taught the Dharma every single day for the rest of his life. The teachings he gave were both detailed and profound, and rich with pith instructions that exposed one's hidden faults. When studying with Khenpo Chokhyab Rinpoche, you would receive within just two or three months the same amount of teachings that you would receive in a year from another teacher because there were no holidays and no weekends.

Khen Rinpoche was utterly equanimous. He treated everyone equally, whether rich or poor, high or low. Sometimes his nephew would visit him, but you would never guess he was a relative. Khen Rinpoche would treat him the same way he treated everyone else. He was not attached to anything at all, and he would speak of this sometimes.

"I really have no attachment to anything anymore, except perhaps to my students," he would say. "Sometimes I feel ever so slightly attached to you lot, to the hope that you will study well, uphold your monastic vows, and become genuine practitioners."

He was a peerless scholar and upholder of the teachings of Mipham Rinpoche, Omniscient Longchenpa, and Rongzom Mahapandita. He would sometimes say, "Even if I had to face the whole of India and Tibet in debate, I would not quake!" This was not pride; this was confidence—confidence stemming from deep realization.

Khenpo Chokhyab Rinpoche embodied the practices of bodhisattvas. He was totally free of arrogance and pride. When students would extol his qualities, he would appear angry (though I do not believe he actually was). He would respond to praise with a reproach: "If you think my simplicity is such a great thing, then why don't you live like this yourself?!" He would dismiss all praise as meaningless flattery, and he accumulated no possessions or wealth. For he had seen "that worldly wealth and glory is futile." For instance, for most of his life he had only one pair of shoes—a handmade pair of traditional leather boots. I now have one of these boots on my shrine and the other boot is with his attendant Drubtob. These boots have been patched five or six times, and they are so old and grimy that anyone else would have thrown them away long ago. I doubt that a dog would even bother sniffing them. As for clothes, in addition to his set of robes, he had only two fur-lined vests. He really was the Milarepa of our age.

I had the great good fortune to stay with Khenpo Chokhyab Rinpoche, on and off, for almost six years, to receive a wealth of teachings from him, and be taken under his wing with great love. Rinpoche had so many accomplished students, like Khenpo Chopon, Khenpo Dawang, and so on, who spent twenty or thirty years by his side. I did not have the merit to spend that much time with Rinpoche, but I was fortunate enough to become one of his closest students.

I have not been able to emulate his qualities or follow his example in any way. Nevertheless, meeting Rinpoche and becoming his disciple was one of the best, most significant things to have happened to me, and it is all thanks to Khenpo Dazer Rinpoche's kindness. I had never even heard of Khenpo Chokhyab Rinpoche before Khenpo Dazer Rinpoche told me about him. After sending me to meet him the first time, Khenpo Dazer Rinpoche sent me back to request teachings on Rongzompa's *Entering the Way of the Great Vehicle.* Over the years, I received that and so many other precious teachings from him. Khenpo Chokhyab Rinpoche was like the bodhisattva Shantideva in his simplicity and like Patrul Rinpoche in his activities. He was a pure bodhisattva, a perfect photocopy of the bodhisattva teachings.

CHAPTER 24

How to Use Objects of Anger on the Path

> 20. If you do not tame the real enemy—your own anger,
> Fighting outer enemies will only make them increase.
> Therefore, with the armies of loving-kindness and
> compassion,
> To tame your own mind is the practice of bodhisattvas.

If you identify your enemy as someone outside yourself and try to conquer them, you will never be free of enemies. On the contrary, more and more enemies will appear. Look at the United States of America. With each war they wage—all in the name of securing peace for their country and its citizens—they create more adversaries, so much so that often US citizens will lie about their nationality when overseas. On the other hand, look at Switzerland with its pacifist policy of neutrality. By avoiding harming others, they have avoided enemies.

As Shantideva said, "There is no misdeed like hatred; / No austerity like patience."[147] Hatred, or anger, has tormented us lifetime after lifetime. It is the main cause for rebirth in the hell realms, it plunders our stores of virtue and destroys our happiness. If, instead of trying to subdue external enemies, we turn our attention inward and focus on subduing our own anger with compassion and love, we will become more peaceful people and our relationships will become more harmonious. This will bring direct benefits in this life, and great benefits in future lives as well.

Moreover, by taming our own mind, we will indirectly help our external enemies tame their minds. For example, Buddha Shakyamuni had a few enemies, such as Devadatta and King Ajatashatru, but they were transformed into friends and devoted followers through his patience, enduring love, forgiveness, and so on.

On the other hand, no matter how much physical clout or political power you might direct at external enemies, you will only create more enemies, and in the end these enemies will destroy you. It is only when we defeat the real enemy—our own anger, the root of all harm—that external enemies will disappear. As Shantideva explains in *Entering the Way of the Bodhisattva*,

> How could one kill belligerent beings
> Who are as infinite as space?
> Vanquishing this one angry mind
> Is like defeating all those foes.
>
> How could there be sufficient leather
> To cover the earth entirely?
> With just the leather for my soles,
> It is as if the whole earth's covered.
>
> Likewise, although I am unable
> To keep external things at bay,
> I'll keep this mind of mine in check—
> What need to ward off anything else?[148]

In certain areas in Kham, there is a type of guinea pig who digs multiple lairs for itself. This guinea pig has a foul odor, and attempting to escape its own stench, the poor animal digs lair after lair but all in vain. It puts itself through so much hardship by digging these long tunnels underground, only to settle there and discover that the awful stench has followed it inside. If we do not turn our focus inward and tame our own minds, and instead we continue trying to manipulate external circumstances, we will be like this poor guinea pig, constantly tiring ourselves out and never finding the peace we are looking for.

How is the inner enemy of anger defeated? Not through physical force but through the forces of loving-kindness and compassion. As taught in Atisha's seven-point causal sequence, the bodhisattva recognizes that all beings have been their loving parents in the past. Wishing to repay their kindness, they give rise to immeasurable loving-kindness (the wish that all beings may have happiness and its causes) and immeasurable compassion (the wish that all beings may be free from suffering and its causes). When all beings have been our kind parents in the past, how could we even think about harming them? Moreover, the bodhisattva knows that so-called enemies and the harm they do are no more than an illusion and a dream. None of it is real, none of it truly exists. In this way, they subdue the anger plaguing their mind. This is the unmistaken approach of the bodhisattvas.

During Buddha Shakyamuni's time, there was a king named Chandapradyota. One day, the king mounted his elephant and journeyed into the woods with his harem of queens. They wandered peacefully along the wood's shaded paths until they reached a beautiful opening where the ground was smooth and soft and carpeted with colorful wildflowers. The sound of trickling streams and sweet birdsong filled the air. The king dismounted and he and his queens enjoyed a picnic together amid this idyllic scene. After eating his fill, the king lay down in the shade of a tree and dozed off.

Soon afterward, the queens saw Arya Katyayana's disciple, the monk Sarana, walking along a path a little way off.

He radiated serenity and inner composure. Enchanted and intrigued, the queens walked over to him and said, "Venerable One, please tell us, who are you? What is your name?" When he told the queens he was Sarana, a disciple of Arya Katyayana, they requested him to teach them some Dharma. When he agreed, the queens suggested they move away from the king, for fear of disturbing his nap. They wandered further into the woods, sat down at the foot of a tree, and there the venerable Sarana began to teach. He spoke with great eloquence and sincerity, filling the queens with faith. They became so absorbed in the Dharma that they completely lost track of time.

When the king awoke, he was perplexed to find himself alone—not a single queen in sight. After some time, he ventured into the forest in search of them. When he found his queens sitting riveted before this handsome monk, drinking in his every word, he was overcome with jealousy. He stormed up to Sarana and demanded that he explain himself.

"What are you doing teaching my queens? Do you have permission to teach a group of women, unaccompanied by another man?"

"I do not," he said.

"Well, are you an arhat then?"

It seems that the king was well versed in the monastic code and knew that while monks are prohibited from teaching laywomen in private, arhats (noble beings, who have directly seen the truth and are thus free of attachment and other afflictions) are exempt from this rule.

"I am not an arhat," he replied.

The king was outraged. He called his ministers and had the monk arrested.

"You have transgressed Buddha's word by teaching my queens unaccompanied. Now you will pay for your mistakes!"

The queens were distraught. They spoke out in Sarana's defense, attesting to his good conduct and the truth of his teaching, but the king was deaf to their words. Maddened by jealousy, he called his guards and had them beat Sarana to a pulp.

Eventually the king called them off and they left Sarana lying, bruised and bleeding, on the ground. Not only had his body been battered but so had his pride. He was enraged by King Chandapradyota's treatment and determined to take revenge. He decided he would return his monastic vows, go back to his kingdom, and use his power as prince to wage war on the king. When he told his teacher, Arya Katyayana, what had happened and what he now planned to do, Arya Katyayana told him to not be reckless, to cultivate patience, but he was immune to all advice. His mind was writhing with anger and thoughts of violent revenge. Arya Katyayana counseled Sarana to at least wait until the morning before taking action.

"Spend one more night here, at the hermitage. In the morning, you are free to go,'" he said.

Sarana then laid his bedding out in a corner of his teacher's room and lay down for the night. Eventually he fell asleep and began to dream. In his dream, he returned to his kingdom, gathered his army, and set out to wage war on King Chandapradyota. He fought a fierce battle. Hundreds of soldiers were maimed and killed. Some had their arms sliced off, some were decapitated, some were stabbed to death. Scores of parents, wives, and children, on both sides of the conflict, were robbed of their husbands, fathers, and sons. King Chandapradyota's kingdom was devastated as houses, roads, and fields were destroyed, and Sarana's own kingdom suffered as well. Contagious illnesses began to spread and food became scarce. A dark cloud descended on both kingdoms, and yet they continued to wage war. Victory on either side was never assured for long. King Chandapradyota and his army would corner Sarana and his troops in a narrow chasm or on the top of a cliff. They would be on the verge of death, then suddenly they would find a way to retaliate and force King Chandapradyota back onto his own land. This went on and on, back and forth, until both kingdoms were painted red with blood. These previously beautiful lands were now littered with corpses and haunted by wounded soldiers, orphaned children, and harrowed widows. Still Sarana was not content. He lusted for vengeance and seethed with pride.

When Sarana woke from this dream, he was aghast.

"To think that I was on the verge of waging war in this way. To think of the horror I could have caused!"

He told Arya Katyayana he had changed his mind and dropped all thoughts of taking revenge. Unbeknownst to him, the dream had been created by Katyayana with his meditative powers. Katyayana then instructed him to train in meditation for seven days. Fueled with renunciation and remorse, he meditated earnestly, morning to night. In the meantime, King Chandapradyota learned of Sarana's identity and was filled with fear.

"I have assaulted the prince of a powerful neighboring kingdom. If I am not careful, this could lead to great strife, even outright war!"

On the seventh day of Sarana's ardent meditation, King Chandapradyota and his retinue traveled to Arya Katyayana's hermitage to make a formal apology. When they arrived, Sarana greeted the king by flying through the air, transforming his upper body into fire and his lower body into water and displaying all manner of miracles. He had attained the state of arhat. King Chandapradyota was filled with faith and confessed his mistakes with heartfelt regret.

You can never bring an end to external enemies by trying to subdue them. It is only by subduing anger, the inner enemy, that outer enemies will disappear. Therefore, it is the practice of bodhisattvas to subdue the real enemy, their own anger, with the powerful armies of loving-kindness and compassion.

CHAPTER 25

How to Use Objects of Attachment on the Path

> 21. Sense pleasures are like salt water;
> The more you drink, the more your thirst intensifies.
> Therefore, to immediately discard all objects
> That trigger attachment is the practice of bodhisattvas.

The "sense pleasures" are the objects of our five senses: pleasant form, smells, sounds, tastes, and textures. These five sense pleasures ensnare us all, whether we are rich or poor, whether we are a human, animal, or another type of being. For example, attached to the sensation of cool mud on their hot skin, elephants wade into swamps and drown. Attached to the sight of light, moths fly into open flames and are burned to death. Enchanted by the sweet sound of music, deer are lured into traps and killed. Enticed by the taste of grubs, fish bite onto hooks and are then reeled in by fishermen. Entranced by the sweet smell of nectar, bees fly into carnivorous flowers. In the same way, beguiled by our attachment to the sense pleasures, we are lured into samsara's snare. And it is not only the sense pleasures that we are attached to. There is also name, fame, and status, our identity, country, family, wealth, and so on.

The bodhisattva sees that the sense pleasures "are just like salty water." If you are thirsty and take a sip of salty water, for a second or two you might feel some relief, but then your thirst will increase. No matter how much you drink, your thirst will only intensify. This is how the sense pleasures affect us ordinary people, those without realization of the natural state.

No matter how much we partake of the sense pleasures, they never bring satisfaction. Even the wealthiest of people are not content. As we know, it is usually the opposite. Even the wealthiest of countries are not satisfied with their economic progress. Look, for example, at the United Kingdom or the United States. They are forever focused on what they lack.

We all have different objects of attachment. Some people are most attached to wealth, others to their spouse or friends. Some parents are so attached to their children that they would literally lose their mind if something happened to them. For others still, it is status and renown. Some desire fame so desperately that they are willing to risk their lives for it, like people who try to reach the peak of Mount Everest in record time and end up dying during the climb. Some are most attached to their spiritual path. But regardless of the object, attachment is attachment. Buddha stated this in no uncertain terms.

Each of us needs to look inward and ask ourselves what we are attached to most of all. In my case, it is my monastery, my students, and the teachings I have received from my precious gurus. This might be virtuous attachment, but it is still attachment and it is therefore an obscuration; it obstructs the attainment of liberation and awakening and so it must be discarded. In short, attachment to the sense pleasures is the cause of samsara. Therefore, we need to recognize attachment when it first arises and drop it right away.

In the past, when bows and arrows were used in warfare, arrowheads would be laced with poison. If you are struck by such an arrow, it is imperative to remove it immediately and treat the wound without delay. There is no time to ask whether the arrow was shot from east, west, north, or south, whether it is made from bamboo, iron, or stone. Such investigations could be helpful in the long term, but not at the moment you are struck. If you want to survive, you need to remove the arrowhead and flush out the wound before the poison spreads through your blood and causes irreversible harm. In the same way, when attachment arises, the bodhisattva must relinquish the attachment immediately, without a moment's delay. It can be helpful to scrutinize one's attachment, to investigate how and why specific attachments arise, what they are associated with, and so on and so forth, but first of all you need to cast the attachment aside. If, instead, you let the attachment linger, it will grow into fixation, and like the arrowhead's poison spreading through your blood, it will cause you grave harm.

In the past, there was an outstanding scholar at Dzogchen Monastery's famed Shri Singha College. He was perfectly learned in the thirteen major treatises as well as the five major sciences.[149] It seems this scholar had become a little arrogant. Arrogance obstructs the dawning of experience and realization, and in general it causes oneself and others a lot of grief. Arrogance, like all emotions, is rooted in attachment—in this case, the scholar's attachment to his knowledge and scholastic prowess.

At the time, the great master Mingyur Namkhe Dorje[150] was presiding as the throne holder at Dzogchen Monastery. One day, quite unexpectedly, he called the scholar to see him.

"You need to leave the monastery straight away," he said. "You must travel to Terkha in Minyak to see Do Khyentse Yeshe Dorje. This is imperative."

Usually, the teachers from Dzogchen Monastery would travel in a large caravan with much pomp and circumstance, but Mingyur Namkhe Dorje told the scholar, "This time you must travel incognito and alone, like an ordinary monk. Otherwise, you'll encounter obstacles." Mingyur Namkhe Dorje was no ordinary lama. The scholar knew this and so he took his instructions to heart. He set off straight away, without telling anyone, and traveled alone and on foot to Terkha, carrying only the most basic provisions in a backpack.

When he finally arrived at Do Khyentse Yeshe Dorje's residence, a puja was being performed. Do Khyentse was a master of tantra who practiced the unconventional conduct of yogis. He dressed like a layman, drank alcohol, smoked tobacco, and so on—a stark contrast to the monastic conduct upheld at Dzogchen Monastery, which was renowned for its strict observance of the monastic code. The scholar was not inspired by what he saw! Nevertheless, he took a seat at the end of the assembly, and honoring Mingyur Namkhe Dorje's command, he stayed firmly put. The puja continued and when they reached the feast offering, or *ganachakra*, the shrine master informed Do Khyentse Yeshe Dorje that there was no meat present and asked him how to proceed. In order to perform a feast offering, a small amount of meat and alcohol are necessary as transformative substances.

Do Khyentse had a small dog on his lap. He had been stroking the dog throughout the puja. Now he picked it up and handed it to the shrine master.

"Here you go," he said.

The shrine master was taken aback, but heeding the master's word, he took the dog. He carried it to the shrine, butchered it, and arranged its bloody flesh with the other ritual offerings. When the scholar saw this, he was revolted. More than that, he was outraged and distressed.

How can this man, acting in such blatant discord with Buddha's teaching, be called a teacher? he thought. *He is a charlatan at best!*

A few moments later, he looked up at Do Khyentse and saw the very same dog sitting comfortably on his lap. He could not believe his eyes. This display of the dreamlike nature of phenomena flooded him with faith.

The view and conduct of Secret Mantra are quite unusual. Being rich in methods that involve little hardship, the tantric teachings make skillful use of "union and liberation" (*tana gana*), as we can see in the life stories of Guru Rinpoche, Do Khyentse Yeshe Dorje, and other realized masters. If the practitioner lacks a high level of genuine realization but nevertheless engages in such conduct, it will amount to nothing more than a fraudulent, shameful spectacle, and there will be serious consequences.

As Khenpo Dazer Rinpoche would say, there are two Tibetan masters in Tibet who were unprecedented and unsurpassed throughout the whole of India and Tibet. The first was the great yogi Milarepa, who was unprecedented and unsurpassed in terms of his liberating life story. The second is Do Khyentse Yeshe Dorje, this peerless mahasiddha with the power to revive the dead. He was, and is, unprecedented and unsurpassed in terms of his yogic prowess.

The scholar was then overcome with faith. He saw Do Khyentse Yeshe Dorje as Guru Rinpoche in person. This experience had freed him from the shackles of his arrogance and his attachment to the reality of appearances. Do Khyentse Yeshe Dorje knew exactly what was going on and knew the scholar had been sent to him by Mingyur Namkhe Dorje to dispel the pride and fixation that was holding him back, and he acted precisely to free him from these obstacles.

Afterward, the scholar stayed with Do Khyentse Yeshe Dorje for some time, and one day Do Khyentse asked him to teach his monks Maitreya's treatise, the *Uttaratantra*.

"After all, you are such an accomplished scholar, and from the esteemed Shri Singha College, no less," he said.

Although the scholar now had great faith in Do Khyentse, he still wondered how learned he was. He thought, *Of course, the master is a realized being, but maybe I am a greater scholar than he is.*

One day, as he was teaching the monks, Do Khyentse Yeshe Dorje appeared outside the teaching hall and began circumambulating it while holding a large staff. When the scholar spotted him, he sat up extra straight. Suspecting that Do Khyentse would listen in when passing by the open door, he began ornamenting his explanation with even more quotations than usual and using ever more eloquent turns of phrase. When Do Khyentse reached the door, he placed his hands on the top of his staff and rested his chin on them.

"Oy! Don't get too puffed up now! My ear, this very ear," he said, pulling on his ear lobe, "has already been to Tushita Heaven and received the *Uttaratantra* directly from Regent Maitreya no less than three times!"

With this, the scholar was stripped naked of his pride. Now free from all lingering attachment to his learning, genuine realization dawned within him, and he went on to become an exceptional practitioner of the Great Perfection.

Khenpo Dazer Rinpoche would sometimes tell us this story. It shows that it really does not matter what the object of your attachment is. Whether it be your body, wealth, status, or learning, your monastic discipline or spiritual accomplishment, attachment to it will delude you and lead you astray. As the eighth-century Indian master Saraha said,

> Whatever you're attached to, just drop it.
> Once this is realized, everything is realized to be just this.

Whatever you are attached to, whatever triggers attachment, just drop it. Cast it aside. When attachment is released, the mind returns to its natural state.

CHAPTER 26

Training in Ultimate Bodhichitta

In Meditative Equipoise, Training in Simplicity Free from Fixation

> 22. Whatever appears is your own mind.
> Mind is primordially free from conceptual extremes.
> Knowing this, to not entertain attributes
> Of perceiver and perceived is the practice of bodhisattvas.

In four clear and succinct lines, this verse condenses the entire meaning of the middle turning of the Dharma Wheel, the teaching of the great mother, the Prajnaparamita. With this verse, we are inquiring into the way things are, as opposed to the way they appear. Here we find a marked difference between Buddha's teachings and many schools of scientific thought. It seems that, until quite recently, the majority of Western scientists believed material substance was the source of all phenomena—both perceived objects and perceiving subjects. In contrast, Buddha explained that all phenomena, including material substance, arise from the mind. "Whatever appears" refers to the external environment and to all living beings. It refers to all possible things, from form all the way up to omniscience—everything that appears and exists. Everything that appears, everything that is experienced, is a projection of one's own mind. Things occur—they manifest—but they lack even the slightest shred of reality. Perceived objects do not exist from their own side.

There are endless passages from Buddha's own teachings and the treatises of great masters that establish this crucial point through examples and rigorous logic. As Omniscient Longchenpa says in *The Wish-Fulfilling Treasury*,

> Intoxicated by the psychedelic datura,
> In the vast gamut of appearances, no matter what arises for us,
> All is hallucination and thus nonexistent;
> The six classes of beings and all delusory appearances,
> Likewise, are pastiches of a mistaken intellect:
> Know every single one as an image of emptiness![151]

Appearances lack true existence; they are projections of the mind. What then is the nature of the mind? The root text answers, "Mind is primordially free from conceptual extremes." One of the four main Buddhist tenet systems is the Chittamatra, or Mind Only, tradition. Followers of this system believe that appearances are projections of the mind, but mind itself truly exists. They assert a nondual, self-reflexive, self-cognizant consciousness that is truly established. However, this is a flawed position; this is not the way things finally, or ultimately, are. The followers of the Middle Way—the pinnacle of the four Buddhist tenet systems—point out the illogical consequences in the Mind Only's position and, using profound logical reasonings, they demonstrate that mind itself is primordially free from, or beyond, all conceptual extremes. As Saraha sings,

> The nature of mind is the universal seed.
> Both samsara and nirvana stem from it.
> Homage to this mind that, like a wish-granting gem,
> Grants all desirable things.

The nature of mind—the causal continuum that is buddha nature, self-arisen primordial wisdom—is the source of all phenomena, of both samsara and nirvana. However, the nature of mind itself lacks reality. Just like the phenomena that appear from it, it is emptiness. It is primordially free—naturally, originally free—from all conceptual extremes.

All conceptual extremes, or constructs, can be condensed into the eight extremes, as explained in *The Root Stanzas of the Middle Way*:

> Everything that arises interdependently
> Is unceasing and unborn,
> Neither nonexistent nor everlasting,
> Neither coming nor going,
> Neither multiple nor single.
> To this teaching that pacifies all concepts and duality,
> The most sacred speech of the fully enlightened Buddha,
> We pay homage![152]

When examined, none of these conceptual extremes can be found to exist. They are mere dependent arisings, mere dependent designations. For instance, when you analyze the notion of arising using the profound logical reasonings taught in the Middle Way treatises, you cannot find "arising" anywhere. It is void of natural existence, void of ultimate reality. And since arising itself does not exist, neither does cessation. For arising and cessation are mutually dependent. Likewise for all the other extremes.

This verse teaching ultimate bodhichitta is the very heart of the text. It is the most essential, profound point from among all the thirty-seven practices. Ultimate bodhichitta is none other than the nature of mind; it is the state of the Great Perfection, the Great Seal, the Great Middle Way. To realize this, we need to purify our obscurations and accumulate vast stores of merit.

It is to this end that we practice the five hundred thousand preliminaries and so on. There are very few students who can realize the natural state straight away, and those few students are only able to do so due to the extensive accumulation and purification they have performed in past lives. I heard that once Khenpo Jigme Phuntsok Rinpoche was introducing the nature of mind to a group of students, but the students just could not understand. He gave the pointing-out instructions again and again, but to no avail. At some point, he just stopped trying and said, "Recite the mani mantra! Just recite the mani mantra!" It was not due to his lack of blessings or skill as a teacher that the students could not understand. It was due to their obscurations and their lack of merit. When the student is obscured and lacks merit, recognition simply cannot take place.

"Attributes" refer to the qualities of shape, color, and so on that characterize material, or external phenomena, and to the notions of positive and negative, pleasant and unpleasant, and so on that characterize mental, or internal, phenomena. The training in ultimate bodhichitta is to rest, free of attributes of a perceiving subject and perceived object, in the natural state of simplicity, the state originally beyond conceptual extremes. As Shantideva teaches in *Entering the Way of the Bodhisattva*,

> And then when neither thing nor nothing
> Remains before the mind,
> Because there is no other way,
> There is no focus—utter peace.[153]

In the Buddhist teachings, a valid cognition is defined as a cognition in which the subject and object are in accord. For example, when you perceive a white conch as white, that is a valid cognition on the conventional level. When someone with jaundice sees a white conch as yellow, that is not a valid cognition because the conch is in fact white. The perceiving subject and perceived object are not in accord.

Similarly, on the ultimate level, a valid cognition is to perceive things as they ultimately are. This is what we are training in here. The bodhisattva understands that dualistic perception does not accord with the ultimate state, and that this discordant perception is the root of samsara and all its suffering. Therefore, it is the practice of bodhisattvas to train the mind in the ultimate state of simplicity, free of all attributes.

To summarize, the first two lines of this verse establish the view—the true nature of all things. The second two lines then explain the meditation—how to familiarize yourself with that view. If you train well in ultimate bodhichitta, you will not need to apply the practices described in the earlier verses, such as the methods for using adverse circumstances on the path. When you become deeply familiar with the ultimate state of simplicity, all afflictions are naturally liberated. In this way, ultimate bodhichitta is a universal panacea. It is the ultimate cure.

Ultimate bodhichitta is the awakened state. There is no higher state of awakening to be found. There is nothing greater to be realized than the natural state beyond conceptual extremes that is taught in this verse. Whether you are practicing the Great Seal, the Great Perfection, the Great Middle Way, or anything else, there is nothing greater to be realized—this is it. This is the ultimate truth that the bodhisattva directly realizes on the path of seeing, the first bhumi, Perfect Joy. As the bodhisattva then traverses the remaining bhumis, advancing from the path of seeing to the path of meditation, their realization of this ultimate truth, the consummate natural state, becomes progressively clearer, deeper, and more complete, until finally it reaches fullness on the path of no more learning, the state of perfect buddhahood.

In *The Wisdom Chapter*, Mipham Rinpoche's commentary on the ninth chapter of *Entering the Way of the Bodhisattva*, he explains the result of directly realizing emptiness: the eight worldly concerns are equalized such that one no longer perceives any difference between them—between gain and loss, praise and criticism, and so on—and love for all beings arises effortlessly. This occurs when one gains direct realization on the first bodhisattva bhumi. However, even us ordinary beings, who have yet to attain realization, should see signs of transformation as we approach emptiness through study and contemplation on the paths of accumulation and joining.

On the path of accumulation, you develop a conceptual understanding of profound emptiness. Then, on the path of joining, you gain ever-deeper experience of emptiness, until this experience matures into direct realization on the path of seeing, the first bhumi, Perfect Joy. As your understanding of emptiness develops, you should become more content and relaxed. This is a natural consequence of understanding emptiness; your fixation lessens, so you become more spacious and at ease. At the same time, you will feel more compassion for others. You will become more benevolent. Your appreciation of the teachings and teachers will grow, and you will develop a deep-seated conviction in the workings of karmic cause and effect. You will understand that ultimately karma does not truly exist—when analyzed, it cannot be found—but on the conventional level of unexamined experience, karma is unfailing. As you familiarize yourself with emptiness, these changes will slowly take place in you, like heat gathering before a fire ignites. You need to develop these signs of progress on the path. If you study and practice but you do not observe such changes within yourself, it is a red flag. Then you need to check your understanding and your practice and ask yourself whether it is the genuine Dharma or not.

Once you have perfectly and directly realized profound emptiness, the state of simplicity that is the realization of all buddhas, there is no longer any distinction between meditative equipoise and post-equipoise. However, until we attain such realization, there is a distinction, and we need to make skillful use of this. We need to familiarize ourselves with emptiness in formal sessions—this is the practice of meditative equipoise. In between formal sessions, we need to use our experiences to bring us closer to realization and to sustain the certainty gained during meditative equipoise—this is the practice of post-equipoise.

Once you have realized the state of equipoise, the qualities of post-equipoise will automatically arise. It is not possible to be realized yet still be bound by attachment and desire. If someone claims that a certain lama is highly realized, but they are still entangled by attachment and aversion, then they are clearly not realized, despite what people say.

In the past, there was a bodhisattva named Ever Weeping (Sadaprarudita) because, in his search for the teachings of Prajnaparamita, he shed so many tears.[154] He had done much study and reflection, and accumulation and purification, but he had still not realized the Prajnaparamita, and this broke his heart. He could think of nothing else, day or night.

One day, the voice of the dakinis resounded from the sky. He must have purified his being quite significantly if he was able to experience this.

"Noble son, do not cry! Travel east and there you will encounter the Prajnaparamita!" the dakinis said.

So, Bodhisattva Ever Weeping set off to the east, and without concern for life or limb, he walked for days on end. He covered hundreds of kilometers but encountered nothing. He persevered and continued walking, but after some time he became disheartened. Once more, he burst into tears. As he sat on the ground weeping, a voice resounded from space: "Noble son, do not weep! Continue to the east to the city Gandhavati. There you will meet the great bodhisattva Dharmodgata and he will teach you the Prajnaparamita!"

Encouraged by this instruction, Bodhisattva Ever Weeping stood up and dried his eyes. *Now that I have precise directions, it will really happen!* he thought. But then he realized he had nothing to offer: *How can I go empty-handed to receive the Prajnaparamita?! I have such scanty merit from my past lives that I have no wealth to give. Well, I will sell myself and use the money as a mandala offering.*

And so, he set off to the nearby marketplace, where he called out, "Man for sale! Man for sale!" but no one wanted to buy him. Feeling desperate and discouraged, once more Bodhisattva Ever Weeping collapsed in tears. When a man walked up to him and asked him what was wrong, the bodhisattva explained the dire straits he was in.

"Well," the man said, "I don't need a man, but I do need some bone marrow from a living human. How about we strike a deal?"

Bodhisattva Ever Weeping was thrilled. He immediately agreed to sell this man his bone marrow. Without a moment's hesitation, the bodhisattva took a sharp knife and began hacking into his thigh. He tore his thigh bone out and was about to smash it against a wall to extract the marrow when suddenly the man intervened.

"Stop!" he said. "I am God Indra. I assumed the guise of a human to test your resolve. Tell me what you wish for and I will grant it! Tell me, what do you need?"

Bodhisattva Ever Weeping said, "What I need is the sacred Dharma of the Prajnaparamita. But I don't think you can give me that."

All the while, from the rooftop of a nearby house, the daughter of a local merchant had been watching this scene play out. She ran down to the bodhisattva and said, "Sir, why are you maiming yourself like this?!" When he told her he was selling his bone marrow so he could request teachings on the Prajnaparamita, she asked, "What is so special about the Prajnaparamita?"

"There is nothing greater than the Prajnaparamita. It is through the Prajnaparamita that buddhahood is realized," the bodhisattva said.

"Well, what is so good about buddhahood?" she asked.

"It is only by attaining perfect buddhahood that you can free all beings from the suffering of samsara," he said.

Inspired by the bodhisattva's example and his profound words, the merchant daughter said, "Let me provide you with all the offerings you need, with gold, silver, precious jewels, and more. And let me accompany you so that I too can receive these sacred teachings." The daughter's family joyfully prepared five hundred carriages and five hundred servants, all bearing copious offerings, and thus Bodhisattva Ever Weeping, accompanied by the merchant daughter, her parents, and servants, set off to see the great bodhisattva Dharmodgata.

When they finally arrived at his residence, they were informed that the great bodhisattva had just begun seven years of retreat.

What little merit I have! Bodhisattva Ever Weeping thought. For the next seven years, with no distinction between night and day, he circumambulated Dharmodgata's palace and made prostrations and prayers.

Then one day a voice resounded from the sky: "In seven days, Noble Dharmodgata will rise from his meditation and proclaim the Dharma!" Bodhisattva Ever Weeping was overjoyed. Immediately he began to prepare the teaching space. He cleaned, swept, and arranged offerings, and to settle the dust he collected water and sprinkled it on the ground. Seeing his devoted efforts, the mara Garab Wangchuk was incensed. He conjured gusty winds so that no matter how many times the bodhisattva dampened the ground, the dust kept billowing up, soiling the offerings and Dharmodgata's throne.

As Noble Dharmodgata's arrival drew nearer and the dust continued to course through the air, Bodhisattva Ever Weeping took a knife, cut open his veins, and began sprinkling the ground with his blood. When Garab Wangchuk saw this, he was overawed and fled. Following the bodhisattva's lead, the merchant daughter and her five hundred companions all did the same, and soon the ground was damp with blood. Witnessing these acts of devotion, God Indra was deeply moved. With his divine powers, he transformed the blood into red sandalwood, whose sweet fragrance replaced the tangy smell of blood.

Finally, Noble Dharmodgata appeared, sat down on the throne, and began to teach. As he took the Prajnaparamita scripture out of its precious casket made of layers of gold, lapis lazuli, and other precious gems, a rain of flowers cascaded down. Like a peacock satiated by the sound of thunder, upon hearing the sacred teachings of the Prajnaparamita, Bodhisattva Ever Weeping's deepest wishes were fulfilled. He and many hundreds of thousands were liberated by realizing the Prajnaparamita and later attained perfect buddhahood.

CHAPTER 27

In Post-Equipoise, Discarding Fixation on the Reality of Objects of Attachment

> 23. When encountering pleasing objects,
> To view them like rainbows in summer skies—
> Lacking reality, however beautiful they appear—
> And thereby relinquish attachment is the practice
> of bodhisattvas.

Rainbows appear in the summer sky, bright and vivid to the eye, but no matter how enchanting they might be, we know they have no substance. We know they lack reality. Likewise, when encountering attractive appearances, the bodhisattva recognizes them for what they are: mere appearances void of true existence, no more substantial than illusions and dreams. They recognize their illusory nature and relinquish attachment to them. The Tibetan word *zhenchak*, translated here as attachment, is a compound of two verbs. *Chak* describes the initial moment of desire, while *zhen* describes the state of attachment, or reification, which that desire develops into if the illusory nature of the object is not recognized and the desire is not dropped.

Often, when we see a handsome mansion, a stunning garden, or someone famous, we gasp, our eyes widen, and we say, "Oh my goodness, look at that!" This is attachment, plain and simple, but we rarely recognize it as such. Khenpo Chokhyab Rinpoche would often point this out to us: This sense of "wow" is simply the outflow of attachment. In such moments, he said, we must remember that appearances, no matter how dazzling they might seem, lack true existence. They are not real. Remember this, then release your attachment into the natural state of simplicity. I took this as a pith instruction, and henceforth I have tried to apply it with mindfulness and vigilance. Now, many years later, I am rarely impressed by appearances—by wealth, beauty, or influence. And if I do get impressed by something—meaning, attached to it—I immediately remember Rinpoche's instruction and let go into a relaxed open state.

Many people seem to believe that reducing attachment will reduce love. Teachers are asked about this repeatedly, especially in Western countries: "If I meditate on emptiness and detachment, surely I will stop caring for my family? Surely I will become irresponsible and aloof?" The very opposite is the case. To the extent that you reduce your attachment, to that extent your love and affection will blossom, deepen, and grow. If someone's love and compassion decrease due to their Dharma practice, it is a clear sign that their practice is flawed. When you are free of attachment, you are free of self-interest. Only then does your love become genuine and pure. Until that point, your love remains laced with hope and fear. It is volatile and self-centered. With a few unpleasant words, this so-called love can turn into hate.

If you consider Buddha Shakyamuni, and likewise Guru Rinpoche, their love for beings is unbridled, unconditional, unmatched. This love stems not from attachment but from realization of profound emptiness.

The revered yogi Shabkar Tsokdruk Rangdrol (1781–1851) grew up with his mother and two sisters in Nyengya, a village in the Rebkong region in Amdo. His family was not rich, but they were comfortable enough. As such, he had been free to pursue the Dharma from a young age. His family rejoiced in his practice. He was respected and loved. He enjoyed wonderful friendships and the security of owning a house, land, and wealth. He had everything most people wish for right there, in the palm of his hand.

And yet, seeing that worldly pleasures have no more substance than rainbows in summer skies, he developed renunciation and resolved to leave his homeland. He knew that if he remained there, beguiled by the comfort of family and friends and the preoccupations of this life, his Dharma practice would be compromised. Thus, at the age of twenty-one, Shabkar decided to leave home and devote himself to authentic practice in the solitude of mountain retreats.

When he told his mother of his plans, she was outraged.

"How can you even think to leave us? You are the only son of the family. One of your sisters is yet to marry. Who will arrange her marriage if you leave? And what about me? Have you thought of that? How am I to live, an old lady all on my own?"

His sister was no more supportive.

"It is a son's responsibility to care for his mother. As a woman, my destiny is marriage," she said. "I don't plan to hang around and become an old spinster. Once I'm wed, I won't be able to care for our mother. Her well-being is your responsibility, not mine."

Shabkar was very skillful. To his sister, he spoke of the shortcomings of marriage and the benefits of staying in one's own home.

"If you marry, you will lose much of your independence," he said. "And who knows if you'll get on with your parents-in-law.

Maybe they'll treat you like a servant. Do you really want to live like that? If you stay here at home, you can enjoy our family wealth and keep your freedom. You'll have the constant love of mother and the support of the community. It will be better for you if you stay at home, and if I go off and devote myself to Dharma, that will benefit all of us."

Shabkar saw that his mother and sister would not give him their blessing if he told them the truth—that he was planning to leave forever, that he might never see them again in this life—so he told them a white lie.

"My beloved mother and sister, I must leave now to receive the Dharma at the feet of Omniscient Ngakyi Wangpo, but I will return in a few years."

His mother was anguished at the thought of his absence, but she finally gave her consent.

On the morning of his departure, his mother and sister accompanied him for a short while, and then they said their tearful goodbyes. Shabkar walked on alone, tears pouring down his cheeks, and when he reached the next pass, he paused and looked back. He saw his mother and sister in the distance, still weeping, and thought, *They think I will return in a few years, but most likely we will never meet again in this life.* His resolve was absolute, but this did not make him immune to grief. He walked on until his mother and sister were out of sight. When he turned back and could no longer see them, he was overcome. He broke down, weeping and wailing until he almost passed out. He had pledged to free himself and all others from the ocean of samsara's suffering, to attain buddhahood for the benefit of all beings. And he had resolved to do what was necessary—to renounce his homeland and apply himself heart and soul to Buddha's teaching. But the anguish of leaving his mother and sister and witnessing their heartache was unbearable.

When he regained his senses, Shabkar rose to his feet and continued on his way. He received the nectar of Dharma from Omniscient Ngakyi Wangchuk and practiced one-pointedly until attaining perfect buddhahood and bringing boundless benefit to beings. Even centuries on, Shabkar's liberating life story remains one of the most influential hagiographies in Tibet, second only to that of the great yogi Milarepa. These enduring waves of benefit stem from seeing through the spectacle of pleasant appearances, from recognizing that they are no more than illusions and so casting attachment aside.

There are no accounts of people gaining realization while remaining attached to their wealth, homeland, family, and friends. Realization is attained by seeing through appearances and discarding all attachment to them. Therefore, it is the practice of bodhisattvas to drop attachment to attractive appearances. This is done by recognizing that they lack reality, that they are no more real than a beautiful rainbow appearing in the sky for a moment, before vanishing without trace.

You might not be able to drop your strongest attachments immediately, but as with all the bodhisattva practices, you should start where you are and do what you can. You need to push yourself a little bit. For instance, if you are stingy, try giving away more than you're comfortable with. Reduce your attachment bit by bit and make aspirations to that end.

CHAPTER 28

Discarding Fixation on the Reality of Objects of Anger

> 24. The various shades of suffering are like your child dying in a dream.
> How tiring to take confused perceptions to be real!
> Therefore, when confronted by adversity,
> To recognize it as confusion is the practice of bodhisattvas.

The bodhisattva understands that all the various shades of suffering that we might encounter are no more real than the appearances in a dream. Adversity refers to unwanted circumstances—physical illness, mental anguish, heartbreak, humiliation, a natural disaster, financial loss, and on and on. No matter how overwhelming they might seem, these experiences are confused perceptions; they are no more real than the death of a child in a dream. How exhausting it is to cling to a dream as if it were real.

When encountering misfortune, remind yourself that this is merely an experience; it is not real. It is nothing more than a confused perception, appearing but lacking reality, just like an illusion and a dream. If you can recall this with conviction, you will be able to relax within the experience and let go, your mind wide open and carefree. This is the approach of the profound view. If you are unable to practice in this way, remind yourself that this adversity is the ripening of your negative karma, and reflect upon impermanence and death. Whether positive or negative, all things are in a state of constant flux, so this adversity will not last. The recollection of karma and impermanence will have a similar effect. It will help you let go within the experience and find a state of inner rest.

It is so important for practitioners to take impermanence to heart. It protects us from many potential pitfalls, such as falling prey to worldly motivations and pretense. When you know, deep in your heart, that life is impermanent and fleeting, you will not be tempted to pursue fame, for example. You will not compromise your integrity because you know that the things of this life are transient and essenceless. For the practitioner, misfortune is more helpful than good fortune. Misfortune is fuel for renunciation, a spur to practice. It was Milarepa's suffering in early life that fueled his motivation on the path, for example.

When you lack familiarity with emptiness, it is difficult to deal with experiences of intense happiness and suffering. If your child falls sick, you are overcome with anxiety. If you feel depressed or bereaved, that mental sensation overwhelms you. However, as you familiarize yourself with emptiness, not just in meditative equipoise but in post-equipoise as well, you will come to understand that happiness and suffering are merely appearances. They are illusory and impermanent; they lack a single atom of reality. Then, through persistent training, you can develop your understanding into experience, and your experience into direct realization.

Yukhok Jadral was an inconceivably sublime master, like Longchenpa incarnate. He was so renowned and revered that almost every lama in Kham and Amdo became his disciple. He was one of Khenpo Dazer Rinpoche and Khenpo Chokhyab Rinpoche's root gurus. Khenpo Dazer Rinpoche did not receive that many teachings from him, but Khenpo Chokhyab

Rinpoche spent many years by his side. He had many incredible disciples, some of whom attained the rainbow body. One of these disciples was Dromton Purba.

Dromton Purba was from a very wealthy family who liked to exercise their power in society. Such people are quick to attract enemies, and Dromton Purba's family was no exception. Dromton Purba had become a disciple of Yukhok Jadral when he was quite young, and ever since he had lived in mountain hermitages away from his family. He was a devoted practitioner who trained in the Great Perfection day and night.

One day a feud broke out between Dromton Purba's family in Serwa and another large family from Towo, whose name I will not mention. The feud became so bitter that Towo declared war on Dromton Purba's family. They gathered an army and descended upon their camp. In a bloody battle, they killed many members of Dromton Purba's family. The Towo army had defeated their enemy, but they were not yet satisfied. They knew that the women, children, and elderly were hiding in the family house, and they knew they were likely to retaliate in the future if they left them alive. So, the Towo army surrounded the family house and set it alight. Those who tried to escape the flames by running outside were shot, stabbed, or beaten to death. The rest were burned alive. Thus, Dromton Purba's entire family was wiped out in a single night.

Several days later, a family acquaintance journeyed to Dromton Purba's hermitage to deliver this shocking news. When they were close to the hermitage, they broke down and began wailing, overwhelmed by their grief. Dromton Purba emerged from his hut.

"What on earth is going on?" he said.

"You won't believe what has happened, lama. It's too horrific to bear! Your entire family has been assassinated. Every single person, your siblings, parents, nieces and nephews . . . they are all dead!"

"What?" Dromton Purba said. "Tell me again."

And so his acquaintance repeated the terrible story from beginning to end. Dromton Purba was silent for a moment. Then he said, "So, the nest of ants has been destroyed," meaning that this display of samsara, like a nest of ants, has been destroyed. That was all he said—no further reaction. He was utterly relaxed, utterly at ease.

Think about how we would react to such news. Most likely, we would be maddened with shock, rage, and grief. We would be losing our senses, passing out, plotting our revenge. But Dromton Purba did not even flinch. He had severed all attachment to reality—and he attained the rainbow body later on.

"This is what a Great Perfection practitioner should be like!" Khenpo Chokhyab Rinpoche would say. To hear of these great masters fills one with inspiration and faith.

Realized masters like this are nothing like us ordinary people. They do not act or see things in the same way. Look at the late Dodrupchen Rinpoche. Several years ago, a Western student sponsored a lot of construction at one of Rinpoche's retreat centers in Nepal. When the work was all completed, a close student took them to see Rinpoche and told Rinpoche how they had funded the building of several dozen retreat huts and sponsored the three-year retreats of a dozen or more practitioners. Most people would expect some acknowledgment after contributing so much—a nice kata and a special blessing perhaps, or at least some words of thanks. But Dodrupchen Rinpoche just nodded and said, "Okay, okay." When they left the room, the student exclaimed, "Dodrupchen Rinpoche has no feelings!" I do not know if they said this in criticism or praise, but when I heard this story later on I thought, *How right they were!* Dodrupchen Rinpoche exemplified the Great Perfection. He had transcended all hope and fear.

Another time, I went to see Dodrupchen Rinpoche in Bangkok. I was able to spend seven days with Rinpoche, by his side from morning till night. It was one of the best weeks of my life. There was a scholar from Derge there as well, a fellow disciple of Dodrupchen Rinpoche. His wife asked us, "Tell me, what is so special about Dodrupchen Rinpoche?" The scholar from Derge summed it up by saying, "Dodrupchen Rinpoche is the embodiment of the Great Perfection. I mean, if you were to place one hundred thousand dollars on the table in front of Rinpoche, he would not even look at it. For him, that wad of cash is no different from a common stone." This was the perfect reply. For the Great Perfection adept, there is no difference between dirt and gold, no difference between foes and friends, no difference between samsara and nirvana.

Post-Equipoise, in Conclusion

In his commentary on *The Seven Points of Mind Training*, Dilgo Khyentse Rinpoche explains that all aspects of practice are included in meditative equipoise and post-equipoise. In meditative equipoise, one familiarizes oneself with the ultimate nature, the state of simplicity beyond all constructs, and in post-equipoise one trains in recognizing all phenomena to be illusions and dreams. When we can merge the view of simplicity cultivated during meditative equipoise with our post-equipoise activities, we will not slip back into mundane experience, the stream of fixation and affliction that characterizes ordinary life.

Sometimes people get so angry that their face flushes and their veins swell. I heard of a lady in Kham who had a violent argument with her daughter and got so angry she passed out. She was taken to the hospital and died there soon afterward. It seems her anger had raised her blood pressure or triggered a heart attack. This is the extent to which ordinary people are overwhelmed by their emotions. However, we are not ordinary people; we are followers of the Buddha. We are studying *The*

Thirty-Seven Practices of Bodhisattvas. We need to recognize that the construct-free state we cultivate during meditative equipoise is also the nature of all post-equipoise experiences. We need to remember this when encountering good fortune and adversity. Then we will not remain ordinary people. And by mingling our practice of meditative equipoise—our confidence in the view—with our post-equipoise practice, both will be enhanced. This is a crucial point. It applies equally to the practice of the Great Perfection and the practice of the Great Seal. If you fail to do this, you could meditate for many years but end up seeing very little improvement in yourself.

Training in the Bodhichitta Precepts

Once the bodhisattva has given rise to bodhichitta and knows there is nothing more meaningful than attaining the state of perfect buddhahood, what is the next step? They will not attain buddhahood by just lying around. They need to train in the precepts of bodhichitta, primarily the six paramitas. This is what Gyalse Tokme explains next.

CHAPTER 29

Training in Generosity

> 25. If those who wish for buddhahood must give even their own bodies,
> What need is there to mention the giving of material goods?
> Therefore, without expecting result or reward,
> To give with generosity is the practice of bodhisattvas.

This tells us that generosity—and, in addition, the remaining five paramitas of discipline, patience, diligence, meditative concentration, and wisdom—must be cultivated in order to attain perfect awakening. The bodhisattva seeking awakening must practice generosity, and in doing so they must give away even their own body, their most cherished possession. Therefore, it goes without saying that they must also give away material goods.

There are many different types and divisions of generosity, one of which is the threefold division of the gift of material things, the gift of the Dharma, and the gift of protection from fear.

The generosity of material things refers to giving food, drink, clothing and the like to others to dispel poverty, discomfort, and physical need.

The gift of the Dharma refers to sharing the Dharma with others. This type of generosity can only be practiced authentically by bodhisattvas on the first bhumi and beyond—noble beings who have realized directly the truth of *dharmata* and so transcended self-interest and the eight worldly concerns. Ordinary beings like us are not yet qualified to practice the generosity of Dharma. Nevertheless, we can practice a semblance of this by introducing others to the path.

To give the gift of protection from fear is to protect the lives of those who are in danger. There are various ways of doing this, such as the traditional practice of releasing lives (*tsetar*).[155] Moreover, if you are in a position of authority, you can use that to prohibit hunting in a certain area or to create a sanctuary for animals. For example, in the Noble Land of India, during King Ashoka's time, one day a group of arhats were flying through the sky above Varanasi. As people stared into the sky in awe, one of the arhat's Dharma robes slipped off and fell to the ground. People thought one of the arhats had fallen and cried out, "A seer has fallen!" But in fact, it was just one of their robes. When King Ashoka heard what had happened, he was flooded with faith and declared the entire area to be a wildlife sanctuary for deer, antelopes, and the like. He named it Deer Forest of the Fallen Seer. This is how Deer Park came about.[156]

The generosity of material goods can be divided further into lesser, middling, and greater types of generosity, with reference to the objects given. Giving food, livestock, medicine, money, and so on to those in need is the lesser generosity of material goods. Giving away one's children and spouse, those closest to you, is the middling generosity of material goods, while giving away one's own body is the greater type of generosity of material goods.

The thought of giving away one's children and spouse might not sit well with modern people. Most likely, it will seem like an outrageous idea: You do not own other people like objects, so they are not yours to give. However, in the past this form of generosity was often practiced by great practitioners. For instance, in the sutras we find many accounts of monarchs, such as Sarvamdada and Drime Kunden, giving up their queens and children for the sake of awakening. However, this was not done by force. Once these monarchs had decided to renounce their kingdoms, wealth, friends, and family, and devote their lives to practice, they consulted their queens and children and asked them what they wished to do. Of course, the culture of the time was markedly different from modern Western culture, but, as you can see from the accounts in the sutras, the queens and children in these instances were courageous and altruistic. They were willing to make great sacrifices for the spiritual path.

In one of Buddha Shakyamuni's past lives, when he was a bodhisattva training on the path, he came across a starving tigress in the mountains, at the site now known as Namo Buddha in Nepal. He offered his body to the tigress to save her life and the life of her cubs. There are many other instances of great bodhisattvas giving their bodies away, such as King Jewel Crest who gave away his crown protuberance, King Drime Kunden who gave away his eyes, King Padma who gave away his flesh, and so on. They made these sacrifices for the sake of awakening, motivated by bodhichitta rooted in loving-kindness and compassion.

Many people are generous, especially with material goods. However, most people give with the hope of getting something in return—recognition or legacy, or perhaps they simply want to feel good. All acts of generosity are to be rejoiced in, but not every act of generosity qualifies as the bodhisattva's generosity. When practicing generosity, the bodhisattva must do so free of all hope for reward, in both this life and the next. This includes all hope for karmic recompense, such as gaining wealth or good health in future lives. The bodhisattva practices generosity motivated solely by the wish to attain perfect buddhahood for all beings' benefit, and they pray that their every act of generosity, however big or small, will be a cause for the awakening of all beings. It is their understanding of emptiness—ultimate bodhichitta—that enables them to practice generosity purely, free of hope for reward.

In one of his five hundred pure rebirths before manifesting perfect awakening, Buddha took birth as a prince called Vishvantara (Universal Liberator).[157] There were two main kingdoms in India at the time, one in the east and one in the south. Vishvantara was born in the eastern kingdom. He was kindhearted and noble-minded. From a young age, he was set on attaining buddhahood. To this end, he was always giving to others. When he came of age, he married an excellent woman named Madri and together had a son named Krishna and a daughter named Jalini.

Vishvantara continued to practice generosity, but at some point he became depressed. His father, the king, said to him, "You have a life of comfort and luxury, a beautiful wife, charming children, and yet you are downhearted. Tell me, what is troubling you?" Vishvantara replied, "Father, our subjects are suffering. Some lack food and drink, some lack clothing and medicine, others lack fields and property. Furthermore, I must by all means attain buddhahood, but in my situation, how can I possibly do so? I cannot bear to see others suffering, Father. Their suffering torments me."

The kind king then asked, "Well, how can you pursue your quest for buddhahood, my son?"

"I must practice generosity, Father," Vishvantara said.

And so, the king gave his son the key to the royal treasury, and Vishvantara was overjoyed. He announced to the kingdom that over the course of several days he would be giving food to those in need of food, medicine to those needing medicine, land to those without land, and likewise livestock, wealth, and more. The kingdom was very wealthy, so he had plenty to give. With a joyful heart, he gave and gave and gave, and soon half the royal wealth had been spent. This made the ministers uneasy. They advised the king that it would be wise to limit the prince's giving and rein him in, but the king paid no heed and let the prince continue giving until there was very little left.

The king had a warrior elephant called Auspicious that was much envied by the neighboring kingdom. In ancient India, armies were composed of four divisions: chariots, elephants, cavalry, and infantry, and the most powerful of all were the elephants. The warrior elephant Auspicious was perfectly trained and incredibly strong, and with weapons attached to his trunk, flank, and limbs he was invincible in war. You could say he was like a nuclear weapon.

When the neighboring kingdom heard that Vishvantara was giving his entire kingdom's wealth away, they decided to send a brahmin to ask for the elephant Auspicious. And Prince Vishvantara, having pledged to practice generosity for the sake of all beings, happily gave Auspicious away. When they heard about this, the ministers were enraged. The king also became irritated and for the first time he chastised his son.

"Son, you have gone too far. You cannot give the kingdom's army away!" he said. Vishvantara replied, "Dear father, these are but small acts of generosity, the gifts of material things. If I were asked to give my life, I would happily give it. Such is the pledge I have made."

Disquiet spread through the kingdom. Eventually it was decided, much to the king's regret, to expel the prince. He knew that if he allowed the prince to remain, there would be civil unrest. With a heavy heart and tear-filled eyes, the king said, "My son, take yourself to the Vindhya Mountain range." And so, Prince Vishvantara, together with his wife Madri and his children Krishna and Jalini—for they insisted on coming with him—departed the kingdom in a chariot loaded with provisions.

The prince's generosity had spread so far that when people saw him coming, they stopped him on the road and asked for clothes, jewels, and food. By the time they reached the mountains, the king had given all their provisions away. After someone asked for the horse pulling their chariot, Vishvantara and Madri dismounted and pulled the chariot themselves. After someone asked for the chariot, they carried their children on their backs.

Eventually they reached the Vindhya Mountain range. The mountains were filled with dangerous animals—with tigers, bears, and snakes—but by sticking together they managed to survive. Over the course of many months, they managed to build grass huts for shelter and find wild fruits and foods to eat. They found wild springs for drinking water and established a simple but pleasant life for themselves. The prince passed much of his time in meditation, while the children played together in the forest and streams. The wild animals slowly became their friends. For several years, they lived a simple but idyllic life.

Nearby there lived an old brahmin who had wed a much younger wife. His wife demanded a servant, and when the brahmin could not provide her with one, she abused him terribly. She declared herself unable to do any work, so the brahmin, despite his old age, was forced to do everything. Eventually the wife said, "Either you provide me with a good servant, or I will leave you! I've heard about this Prince Vishvantara who has pledged, for the sake of buddhahood, to give whatever is asked of him. I hear he has two children, so why not ask him for them?" Desperate not to lose his young, beautiful wife, the old brahmin set out, leaning heavily on his walking stick, on the long walk to Vishvantara's hermitage.

When the brahmin finally arrived, Krishna and Jalini were playing joyfully in a stream, surrounded by peacocks and deer. Vishvantara was immersed in meditation at the foot of a tree, with an aura of blessings radiating out from him. Madri, the prince's wife, had gone deeper into the forest to forage for fruit. When the brahmin approached Vishvantara and made his request, the prince was taken aback. He could not, would not, break his vow to give whatever was asked of him, and yet the thought of being parted from his children, and the thought of the fear and pain they would suffer, was overwhelming. A tight pain seized his heart, tears flowed down his cheeks. Krishna and Jalini begged their father to be allowed to see their mother one last time before being sent away. But the brahmin would not allow it. He tied the children's wrists up and led them away, like two small prisoners.

When Madri arrived back at the hermitage later that day, she could sense that something was wrong. The birds had been silent all afternoon, and the animals had gone into hiding, as if they were sick. "Where are our children?" she asked Vishvantara, her heart trembling in her chest. When he told her what had happened, she fainted from the shock.

Vishvantara tried to console Madri and reminded her of his vow—his promise to give whatever is asked of him for the sake of attaining buddhahood for all beings. "If someone were to ask for you, you know I would give you away as well," he said. Madri was stricken with grief at the loss of her children, but she rejoiced in her husband's noble pledge. Soon, another brahmin appeared. He asked Vishvantara to give him his beloved wife Madri as a servant. Madri willingly agreed to go, and so the prince gave her away. Now he would be all alone.

As soon as he had given Madri away, the brahmin before him disappeared and in his place the god Shakra appeared. Shakra had assumed the guise of this brahmin to put the prince to this final test. Delighted by Vishvantara and Madri's extraordinary generosity, he said he would grant them whatever they wished. Bowing down to Shakra, Vishvantara said, "Please, ensure my children never suffer from hunger. Ensure they return to their grandparent's kingdom, and grant your blessings that we are all reunited in our homeland before too long."

God Shakra then made the brahmin go insane so that he unwittingly went to the king's city Vishvapuri and tried to sell the children there. The king's ministers immediately recognized the children. They saved them from servitude and reunited them with their grandfather, the king. Shortly afterward, the king died, and the ministers invited the prince back to the kingdom, where he was enthroned and continued to practice generosity. Thus, Vishvantara, Madri, and their children were reunited, just as the prince had wished. Vishvantara became known as King Sarvamdada, Giver of Everything.

That is how the bodhisattva practices generosity for the sake of awakening; they give unstintingly. Hearing such stories should inspire us. It should help us strengthen and upgrade our own generosity. You do not need to be rich to practice generosity. You can be generous with whatever you have, such as time, energy, privilege, knowledge, care, attention, and so on.

Moreover, as Karma Chakme teaches in his *Mountain Dharma*,[158] when you encounter beautiful sights, tastes, scents, and so on, you can offer them to the buddhas and bodhisattvas. A stunning hotel, exquisite jewelry in a shop window, or breath-taking scenery—all of this can be offered up to the Three Jewels. If you do so sincerely and without attachment, it will become a pure and excellent offering. But you need to offer without attachment. This means that if you make an offering of a beautiful waterfall, you need to really imagine that the offering has been received and then let go. If you continue to look at the waterfall and marvel at its beauty, you have not really offered it up. This is a very important point. Once you have offered something, whether material or imagined, you must cut all ties of attachment to it.

CHAPTER 30

Training in Discipline

> 26. If, lacking discipline, you cannot benefit yourself,
> To think of benefiting others is laughable.
> Therefore, to observe discipline
> Free of samsaric motives is the practice of bodhisattvas.

There are different levels of discipline: the outer discipline of the personal liberation vows, the inner discipline of the bodhisattva trainings, and the secret discipline of the Secret Mantra samayas. In the context of *The Thirty-Seven Practices of Bodhisattvas*, we are looking at the discipline of bodhisattvas, which is composed of the discipline of binding negative conduct, the discipline of gathering virtuous qualities, and the discipline of benefiting others. To observe these three types of discipline is the practice of bodhisattvas. As taught in *The Treasury of Abhidharma*,

> Observing discipline, and having studied and
> contemplated the teachings,
> One applies oneself intensively to meditation.

It is with a foundation of authentic discipline that one should engage in study, and with a foundation of study that one should then contemplate. Then one should internalize one's study and contemplation by training diligently in meditation. This is the sequence in which we should apply ourselves to the path. Without a sound foundation of discipline, our study, contemplation, and meditation will not bear fruit, just as an uncultivated field will not yield an abundant harvest. As Nagarjuna explains,

> Just as the earth's the base for all that's still or moves,
> On discipline, it's said, is founded all that's good.[159]

Discipline is like the earth. The earth contains great riches, such as gold, silver, copper, and so on. It is "the base," or support, "for all that's still or moves"—for precious animals such as tigers, leopards, elephants, and horses and for human existence, as well as all luxuries and material wealth. Similarly, the excellence of the inner bodhisattva trainings and the Secret Mantra samayas rests upon the outer personal liberation vows.[160]

Therefore, the first aspect of a bodhisattva's discipline is the discipline of binding negative conduct, which is to abandon harming beings and the basis for this. This aspect of discipline includes all the outer personal liberation vows of the Lesser Vehicle, such as the 253 vows of a fully ordained monk, the 364 of a fully ordained nun, the 33 vows of novice monks and nuns, and the five precepts of lay practitioners.[161] The bodhisattva observes the very same personal liberation vows as the shravakas and pratyekabuddhas, but the motivation with which they do so differs. Their vast bodhichitta motivation transforms the personal liberation vows into an aspect of bodhisattva discipline.[162]

If you lack self-discipline, you will be unable to benefit yourself. You will be unable to fulfill even short-term, personal goals such as attaining a human rebirth or the partial awakening of a shravaka- or pratyekabuddha-arhat, so to wish to benefit all beings is a joke. This would be like someone drowning in a river trying to pull another drowning person onto dry land.

The discipline of gathering virtuous qualities refers to gathering stores of merit and purifying obscurations. The bodhisattva achieves this primarily by engaging in the ten virtuous actions and the six paramitas in vast and varied ways.

The third aspect of the bodhisattva's discipline is benefiting other beings. The most supreme of all the buddhas' benevolent activities is the turning of the Dharma Wheel. They do this through the four means of magnetizing: being generous, talking pleasantly, teaching accordingly, and practicing as they preach. To begin with, the buddhas and bodhisattvas attract disciples with generosity. Then they converse with them in pleasant and meaningful ways. They practice as they preach and, with a pure motivation unsullied by a single drop of self-interest, they guide students in the ultimate teachings of the Great Vehicle—the teachings of definitive meaning that lead to perfect, omniscient buddhahood. This is the discipline of benefiting beings.

We can see these three aspects of discipline in the awakened deeds of Buddha Shakyamuni. When training on the path in his previous lives, Buddha renounced worldly life and established a firm foundation of discipline. He then gathered vast stores of merit for three countless eons through the practice of the six paramitas. Finally, Buddha attained perfect awakening at Bodh Gaya, and then at Varanasi and other places, he turned the three turnings of the Dharma Wheel for countless beings.

My root guru, Khenpo Dazer Rinpoche, embodied discipline in the same way. He maintained immaculate discipline throughout his life. As a young boy, he took the vows of a novice monk. As a young man, he traveled with his close Dharma friend, the renowned Khenpo Jigme Phuntsok Rinpoche, to Mani Lama Pema Siddhi's residence in Golok and received the vows of a fully ordained monk. Mani Lama was a great saint, an emanation of Avalokiteshvara whose appearance had been prophesied in the scriptures, where it is stated that he would lead tens of millions of beings to the pure realms.

Henceforth, Khenpo Dazer Rinpoche maintained his monastic vows purely and perfectly. Even through the turbulent years of the Cultural Revolution, when basic food, clothing, and shelter were rarities and monks and nuns were forced to transgress their precepts by working the fields and so on, Khenpo Dazer Rinpoche was able to maintain his monastic discipline and was not parted from the three Dharma robes. He ascribed his good fortune to the kindness of the lamas of Dzogchen Monastery and his root guru, Omniscient Botrul Rinpoche.

Around 1961 Khenpo Dazer Rinpoche arrived in Kalimpong, India, and as soon as he could, he established, for the monastics living in exile, the three foundations for all monastic training—*sojong* (the purification ceremony), *yarne* (the rainy-season retreat), and *gagye* (the ceremony that concludes the rainy-season retreat). The late Kyabje Dudjom Rinpoche acted as the sponsor, while Khenpo Dazer Rinpoche acted as the preceptor. This was the first time that *yarne* had been held in the refugee communities in India. In subsequent years, in Sikkim, Bhutan, Nepal, and other locations, Khenpo Dazer Rinpoche bestowed the novice vows on many thousands of monks and the full monastic vows on many hundreds. These days, you will find students of Khen Rinpoche in almost all the monasteries and *shedras* (monastic colleges) in India. In this way, Khenpo Dazer Rinpoche revived the fading embers of monastic discipline for the benefit of future generations.

He had not the slightest interest in name or gain. He was untouched by the eight worldly concerns. He was a genuine renunciant who lived in perfect adherence with the monastic code. His simplicity was surpassed only by that of Khenpo Chokhyab Rinpoche. I doubt very much we could find any contemporary lamas that match their example.

When Khenpo Dazer Rinpoche fell ill toward the end of his life, he was not interested in getting medical treatment, but when we, his students, pleaded with him, he eventually agreed to visit a hospital in China, since there were no hospitals nearby. Once Khen Rinpoche had agreed, there then came the question of covering the medical expenses. Khenpo Dazer

Rinpoche had an old red leather wallet from Kalimpong, and he told me to look in there for some money. I opened the wallet and found thirty-five Chinese yuan.

"Is this all you have?" I said, to which Khen Rinpoche replied, reproaching me, "You think I've been hoarding money?!"

Thirty-five yuan would not even cover the bus ticket from Khen Rinpoche's hermitage in Kham to the hospital. All Khen Rinpoche's students then got together and pooled whatever little money we had. Most had just fifty or one hundred yuan—all Khen Rinpoche's monk disciples were real medicants back then. A few of us had a little more, and eventually we managed to gather five thousand yuan, just enough to get Khen Rinpoche to the hospital and cover the first few weeks of treatment. We told Khen Rinpoche we would gather whatever other funds were needed in due course.

Khen Rinpoche traveled to Tridu Hospital accompanied by his two nephews. At first, he seemed to be responding well to treatment, but then one day his health declined. His nephew Rikter had gone out to do some chores, while his other nephew Lungtok Nyima stayed by his side. At some point, Khen Rinpoche told Lungtok Nyima to leave him for a while, so he stepped outside. Once he had left the room, he heard Khen Rinpoche clap his hands three times, then shout "PHAT!" Lungtok Nyima rushed back inside and saw Khen Rinpoche sitting upright on the hospital bed. He had passed into parinirvana.

I had stayed back at the hermitage and had been teaching *The Ornament of the Middle Way* to some of the other monks. Shortly before he passed, we had received a message from the hospital that Khen Rinpoche was slowly recovering and that we need not worry. We had just completed the text, so we were celebrating—celebrating the completion of the teachings and most of all our precious guru's good health. As we were drinking tea and enjoying ourselves, a round rainbow, a perfect *bindu*,[163] appeared in the sky. We all marveled at it, and I thought to myself, *Either a nirmanakaya is taking birth or a great master is passing away.* We found out later that Khen Rinpoche had passed away at that same moment. Several days later, his holy body was brought back to the hermitage.

Khenpo Dazer Rinpoche left behind the following possessions: five or six blocks of butter in his pantry, three or four gold-plated statues (including a Manjushri statue containing relics of Mipham Rinpoche, which was offered to Dzogchen Monastery), one set of silver offering bowls, one silver lamp, one copper lamp, and one set of old robes. Khen Rinpoche had no change of robes to wear on special occasions, unlike most other monks. He simply wore the same set of robes year in, year out, until they fell apart. Khenpo Tsering Zangdrub of Rahul Monastery said to me once, "Our Khenpo Chokhyab Rinpoche was a true renunciate, but Khenpo Dazer Rinpoche was just the same, maybe even more so, don't you think?" What he said was true. The only difference between them was that Khenpo Dazer Rinpoche had several statues and a set of silver offering bowls.

Khen Rinpoche arrived in Sikkim in the early 1960s and established a shedra there at the command of Ponda Khen Rinpoche.[164] Later on, Khen Rinpoche traveled to Bhutan and stayed for nine years at Tarpa Ling, the seat of Longchenpa, bestowing a wealth of teachings on the local practitioners. Kyabje Penor Rinpoche[165] later invited Khen Rinpoche to Namdroling Monastery in India, where Khen Rinpoche taught many major treatises for a year or more. From India, Khen Rinpoche traveled to Tibet to the famed Dzogchen Shri Singha Shedra, which had just been rebuilt, and taught there for five or six years. Khen Rinpoche then traveled to Rahor Monastery in his homeland, where he reestablished the practice of yarne. In his latter years, he lived at a hermitage in Yarlung, near Dzogchen. Many of Khen Rinpoche's students are now great teachers in Tibet and many others are still living in Sikkim and Bhutan.[166]

He was overflowing with faith and pure perception and utterly free of sectarianism. You only had to spend time with

Khen Rinpoche to see the reverence he held for Je Tsongkhapa and his followers, for the Sakya forefathers such as Sakya Pandita, for Marpa, Mila, and Gampopa, whose life stories he would recount repeatedly, and of course for Omniscient Rongzompa, Longchenpa, Mipham Rinpoche, and Jigme Lingpa. My own lack of sectarianism is thanks to Khen Rinpoche. That said, when it came to the various tenet systems, he was uncompromising and unwavering in his presentation of the wisdom intent of Omniscient Rongzompa, Longchenpa, and Mipham Rinpoche.

Though he was utterly free of pride, he often said, with assured dignity, "I don't have any special qualities, except for the fact that when I die, I can die cloaked in my saffron Dharma robe. This is my greatest accomplishment."[167] He would advise us to observe discipline purely, for upon this basis of discipline all other excellent qualities will arise, and again and again, he would quote these words of Vasubandhu:

> Observing discipline, and having studied and
> contemplated the teachings,
> One applies oneself intensively to meditation.

It seems this was the influence, or tradition, of his guru, Botrul Rinpoche, for Khenpo Chokhyab Rinpoche would also recite these lines frequently. He placed great importance on the observance of discipline, and he embodied this himself. As we have seen, there is no Dharma that is not included within discipline: the discipline of binding negative conduct, gathering virtuous qualities, and benefiting beings. There is so much merit and benefit to keeping the monastic vows. A fully ordained monk or nun is an incredibly precious thing. The ordained sangha is the foundation of the teachings—Buddha said this himself. And the higher tantras state that the supreme vajra holder is one who upholds full monastic vows.

Khen Rinpoche lived like an ordinary monk and maintained a strict routine. He would rise early every day, complete his practice session, then perform the water-torma offering (*chutor*) and *The Mountain Smoke Offering* (*Riwo Sangcho*). He would teach the scriptures until noon and study and contemplate throughout the afternoon. Then, in the evening, he would perform *dharmapala* offerings[168] and the offering of *sur*.[169] This was his daily routine, month after month, year after year. My own daily practice of making a smoke offering in the morning and a *sur* offering in the evening comes from his example. He gave teachings every day for most of his life, firmly planting the unique tradition of Ju Mipham Rinpoche and the wisdom intents of Omniscient Rongzompa and Longchenpa. In this way, he embodied the discipline of benefiting beings.

Khenpo Dazer Rinpoche said a practitioner should proceed in the way a rich person gathers wealth. In the olden days, a wealthy person would give importance to all their assets, large and small, from valuable livestock to a single needle and thread. In the same way, a practitioner should aim to do long retreats and engage in extensive study and meditation, and they should pay equal attention to smaller positive deeds, such as reciting a few mani mantras, circumambulating a stupa, lighting a single butter lamp, and so on.

Khenpo Dazer Rinpoche observed karmic causality so finely. For instance, he kept two envelopes for storing offerings: one was for offerings made by the living, and the other was for offerings made in request for prayers and guidance for the dead. He would use the offerings made by the living for food and other basic provisions, but he would never touch the offerings made for the dead. With this money, he would either offer butter lamps, sponsor the printing of texts, or sponsor the recitation of *The King of Aspiration Prayers*. I never saw anyone be so careful with their offerings. Maybe there were practitioners like this in the past, maybe there are some nowadays, but I have never seen anyone as vigilant as Khen Rinpoche. Similarly, he was incredibly careful in his daily actions. For instance, Khen Rinpoche would always urinate on a rock. (We did not have indoor toilets in Kham back then.) When I asked him why he did this, because it certainly was not comfortable, he said, "If you urinate directly on the ground, you might kill insects. If you urinate on a rock, you can avoid committing such harm."

Khenpo Dazer Rinpoche was a triple-vow vajra holder, a master who could maintain the vows of each of the three vehicles simultaneously and without conflict. He upheld the outer personal liberation vows, the inner bodhisattva trainings, and the Secret Mantra samayas. He was perfectly learned, righteous, and kind.

Khenpo Chokhyab Rinpoche would sometimes tease Khenpo Dazer Rinpoche by saying, "Well, he hasn't gone overseas and gotten rich, nor has he gathered many students." Khenpo Dazer Rinpoche himself would talk about his decision not to travel overseas, to Europe, America and so on. It was not for lack of invitations. He was invited as early as the seventies by Tulku Kunga, and later on Tulku Pema Wangyal Rinpoche invited him to France, but each time he declined.

He would say to me, "You will find yourself overseas, you just wait! Be sure to never stay overseas for more than three months at a time. There's not much benefit in lamas and monks traveling to foreign countries. There are only two people who can bring benefit in that way: Dilgo Khyentse Rinpoche and Dudjom Rinpoche. This is because they have freed themselves through realization and have the power to free others through compassion. Therefore, they bring benefit to everyone who sees, hears, or thinks of them." Of course there were other great masters alive at the time, such as Dodrupchen Rinpoche, Trulshik Rinpoche, and Penor Rinpoche, but this was Khen Rinpoche's perspective and this is what he would say.

Khen Rinpoche's root guru, Omniscient Botrul Rinpoche, had told him, "In the future, there won't be many opportunities to teach the Dharma, so apply yourself to practice in retreat." Accordingly, wherever Khen Rinpoche went, he would stay in retreat. He would teach once a day, but for the rest of the time he maintained his solitude and practiced day and night. He devoted his entire life to study and practice. He never separated these two.

When he was a student himself, he endured many hardships, together with his Dharma brother Khenpo Chokhyab Rinpoche. They had very little food, no proper shelter, and they often had to walk through snow-filled valleys without any shoes. One time when he was staying at Shechen Monastery and the snowfall began, Khen Rinpoche took shelter in a makeshift hut. Accommodation and food was not automatically provided to students back then. At night, Khen Rinpoche would lay some pieces of wood over the hut's open roof and drape his shawl over the wood to create an enclosure. Then, in the morning, he would shake the snow off his shawl, put it on, and walk to class. At the time, Khen Rinpoche's kitchen contained only a clay cup and small kettle. He would cover these with a piece of cloth when he left the hut, but crows would come in during the day and upturn everything, creating even more difficulties. These are just some of the hardships Khenpo Dazer Rinpoche endured for the sake of the Dharma. As taught in *The Words of My Perfect Teacher* and other texts, the practitioner should be willing to get by with the bare minimum of clothing and food. Khenpo Dazer Rinpoche and Khenpo Chokhyab Rinpoche really practiced this. I am not exaggerating at all; his other students can confirm the truth of my account.

Khen Rinpoche was free of short-term samsaric aims—meaning, the eight worldly concerns and all mundane motivations, such as observing discipline to ensure rebirth in the human and god realms. Motivated by bodhichitta, he upheld to perfection all three aspects of discipline.

CHAPTER 31

Training in Patience

> 27. For the bodhisattva who desires the joys of virtue,
> All who harm them are precious gems.
> Therefore, to cultivate patience toward all,
> Without resentment, is the practice of bodhisattvas.

Entering the Way of the Bodhisattva states,

> There is no misdeed like hatred;
> No austerity like patience.[170]

Patience has so many benefits. It is one of the best ways to accumulate merit and is even more powerful than maintaining discipline and practicing generosity.[171] Anger, on the other hand, is the most destructive of emotions. As Shantideva said,

> One moment's anger shatters all
> Good acts accumulated
> In a thousand eons, such as giving
> Or offering to the buddhas.[172]

A single moment of anger can destroy a thousand eons of merit. From among the three poisons of attachment, anger, and ignorance, anger is the worst. Attachment and ignorance create negative karma and perpetuate samsara, but they do not destroy previously accumulated virtue. Anger not only creates negative karma; it also destroys virtue.

As with the other paramitas, there are many different types and divisions of patience, one of which is the threefold division of patience in the face of ingratitude, patience of enduring hardships for the sake of the Dharma, and patience of not fearing profound reality.

As for the first, ingratitude is very difficult to bear. If you are a parent, your children might sometimes be rude and ungrateful. Despite your love and care, they might treat you like an enemy. If you can cultivate patience in the face of such ingratitude, you will accumulate great merit.

The best example of the second type of patience, the patience of enduring hardships for the sake of the Dharma, is Jetsun Milarepa, who, as stated above, endured beatings and ridicule from his teacher, Marpa.

Third, the patience of not fearing profound reality refers to being able to comprehend the meaning of emptiness, the illusory unreal nature of all phenomena.[173] Such teachings fill some people with hesitation and fear. There are stories of shravakas hearing these teachings and becoming so terrified and overwhelmed that they immediately had a heart attack and died. Likewise, there were people in the past, and also today, who claim that the Great Perfection and the Great Seal are not genuine Buddhist teachings but are the nihilistic teachings of Hashang, that they are an incorrect, perverted view.[174] When people make these mistaken claims, it shows they are lacking this third type of patience—patience toward profound emptiness. Their minds are not large enough to accommodate the vast meaning of profound emptiness.

In the past, two shravaka practitioners came to receive teachings from Lord Atisha. To begin with, Atisha taught the divisions of the aggregates, elements, and sense sources, the principle of karma, the emptiness of the personal self, and so on. They were so delighted with these teachings that Atisha continued to instruct them. He moved on to the Great Vehicle teachings, explaining the profound emptiness of all phenomena from form up to omniscience. But they could not bear to hear such things. They became terrified and overwhelmed. Placing their hands over their ears, they pleaded with Atisha to stop. In response, Atisha shook his head and with a weary heart said, "Discipline alone is not enough, is it?" Without the courageous heart of bodhichitta, discipline on its own is not much use.

For the bodhisattva who is seeking awakening, and who is seeking a great mass of virtue to that end, there is no greater quality than patience. For by generating patience in the face of harm, hardships, and profound reality, you can quickly amass great stores of merit and purify eons' worth of obscurations and misdeeds at the same time.

This is also the reason why there is nothing more valuable to bodhisattvas than those who do them harm. "All who harm them" refers to everything that causes one difficulty, such as enemies, harm doers, and irritants, including sickness and bad luck. The bodhisattva acknowledges that these are all the result of their own past karma, and they welcome them. For without these sources of harm, they would have no opportunities to cultivate patience, thereby gathering merit, purifying misdeeds, and progressing on the path. Therefore, the bodhisattva cultivates patience "free of resentment," meaning free of malice, hatred, and spite. They do this "toward all," meaning toward all objects of patience without exception—everyone and everything that causes them harm.

Once, a monk from Amdo came to receive teachings from the Great Perfection master Yukhok Jadral. He claimed to have transcended anger and perfected patience, which is no small feat. After all, patience is only truly perfected on the third bhumi, Luminous. Eventually his audacious claims reached Yukhok Jadral, who went to see him one day.

"I hear you have transcended anger. Is it true?" he asked.

"It is indeed," the Amdo monk said.

"I see," Yukhok Jadral said and left it at that.

Yukhok Jadral liked to test people in strange ways. A few days later, Yukhok Jadral called one of his other students who lived in a room near the Amdo monk.

"Later today, when this monk is in his room, go out to fetch water and ask him to keep an eye on your room," he said. "Shortly after you return, tell him you had five or six silver coins stored under your mattress, but you just checked and they're no longer there. Ask him if anyone passed by while you were out fetching water. If he says that no one passed by, then confront him. Say, 'Well, in that case, the thief must be you!' If he denies it, raise the pressure. Say that, without a doubt, it must have been him. Swear on your life that you had those coins under your mattress. If he gets angry, bring him to me."

The monk did just as Yukhok Jadral said. When he accused the Amdo monk of stealing the coins, the Amdo monk said, "Please don't say that. I am a monk. I would never steal." He did not seem angry at all.

"Monk or not, you have taken my money!" the monk replied. He carried on accusing him, saying that it must have been him, it could not have been anyone else, and that he should not lie about it. At this point, the Amdo monk started to get a little agitated. The monk then called the disciplinarian and the two monks explained the whole scenario to him, but it was just the word of one monk against the other, so no conclusion was reached. By now, the Amdo monk was a little tetchy.

"Well, we will have to take this to Yukhok Jadral," the disciplinarian said.

Before their teacher, the Amdo monk attested to his innocence again: "I would never steal, Rinpoche. I am a monk!

Furthermore, I would never steal in the presence of you, our precious guru, the Wish-Fulfilling Jewel."

He swore on his life that he was innocent. Yukhok Jadral heard him out, then he said, "You know, despite what you say, I'm quite sure you did it. This monk over here, I know him well, and he is very honest. In spite of what you say, it seems you are a thief."

Looking around the room, the Amdo monk saw the disciplinarian, the monk, and several others all staring at him reproachfully. His cheeks began to blush, his muscles began twitching, and indignation welled up in him. Finally, he exploded: "How dare you falsely accuse me?! I am not a thief!" he yelled. Then he turned to the disciplinarian and the monk and started laying into them.

At this point, Yukhok Jadral raised his voice: "Hey! Forget it, forget it. Cool down! You claim to have perfected patience, but it looks like you are still subject to anger after all," he said.

He then gave the Amdo monk a real dressing down: "You are nothing but a charlatan! You claimed to be a third-bhumi bodhisattva, but look at you now! I set this whole saga up just to test you, and you have done a good job of exposing yourself." The lama was so ashamed when he heard this, he almost dissolved into the ground.

"You think the third bhumi is something easy to attain? If you just lie around in your homeland, eating meat, butter, and cheese and bathing in the sun, of course you won't feel anger. Anger arises when triggered—when there are triggers! You are a liar and a fraud. Tomorrow you will pack your bags and leave." With that, he expelled the monk from his community.

On the other hand, Yukhok Jadral had a student who was renowned in the community for his patience. He was said to be utterly free of anger, free of jealousy and pride, and many of his fellow students would praise him. One of Yukhok Jadral's students was a rather plump monk from a wealthy family in Amdo, and when he heard this monk being lavished with praise, he became suspicious and perhaps a little jealous.

"Come on, everyone gets angry sometimes. I don't believe it. I'm going to test this guy out," he said to himself.

One day, when this plump monk saw his much-praised Dharma brother walking down to the latrine, he followed him. This was not a proper toilet with plumbing and so on, but an open latrine, the ground wet with urine and feces. When the patient monk was not looking, he shoved him from behind. The monk stumbled but regained his balance. He did not seem at all irritated. He just chuckled to himself. The monk then shoved him a second time, with more force. The patient monk almost fell over, but he managed to steady himself. His skirt had fallen into a puddle of sewage and was a little soiled. But again, he just chuckled to himself and gave the other monk a smile. The monk then shoved him a third time, with all his might. The patient monk toppled to the ground, face down in the muck. He scrambled back onto his feet, but his robes were completely soiled, dripping with muck. Once more, he chuckled to himself and gave the monk a smile. The Amdo monk was astonished and tears welled up in his eyes.

"It's really true, you have perfected patience!" he said, and from that point on, he had tremendous faith in him. For the many years the Amdo monk lived at Yukhok Jadral's hermitage, he supported this monk and Dharma brother financially and showed him great respect. Being from a wealthy family, he had a very nice house, and he hosted his Dharma brother there and looked after all his needs.

CHAPTER 32

Training in Diligence

> 28. Merely for their own sake, the shravakas and pratyekabuddhas
> Exert themselves like someone extinguishing a fire in their hair.
> Seeing this, to develop diligence, source of virtues,
> For the benefit of all beings, is the practice of bodhisattvas.

Diligence is defined as taking delight in virtue. As Shantideva explains,

> Diligence is a zest for virtue.[175]

Simply working hard does not qualify as a bodhisattva's diligence. Diligence is the application of joyful effort in virtuous activities.

The shravakas and pratyekabuddhas who follow the Lesser Vehicle strive for liberation from samsara, a state of cessation that is a partial awakening that benefits oneself alone. To this end, they maintain their full monastic precepts and, content with the bare necessities, adhere to solitary places where they plant the victory banner of accomplishment. In this way, they embrace hardships for several lifetimes in pursuit of liberation for their personal benefit alone.

Imagine that a young woman is preparing for a party. She oils her hair, applies her makeup, and puts on her dress. She sprays some perfume on her wrists, looks in the mirror one last time, and is about to step out of the house when suddenly a spark from a candle flame sets fire to her hair. How would she react? Without a second thought, she would be patting her hair and extinguishing the fire. It is with this kind of urgency that the shravakas and pratyekabuddhas apply themselves to their path—a path aimed at a limited state of awakening for their own benefit alone. Seeing this, the bodhisattva—who is seeking perfect buddhahood, the source of all virtues, for the benefit of all countless beings—strengthens their diligence on the path. Buddhahood is attained through diligence, as the great yogi Milarepa said.

The scriptures describe three types of diligence: armor-like diligence, applied diligence, and insatiable diligence. Armor-like diligence is the determination to persevere in your practice, regardless of the difficulties you encounter. Look at how Buddha Shakyamuni, Milarepa, Longchenpa, and others endured hardships in their pursuit of buddhahood. Longchenpa, for example, sustained himself for several months with twenty-one mercury pills.[176] Likewise, when Pema Dechen Gyalpo (the first Degyal Rinpoche) spent nine years practicing *nyungne* (the fasting practice of Avalokiteshvara) at Riprup Mountain, whatever small alms of food he received from his family and the local people he would give away to the wild animals. In this way, he immersed himself in the practice of Avalokiteshvara, the Great Compassionate One. It is said that at one point his body grew so emaciated that the sunrays would shine straight through the palms of his hands. For the entire nine years, he sustained himself on boiled inner tree bark and nothing else. He had extraordinary meditative experiences and direct visions of many wisdom deities during this time.

Take inspiration from their examples, and donning the armor of determination, be willing to sacrifice good food, clothing, and reputation for the sake of the path. We should not feel discouraged, thinking, *Well, the great masters of the past were emanations of the buddhas and bodhisattvas. I'm just an ordinary person, so there's no way I can endure the sorts of hardships they did.* We need to draw inspiration from their examples and resolve to practice with the same—or even greater—determination. We need to toughen up a little so that we are not put off by small hardships, like not getting good food or comfortable clothes. This armor of determination is like a bulletproof vest; it protects you from discouragement.

Applied diligence is a remedy for procrastination. It means to apply yourself to the practice of the six paramitas and to make your practice your priority. These days, people are forever making excuses for themselves and putting off their practice. You might think, *Well, I am still quite young, so I'll do a three-year retreat, but I'll do it in the future when I have some savings*, and so on. In this way, you delay your practice, and the days, weeks, months, and years of your fleeting life slip through your fingers like sand. Procrastination is a major obstacle. As Omniscient Longchenpa said,

> Worldly preoccupations never end until the moment
> we die.
> But they end when we drop them—such is their nature.[177]

That is the truth, but most people cannot accept it. Applied diligence is to apply yourself immediately to practice in whatever way you can, just like a coward seeing a snake in their lap and jumping to their feet without a moment's delay.

Insatiable diligence is to continue exerting yourself in virtue, without feeling satisfied with what you have accomplished thus far. We should learn to be satisfied with our worldly activities because there is nothing meaningful to be gained from them, but we should never be satisfied with our Dharma practice. You might think that since you have completed the five sets of one hundred thousand preliminaries (*ngondro*), a three-year retreat, or several years of study, you have done enough. Or perhaps you feel satisfied with yourself for maintaining your monastic vows or for accumulating ten million vajra-guru mantras. Such an attitude is of no use. We need to keep applying ourselves until we reach perfect buddhahood. Once we reach perfect buddhahood, then we can stop. But until then, we should practice the way a yak eats grass: While taking one mouthful, he is already eyeing up the next. So, when practicing the preliminaries, you should already be thinking about what practice you will do next—the practices of generation and completion, of trekcho and togal, and so on.[178] Otherwise, if you do a small amount of Dharma, such as a three-year retreat, and then feel you can lie back and rest on your laurels, you will be like someone with a liver problem: They eat a little and then feel nauseated and lose their appetite. We need to have an insatiable appetite for Dharma.

Before Milarepa met his guru Marpa Lotsawa, he studied black magic under the famed sorcerer Yungtun Trogyal and caused the death of thirty-five people. Later, seeing the suffering he had caused, he was filled with remorse. A lama then foretold that Milarepa's destined guru—the guru with whom he had a karmic connection from past lives—was Marpa Lotsawa, and so Milarepa set off in search of him. Due to his previous karma and aspirations, the moment Milarepa saw Marpa, all his ordinary thoughts and perceptions came to a halt.

When Milarepa told Marpa his story, Marpa replied, "Well, it seems you are a great sinner, just as you say. I have excellent Dharma, the teachings of Naropa that can deliver one to buddhahood, the state of the Great Seal, in a single body and life. That said, excellent Dharma alone cannot do the job. It all depends on your own diligence and faith. If you can work hard, there is no doubt that you can reach buddhahood through these teachings, but you need to work hard. In the past, the great pandita Naropa underwent twelve great hardships at the feet of his guru, Tilopa." Marpa then told Milarepa the life story of Naropa and how he had followed Tilopa. He then gave Milarepa the refuge vows and five precepts, since refuge is the entryway to all Dharmas.[179]

After granting Milarepa the refuge vows, Marpa told him that he needed to build several towers for his son, Dharmadode, and to this end Milarepa was set to work. With his bare hands, he built four towers—one round tower, one crescent-shaped tower, one triangular tower, and one square tower representing the four activities. Milarepa's hands, arms, and back became covered with calluses and wounds constantly seeping pus and blood, but still he persevered. This was armor-like diligence. In his hagiography and his collection of songs, you can learn more about the hardships Milarepa embraced for the sake of Dharma, for the sake of attaining the state of the Great Seal in a single body and life. Similarly, you can look at the life story of Marpa Lotsawa and how he endured hardships at the feet of his guru, Naropa. These are examples of armor-like diligence.

After enduring those hardships for the sake of Dharma, Milarepa went to Trakar Taso, Tsari, Mount Kailash, and other such places, and devoted himself, night and day, to practice. Lacking provisions, he sustained himself on a diet of wild nettles to the point that his skin turned green and became covered with nettle fur and it was difficult to tell if he was a human or a ghost. This was applied diligence.

Milarepa continued to practice in the mountains with insatiable diligence until attaining the state of perfect buddhahood. Until that point, he was never satisfied with the amount of practice he had done or with his signs of accomplishment. By training in the subtle channels, winds, and essences, he gained mastery over the elements. He could not be burned by fire, swept away by water, and so on. The warmth of bliss pervaded his body and he was able to sustain himself through meditation, without the need for ordinary food and drink. By continuing to exert himself, he eventually reached the consummate state of the Great Seal and attained perfect buddhahood. With his unrelenting diligence, he achieved this in a single body and a single life.

Think of how many beings have attained buddhahood in the centuries since by following Milarepa's teachings and example. Think of how many beings right now are setting out on the path to buddhahood inspired by Milarepa's life. It was through his diligence that Milarepa attained perfect buddhahood, the source of all excellent qualities. It was through his diligence that he became an enduring source of benefit for beings. As Milarepa himself said, "I attained buddhahood through diligence. You wander in samsara due to laziness."

At one point, Ngenzong Tonpa, one of Milarepa's disciples, said to him, "Precious Guru, the diligence with which you practiced and the hardships you endured are difficult for us ordinary people to conceive of, let alone emulate. Without doubt, you must be an emanation of a buddha or a great bodhisattva. Please, tell us whose emanation you are. Tell us which great being you were in the past."

Milarepa replied, "My son, your pure perception is admirable, but with these words you denigrate the sacred Dharma. If you receive the sacred Dharma, such as the instructions of the Great Seal, and you train in them with unwavering diligence, as I did, there is nothing to stop you, or any other ordinary being, from becoming just like me and attaining the awakened state of Vajradhara in this very body and life."

One day, as a parting instruction to his heart son Gampopa, Milarepa turned around, raised his lower robe, and revealed his bare buttocks. They were covered with thick calluses, like the butt of a monkey, from having sat for so many years in meditation. Milarepa said, "Whether you become a buddha or not depends on diligence. If you have diligence, you can free yourself without a doubt."

CHAPTER 33

Training in Meditative Concentration

> 29. Knowing that the afflictions are conquered
> By deep insight grounded in calm abiding,
> To train in concentration that utterly transcends
> The four formless states is the practice of bodhisattvas.

As Shantideva explains,

> Realizing that afflictions are destroyed
> By shamatha and insight in conjunction,
> First seek out shamatha, which comes from joy
> For having no attachment to the world.[180]

This verse from *The Thirty-Seven Practices* is very similar to the above verse from *Entering the Way of the Bodhisattva*. That said, since it is the distillation of the latter's entire chapter on meditation, and of the words of Buddha himself, Gyalse Tokme's verse is even more precious and profound.

The bodhisattva must cultivate a concentration that is the unity of calm abiding (*shamatha*) and deep insight (*vipashyana*), and to do so, they must free themselves from worldly ties by shunning all external and internal busyness. External busyness refers to disturbing noise created by animals, humans, machinery, and so on, all forms of hustle and bustle, whether it be in the city or countryside. Amid such busyness, the mind cannot settle, and so calm abiding cannot develop. Therefore, the bodhisattva seeks out quiet, solitary places, as Khandro Yeshe Tsogyal describes in her prayer to Guru Rinpoche:

> In charnel grounds, hermitages, retreats amid the snows,
> And other secluded places with all perfect qualities,
> Let the quintessence of deep meditation
> Be my constant practice.[181]

Internal busyness refers to the eight worldly concerns and all activities connected to them. If your body is in the mountains but your mind is wandering through city streets, concentration will not develop. So, remove your body from hustle and bustle, and remove your mind from discursive thought. This is an important prerequisite for cultivating meditative concentration. For the actual practice itself, one needs to discard the five flaws using the eight applications and thereby progress through the nine stages of resting the mind. These important points are taught in *The Ornament of the Mahayana Sutras* and other texts.

The bodhisattva must cultivate meditative concentration in which calm abiding and deep insight are a natural unity. It is only this type of meditative concentration that can overcome, or uproot, the afflictions once and for all. In this context, "afflictions" include both the afflictive obscuration, which prevents liberation, and the cognitive obscuration, which prevents the omniscient state of perfect buddhahood. The two obscurations cannot be overcome by calm abiding alone—one needs deep insight. But, without the stability of calm abiding, deep insight will lack strength. As Longchenpa explains in *Finding Rest in the Nature of the Mind*,

> When there is no calm abiding,
> Deep insight is a state of moving thought.
> Deprived of insight,
> Calm abiding is a neutral and amorphous state.[182]

The unity of calm abiding and deep insight is the unity of compassion and emptiness; calm abiding is compassion, and deep insight is the realization of emptiness.

There are many types of meditative concentration, but they can all be condensed into the following three categories: the childish concentration of ordinary beings, the clearly discerning concentration of the worldly mind, and the excellent concentration of the *tathagatas*. The childish concentration of ordinary beings is practiced by those who have not yet entered Buddha's teachings. The bodhisattva, who wishes to attain liberation and buddhahood, trains in the latter two types of meditative concentration.

Generally speaking, meditative concentration is defined as a mind focused unwaveringly on a virtuous object. One can practice calm abiding using any focal object, such as a stone, a piece of wood, the syllable AH, or one's breath. However, Mipham Rinpoche extolled the virtues of using an image of Buddha Shakyamuni because of the blessings of Buddha's form.[183] In any case, the practice of calm abiding involves placing the mind one-pointedly on one's chosen focal object. By training persistently in this, the mind becomes increasingly focused and pliable, and traversing the nine stages of resting the mind, one reaches the one-pointed mind of the desire realm, thereby perfecting calm abiding.

The practice of calm abiding is not unique to the Buddhadharma. Many Hindu and other traditions practice similar techniques, and as a result they can attain miraculous powers, such as the ability to levitate, fly, or sustain themselves without food. However, these are merely common siddhis.

They might bring some temporary benefit but they will never lead to liberation or buddhahood. Unless these meditations are infused with deep insight into emptiness, they remain the childish concentrations of ordinary beings.

If you train diligently and correctly in meditation, the meditative experiences of bliss, clarity, and nonthought will arise. This is inevitable. For bliss, clarity, and nonthought are natural qualities of the mind. If you fixate on these experiences, they become causes for rebirth in the three realms: Fixation on the experience of bliss—intense physical or mental bliss that brings all other sensations and thoughts to a halt—leads to rebirth in the desire realm. Fixation on the experience of clarity, when the mind or your other senses become exceptionally lucid, even prescient, leads to rebirth in the form realm. Fixation on the experience of nonthought, when thoughts and emotions come to a temporary halt, leads to rebirth in the formless realm. Whether you are practicing calm abiding, the Great Perfection, the Great Seal, or another type of meditation, if you become attached to any of these experiences of bliss, clarity, and nonthought, your meditation will remain the childish concentration of ordinary beings. It is very important to understand this. There seem to be many contemporary practitioners unwittingly falling into this trap.

As Buddha taught,

> First you must educate yourself.
> Then you must go to the forest and practice there.

At the outset, we need to study in order to gain a genuine understanding of what meditation is, how and why it is practiced, and so on. Then we need to bring our study to fruition through practice. As Zurchung Sherab Trakpa says in his *Eighty Chapters of Personal Advice*, if you do not realize the natural state, meditating year after year will just turn you into a scarecrow.

The practice of calm abiding alone can never lead to liberation and buddhahood. To attain liberation and buddhahood, we need to realize the natural state of all things. And to do that, we need to accomplish the unity of calm abiding and deep insight.

The clearly discerning concentration of the worldly mind and the excellent concentration of the tathagatas are transcendental types of meditation—they lead beyond the wheel of samsaric existence to liberation and the omniscient state of perfect buddhahood. These meditative concentrations are the unity of calm abiding and deep insight, the unity of compassion and emptiness and so forth, and they are unique to the Buddhist path. As Nagarjuna taught,

> Emptiness with a core of compassion—
> This is the route to awakening.

The clearly discerning concentration of the worldly mind is practiced by beings on the paths of accumulation and joining. As taught in *The Ornament of the Mahayana Sutras*, *The Ornament of Clear Realization*, and other texts, first one should study and reflect upon the view of the four truths with their sixteen aspects of impermanence and so on. Then one should meditate on the four applications of mindfulness and so on.[184] In this way, one develops an understanding of emptiness hand in hand with compassion for all those who have not yet realized the true nature of things. On the paths of accumulation and joining, one cultivates a mental image, or conceptual understanding, of emptiness. At this point, emptiness is viewed as an antidote for the afflictions of attachment, aversion, and so on. As such, there is a subtle attachment to emptiness, which, like all attachment, must eventually be abandoned to reach buddhahood. Nevertheless, at this stage of the path, it is an effective, and very necessary, antidote.

In the vehicle of characteristics, the clearly discerning concentration corresponds to the patience of not fearing profound reality, while in the context of the Vajra Vehicle it corresponds to illustrative luminosity and so on.

The excellent concentration of the tathagatas is the meditative concentration of noble beings, from the first bodhisattva bhumi, Perfect Joy, up to the state of perfect buddhahood. It involves direct realization of the natural state beyond all constructs and extremes. In this sense, this type of meditative concentration is the same as *prajna*, or wisdom.

It cannot be said enough that calm abiding is indispensable for developing deep insight. Calm abiding is the foundation for all practice. It is as crucial as soil. A firm foundation of calm abiding will aid a Vajra Vehicle practitioner in their generation stage practice, and when generation stage practice progresses, in turn, completion stage practice will automatically progress. In *The Noble Sutra of Recalling the Three Jewels*, a perfect buddha is described as "endowed with wisdom and worthy of reverence" or, more literally, "endowed with wisdom and with feet." Mipham Rinpoche explains in his commentary on this sutra that "wisdom" refers to the view as realized through deep insight, while "being worthy of reverence," or "endowed with feet," refers to calm abiding. Both are indispensable, like eyes and legs. The result of having the eyes of deep insight and the legs of calm abiding is the state of the perfect Buddha, the *sugata*, or "bliss-gone one."

The Vajra Vehicle practices of the generation and completion stages, with the three samadhis, the visualization of deities, mantra recitation, and so on, are all forms of meditation. It is important to understand this. Sitting with one's eyes closed while focusing one-pointedly on the breath is a form of meditation. The Great Perfection practice of togal with its various postures and gazes—and likewise the meditations on the subtle channels, winds, and essences, and so on—are also forms of calm abiding and deep insight. As Jigme Lingpa explains,

> There are two ways whereby [beginners] are instructed
> In both calm abiding and deep insight:
> As having the same nature or as different.[185]

One accomplishes such meditative concentration by planting the victory banner of accomplishment in solitary places. In short, by applying yourself diligently and wholeheartedly to practice. Even our teacher Buddha Shakyamuni needed to gather great stores of merit for three countless eons and then renounce his kingdom and practice austerities before he attained perfect buddhahood. (From the Great Vehicle perspective, Buddha Shakyamuni was already awakened long before he appeared in this world; he went through the process of training on the path not for his own benefit but as a compassionate display for the benefit of other beings.) To this end, knowing that one cannot reach buddhahood while entangled by worldly concerns, he abandoned his kingdom, his loving family, and the security of status and wealth. Then, on the banks of the Niranjana river, he engaged in austerities, such as partaking daily of no more than a single grain of rice and several drops of water, for six years—austerities so severe and intense that even the gods were overawed.

In short, buddhahood is attained through deep insight infused with calm abiding, but without calm abiding, deep insight cannot dawn. How then does one accomplish calm abiding? By following in the footsteps of all the awakened ones of the past and adhering to solitude. Every accomplished practitioner has demonstrated this truth. This is a hallmark of the life story of every awakened being.

The modern Nyingma master Lama Kunga Palden[186] was a disciple of Orgyen Tenzin Norbu,[187] who was one of Patrul

Rinpoche's best disciples, and the brother of Gyalse Shenpen Taye. Khenpo Shenga Rinpoche[188] and Lama Kunga Palden were Orgyen Tenzin Norbu's two most brilliant disciples. According to Khenpo Dazer Rinpoche, these two heart disciples were equally erudite.

One day, Orgyen Tenzin Norbu and his two disciples visited the Derge Printing House. Placing the thirteen major treatises on the crown of Khenpo Shenga Rinpoche's head, Orgyen Tenzin Norbu said, "Devote yourself to study and teaching. It won't help to sit around in the mountains eating shit." Those were his actual words. "Establish as many shedras as you can, compose commentaries for the thirteen major treatises, and focus on teaching others without stop."

From that moment on, Khenpo Shenga Rinpoche obeyed his guru's instruction. It is said that he taught and studied every day for the rest of his life, without even one week's break. Khenpo Shenga Rinpoche composed commentaries on all thirteen major treatises and established 108 shedras, not just for the Nyingma tradition but for the Kagyu, Sakya, and Geluk traditions as well.

Orgyen Tenzin Norbu said to Lama Kunga Palden, "We are living in the degenerate age. If you do not tame your own mind, it won't help to spend your time studying and teaching. So, adhere to solitude and devote yourself to practice." Accordingly, Lama Kunga Palden spent the rest of his life practicing in mountain hermitages. For many years, he stayed in strict solitary retreat. Later on, when students began to gather around him, he maintained his solitude by having them live several kilometers away from him. His focus was the Great Perfection practice of *The Guru's Inner Essence* (*Lama Yangtik*), by means of which he cultivated the perfect unity of calm abiding and deep insight, cutting through to primordial purity and leaping over to spontaneous presence.[189]

He lived in utmost simplicity, shunning all types of busyness, renouncing all worldly concerns. He made do with the simplest of clothing, the simplest of food, and focused entirely on his practice—accomplishing the unity of calm abiding and deep insight—in accordance with his guru's command. He did not even keep a vajra and bell. He was focused entirely on meditation. He stayed in dark retreat for many months, and he also meditated for long periods on incredibly high, windblown mountain peaks. In this way, he gained accomplishment and became one of Orgyen Tenzin Norbu's supreme disciples.

CHAPTER 34

Training in Wisdom

> 30. In the absence of wisdom, perfect buddhahood
> Cannot be attained by the other five paramitas alone.
> Therefore, to cultivate wisdom combined with skillful
> means
> And free of the three spheres is the practice of bodhisattvas.

The teachings on wisdom are the most precious of all Buddha's teachings. For without wisdom, it is not possible to reach awakening. Without wisdom, it is not even possible to accomplish worldly deeds. The wisdom we are concerned with here is genuine wisdom, the nonconceptual wisdom of the noble ones—the realization of profound emptiness, the true nature of all things. The paramita of wisdom is defined as nonduality, or unity, the state of emptiness. By contrast, worldly wisdom is afflicted wisdom. For example, scientists might use their intelligence to create weapons. This requires a tremendous amount of wisdom, but the result is negative, and the motivation too.

As explained in the previous verse, the bodhisattva must train in the unity of calm abiding and deep insight. Without calm abiding, deep insight becomes unstable and weak. At the same time, calm abiding alone cannot uproot the afflictions. For instance, you need an axe with a sharp blade and good technique to chop wood. You need to have a firm grip on the handle and to focus your eyes on your target. Otherwise, you end up like me when my father would send me out to collect firewood. I would hack away at a branch for an age but make nothing more than toothmarks on the wood and blisters on my palms. Deep insight is like a sharp blade, and calm abiding is like the good technique. Deep insight, the sharp blade of wisdom, is the most vital quality of all. Without wisdom, the other five paramitas of generosity, discipline, patience, diligence, and meditative concentration cannot be perfected and awakening cannot be attained.

When generosity is not embraced by nonconceptual wisdom (wisdom that is free of the three conceptual spheres of agent, action, and object), it generates karma conducive to merit that can ripen as rebirth in the higher realms of gods and humans, but it does not, and cannot, generate karma conducive to liberation (the karma that leads to liberation from samsara and the attainment of omniscience). This likewise applies to the other paramitas. Only when the first five paramitas are embraced by the sixth paramita of wisdom do they become actual paramitas—practices that lead one beyond the extremes of existence and peace.

"Combined with skillful means" refers to wisdom being endowed with generosity, discipline, patience, diligence, and meditative concentration. These first five paramitas are skillful means; the paramita of wisdom, free of the three conceptual spheres, is the outcome of those skillful means. Therefore, it is the practice of bodhisattvas to cultivate the wisdom that realizes emptiness—wisdom that transcends the three conceptual spheres and is replete with skillful means.

In the general Great Vehicle teachings, buddhahood is taught to be composed of the two *kayas*—the *rupakaya* and the dharmakaya.[190] The store of merit with concepts leads to the rupakaya, and the store of wisdom without concepts leads to the dharmakaya. From among the six paramitas, generosity, discipline, and patience are the specific means for accomplishing the rupakaya, while meditative concentration and wisdom are the specific means for accomplishing the dharmakaya. Diligence assists them all. Without diligence, none of the other paramitas can be perfected; they cannot lead to the attainment of perfect buddhahood. As the famous dedication prayer states,

> Through this virtue, may all beings
> Perfect the stores of merit and wisdom
> And attain the two sublime kayas
> That arise from merit and wisdom.

And, as Shantideva explains in the wisdom chapter of *Entering the Way of the Bodhisattva*, after teaching the other five paramitas,

> The Sage taught all these preparations
> For the sake of wisdom,
> So those who wish to pacify
> Suffering should develop prajna.[191]

There are three aspects, or types, of wisdom: the wisdom of study, the wisdom of reflection, and the wisdom of meditation. The wisdom of study refers to studying the scriptures and receiving teachings. The wisdom of reflection is to think deeply about what one has learned and thereby gain conviction in those teachings. By sustaining this state of conviction through meditation, you deepen your familiarity with the natural state, and by training persistently in this way, you can gain direct realization. This is the wisdom of meditation. An example of someone who attained the wisdom of meditation is Noble Nagarjuna. He was able to pass directly through solid matter, to walk through pillars and buildings, as a result of realizing emptiness. As Shechen Gyaltsab Rinpoche explains in his annotations to Zurchungpa's *Eighty Chapters of Personal Advice*,

> Now, by recognizing that appearances are the mind, the mind is empty, emptiness is nondual, and nonduality is self-liberating, one clears away all misconceptions about the outer, inner, secret, and absolute.[192]

From among the three wisdoms of study, reflection, and meditation, the wisdom of meditation is the most important and powerful. It is the wisdom of meditation that gives birth to genuine realization, and from realization, knowledge will spontaneously arise. For example, Omniscient Jigme Lingpa undertook very little formal study, but through his diligent meditation practice, wisdom burst forth within him, and he then became knowledgeable about everything.

In *The Perfection of Wisdom in Eight Thousand Lines*, Buddha taught,

> The blind, even when numbering in the millions,
> Cannot see the way, so how will they ever reach their destination?
> Without wisdom, the five other paramitas are blind;
> On their own, they cannot reach awakening.
> Once they are embraced by wisdom,
> They gain sight and become worthy of their name.

Imagine a large group of blind people standing in the middle of an empty plain. There is a path leading out of the plain to their chosen destination, and all the blind men and women are fit and strong. However, because they cannot see, they cannot orient themselves—they cannot find the path and set off. The paramita of wisdom is like eyesight; the paramitas of generosity and the rest are like legs, arms, and so on. Without the eyes of wisdom, we cannot direct the paramitas of generosity and so forth to the goal of awakening.

Early one morning, I was walking to Boudhanath Stupa in Kathmandu to do circumambulations (*kora*). I passed a long line of young men and women walking, one after the other, with a hand on the shoulder of the person in front of them. They were walking calmly and happily and were talking among themselves. I did not realize at first that all these people were blind. At the beginning of the line was a sighted person. Linked together in this way, the leader was guiding the entire group of blind people down to the stupa. Without the help of that one sighted person, the others, despite their number, would not be able to guide themselves to their destination.

In *Introduction to the Middle Way*, Chandrakirti explains,

> A single man endowed with eyes
> Can lead unseeing multitudes with ease to where they
> wish to go.
> And so it is with wisdom, here;
> It takes the sightless virtues, guiding them to Victory.[193]

When you cultivate the wisdom of study and reflection and thereby infuse the skillful means of generosity and so on with an understanding of emptiness, you are like a blind person gaining sight. You can find your direction and set off on your way.

On the other hand, wisdom on its own, divorced from skillful means, will not lead to awakening. These two—skillful means and wisdom—must go hand in hand. This is the path to buddhahood—the path of unity, the path of interdependence that transcends the extremes of permanence and nihilism. As taught in the Great Perfection tantra, *The Omnipotent Monarch*, Samantabhadra is the appearing aspect of skillful means, and Samantabhadri is the emptiness aspect of wisdom. When Samantabhadra is not united with Samantabhadri, the accumulation of merit through skillful means becomes the work of mara because it is laced with attachment to reality.

To reiterate, all the practices of skillful means—namely, the first five paramitas—must be embraced by wisdom because they alone cannot lead to awakening. This is the crucial point. Wisdom is the main factor that leads us to awakening, that makes the attainment of awakening possible. Wisdom is taught in increasing depth and breadth in the ascending vehicles, in accord with the capacities of practitioners. For instance, the ultimate state of emptiness beyond all conceptual extremes, which is taught in the vehicles of characteristics, is realized more swiftly and easily through the Vajra Vehicle's path of skillful means. And in the Great Perfection, natural awareness, self-arisen primordial wisdom, can be realized directly and immediately, without the need to gather stores of merit for many countless eons. The awakened state attained through the paths of sutra and mantra does not differ; there is only one perfect buddhahood. However, due to differences in the profundity of wisdom, and the presence or absence of skillful means, there arise differences in the duration and nature of the paths that lead to awakening. The more penetrating the wisdom, the more swiftly the path is traversed and the goal achieved.

Training in the Four Practices Taught in the Sutras

The following four practices were taught by Buddha Shakyamuni in sutras such as *The Heap of Jewels* and *Inspiring Determination*. The Kadampa masters then extracted and distilled them for our benefit. However, it is not only these four practices that come from the sutras—the entire content of *The Thirty-Seven Practices of Bodhisattvas* comes from the sutras. As explained earlier, this teaching is a distillation of *Entering the Way of the Bodhisattva*, which Shantideva himself described as a condensation of Buddha's sutras.

CHAPTER 35

To Scrutinize Your Own Confusion and Give It Up

> 31. If you do not examine your own confusion,
> You might, in the guise of Dharma, act contrary to it.
> Therefore, to continuously examine your confusion
> And give it up is the practice of bodhisattvas.

There is nothing more important for practitioners than this. We must constantly examine our own confusion and faults and thereby rid ourselves of them. We are followers of Buddha. We are training on the bodhisattva path. But we need to ask ourselves, are our actions really the actions of a practitioner? Are we really living in accord with the Buddhadharma? These days, there are so many so-called practitioners whose behavior is in complete discord with the Dharma. Most often, this hypocrisy stems not from a lack of knowledge but from a lack of self-scrutiny.

Therefore, it is the practice of all bodhisattvas to examine oneself constantly, day and night. You need to examine the way you walk, the way you talk, the way you think, your every action of body, speech, and mind. You need to ask yourself, *Are my words, thoughts, and deeds truly in accord with the Dharma or not?* And when you see confusion or flaws in yourself, you need to do whatever you can to rid yourself of them.

In the past in Tibet, there was a Kadampa geshe called Ben Kungyal. He lived in a hermitage in the mountains, where he engaged night and day in profound practice. He was a genuine bodhisattva practitioner who maintained mindfulness and vigilance and was always examining his mind. His sponsor would visit him once a month or so on auspicious days and bring him provisions, such as barley flour, butter, and tea.

One day, Geshe Ben was looking down into the valley, and in the distance he saw his sponsor making his way up the mountain, leading a mule loaded with provisions. Geshe Ben immediately went back into his hut and started to clean his shrine. He dusted everything off, polished his offering bowls, filled them with fresh water, and arranged everything neatly. He even sent a young student a little way down the mountain so he could be informed when his sponsor was nearby. When he got the sign that his sponsor was just a few minutes away, he lit a stick of incense and made some final adjustments. For a moment, he marveled at the pleasing sight of his pristine shrine.

At that very moment, his habit of introspection kicked in. He looked at his mind and saw himself playing the worldly game of keeping face. He saw, to his alarm, that he had not cleaned his shrine as an offering to the Three Jewels—he was just trying to impress his sponsor. Seeing this, he bent down, scooped up a handful of dirt, and hurled it at the shrine.

"Take that, you lousy worldly concerns!" he said. A minute later, his sponsor arrived at the door. He was astounded to see a cloud of dust hanging over the geshe's shrine.

"What on earth happened?" he said. Geshe Ben simply welcomed him and did not explain.

Later on, when Padampa Sangye heard about this, he proclaimed that, from among the hundreds of thousands of offerings made in the Snowy Land of Tibet, the most virtuous of all was this offering of dust by Geshe Ben because it was utterly free of hope and fear, free of the eight worldly concerns.

If an action serves to erode your attachment—and likewise your anger, jealousy, ignorance, or pride—it is a virtuous action, regardless of how it might appear. Similarly, no matter how meritorious an action might appear, if it does not remedy the mental poisons, it is not virtuous. *Treasury of Precious Qualities* says,

> A healing root will yield a healing plant—
> What need is there to say what poisoned roots produce?
> Intention, good or ill, dictates the act's effects
> And not the size of the apparent right or wrong.[194]

Here is another short story to illustrate the same point. My brother Shiva Rinpoche was once in Taiwan visiting Dungse Thinley Norbu Rinpoche. Shiva Rinpoche was sharing a hotel room with a fellow disciple called Mr. Tan. At the time, Shiva Rinpoche would usually sleep in until six or seven in the morning, but now he thought, *Well, Mr. Tan is a disciple of Dungse Rinpoche, so no doubt he gets up very early to practice. I better do the same, or what will he think?!* And so, Shiva Rinpoche set his alarm for 3 a.m. Likewise, Mr. Tan thought, *Well, Shiva Rinpoche is a tulku and practitioner, so no doubt he gets up very early to practice. I better do the same, or what will he think?!"* So he set his alarm for half past two!

When the alarms went off, one after the other, they both forced themselves up and sat on their hotel beds doing their practice through the early hours, trying very hard not to fall asleep. Later that day, when they were both drowsy from lack of sleep, the truth came out. They were both trying to impress the other; their motivation in getting up early to practice was not at all sincere. My late brother told me this story himself. He was always very honest. It is a very funny story, but, needless to say, we should not act like this. Most especially, we should never boast about or flaunt our practice; that is one of the four causes for exhausting virtue.[195]

CHAPTER 36

To Give Up Speaking of Bodhisattvas' Faults

> 32. If, under the sway of afflictions, you speak of
> Other bodhisattvas' faults, you will damage yourself.
> Therefore, to not speak of the faults of anyone
> Who has entered the Great Vehicle is the practice of
> bodhisattvas.

If under the sway of afflictions—such as anger, attachment, ignorance, jealousy, and pride—we criticize other bodhisattvas, accuse them of wrongdoings, or point out their faults, we are creating terrible karma. We are damaging ourselves. As Karma Chakme writes in his famous prayer, *Aspiring to be Reborn in Sukhavati*,

> Worse than killing all beings in the three realms
> Is the slandering of bodhisattvas.
> I openly confess these pointless misdeeds!

Buddha himself said that disparaging a bodhisattva creates even more negative karma than killing every single being in the three realms. A bodhisattva is someone who has devoted their entire being, from now until the end of time, to benefiting all beings in all ways, without the slightest discrimination.

Therefore, to harm a bodhisattva creates tremendous negativity. As Shantideva teaches in *Entering the Way of the Bodhisattva*,

> Anyone else who thwarts [a bodhisattva's] merit
> Even a moment will be born
> Endlessly in the lower realms
> Since they've decreased all beings' welfare.
>
> If one who spoils the happiness
> Of even a single being is ruined,
> Why mention ruining the well-being
> Of infinite beings throughout space?[196]

These, and other such statements, all stem from Buddha's own words. Bodhisattvas are very powerful objects! The benefits of assisting or honoring them surpass thought. This is the case whether they be ordinary bodhisattvas on the paths of accumulation and joining or noble bodhisattvas on the paths of seeing and meditation. Just as assisting bodhisattvas creates tremendous merit, criticizing or harming bodhisattvas creates tremendous negativity. Moreover, once we have taken the bodhisattva vow, the strength of our virtuous actions increases, and the strength of our unvirtuous actions too, so it is extremely important to be careful about we say, think, and do.

We must remember that we cannot see others' minds and we cannot fathom the vast activities of the buddhas and bodhisattvas. We cannot say with any certainty who is who, for the noble ones emanate for beings' benefit in all manner of ways. All too often we project our own negativity onto others because of our own lack of mindfulness and vigilance.

Even if it seems that a certain bodhisattva really does have faults and flaws, it is not our place to speak of them. That is the job of their spiritual teachers, not us. As Patrul Rinpoche said, "When in company, guard your mouth. When in crowds, guard your hands." It is best not to talk too much. By curbing our speech, we automatically avoid a lot of negativity. Moreover, it is important to cultivate pure perception—most especially for our own teachers and tradition, but also for all Buddhist traditions and all other religions too.

In the past, there were two monks living on neighboring mountainsides in Tibet. They were both dedicated practitioners and fully ordained monks. They were supported by the same sponsor, a local layman who had equal faith in the two of them. They lived in their respective hermitages for several years, passing their days in diligent practice. Each of them had a younger monk attending them.

One day, one of them heard from a local acquaintance that the neighboring monk had lost his monastic vows and taken up with a woman. When he heard this news, he told his young attendant, "My friend, make us some delicious tea. I have some great news for us!" A little while later, the attendant came in bearing two cups of fragrant, steaming tea.

"Do tell me, what is the good news?" he said.

"Well," the elder monk said, rubbing his hands together. "It seems our neighbor has broken his vows and hooked up with a girl!"

"Oh," the attendant said, awash with sadness at this news. "Well, what's the *good* news then?"

"What do you mean?! That *is* the good news! Now that he's fallen from virtue, we will get twice the attention from our sponsor."

When Padampa Sangye heard of this, his face fell. He said the monk who rejoiced in the other's downfall created more nonvirtue than the monk who had broken his vow. Jealousy is a vicious and destructive emotion. We need to be especially vigilant of jealousy toward our fellow Dharma brothers and sisters. Jealousy pollutes Dharma practice. It turns virtuous deeds into unvirtuous deeds and poisons the mind. As Lord Gampopa said,

> Unless you practice the Dharma according to the Dharma,
> Dharma itself becomes the cause of evil rebirths.[197]

CHAPTER 37

To Give Up Attachment to the Households of Sponsors

> 33. Offerings and respect may bring discord
> And cause study, reflection, and meditation to decline.
> Therefore, to give up attachment to the households of
> Sponsors and friends is the practice of bodhisattvas.

This point is directed at renunciates, meaning monastics and practitioners who rely on the support of sponsors. In Tibet and China, and many other areas in Asia, there is a long-standing tradition of sponsoring practitioners and making offerings to teachers, monastics, and sanghas on behalf of the living and dead. This is a wonderful tradition that generates vast stores of merit for all involved. It seems that this tradition has not yet taken root in Western countries, but maybe it slowly will.

If you are a renunciate, a certain sponsor might offer you food and financial support. If that same sponsor starts supporting one of your Dharma siblings, you might feel jealous and threatened. Such jealousy, or rivalry, could lead to discord between you and your Dharma sibling. This discord would consume your attention and so cause your study, reflection, and meditation to decline. Therefore, it is the practice of renunciate bodhisattvas to give up attachment to the households of sponsors, and also the households of family and friends. To this end, renunciate bodhisattvas should not spend too much time in these households. They should maintain their distance, thereby preventing attachment from taking hold.

If you are a layperson, this verse will not be directly relevant to you. Nevertheless, rivalry can always arise between Dharma siblings, or between students and their teachers, due to attachment to honor and gain. We must all be on guard against this.

Gen Riksang Dorje Rinpoche[198] was a senior disciple of the first Degyal Rinpoche and, later, of Dudjom Rinpoche as well. He was born in Pari in Amdo. During his youth, he studied at a monastery in his homeland and became well versed in the scriptures. He then traveled to Central Tibet, where he stayed for some time before traveling to Ngari, where he met Degyal Rinpoche, in whom he felt tremendous faith. Gen Riksang Dorje stayed by Degyal Rinpoche's side for many years, receiving teachings and practicing intensively. He had woodblocks carved for the liturgies and texts used by the Namkha Khyung Dzong tradition. It is largely due to this act of kindness that these texts were preserved in full for the later generations. After Degyal Rinpoche's passing, Gen Riksang Dorje went to Kongpo and spent many years there with Kyabje Dudjom Rinpoche. It seems he completed a three-year retreat during this time, though I am not sure exactly where.

He was the main student to request the blessed *Mountain Dharma*[199] from Dudjom Rinpoche. In the colophon of this text, Dudjom Rinpoche describes him as "one diligent in practice, endowed with the jewel of unshakable devotion." This is not a small compliment when coming from Dudjom Rinpoche; it shows us the kind of practitioner he was.

Later on, Gen Riksang Dorje traveled to Humla, Dolpo, Pokhara, Mugum, and other Himalayan regions, living almost constantly in retreat. He never settled in one place. As soon as he became familiar with his sponsors and the local people, he would move on—precisely to prevent attachment from taking root.

In his seventies and eighties, when he was no longer strong enough to walk long distances, he settled at Nangkyi (Nagi Nunnery) in Shivapuri, Nepal. He spent the remaining last twelve or so years of his life there, practicing one-pointedly until taking his last breath. Gen Riksang Dorje embodied the buddhas and bodhisattvas' practice of giving up attachment to the households of sponsors, family, and friends. As we can see from the story below, he was following the example of Buddha Shakyamuni, who was utterly free of attachment to his patrons.

Buddha Shakyamuni and a large group of disciples once traveled to a nearby kingdom. The local king and his minsters gave them a very poor welcome and showed little hospitality and respect. Some of Buddha's students suggested they move elsewhere. What was the use in staying here, in the land of a king who so clearly did not value Buddha's presence? After all, the neighboring kingdoms were lining up to host Buddha and the sangha and mourning their absence. But despite their entreaties, he chose to stay put.

The local king knew Buddha was honored by the neighboring kingdoms. He knew they hosted him and his students with great reverence. Personally, though, he did not see why Buddha was so special, and so he had not offered him and his sangha any assistance at all. Nevertheless, as the days and weeks passed by, the king grew curious. *What's going on with this man?* he thought. Despite the poor living conditions and blatant lack of respect, Buddha continued to follow his daily routine of teaching when requested, going on his daily alms round, and so on. He did not complain or take offense. Buddha's humility began to erode the king's critical lens, and he began to glimpse with his own eyes the Buddha's lack of aggression, attachment, and pride. He could not help but feel some faith in this man.

Eventually, the king began offering food and hospitality to Buddha and his disciples. He expressed remorse for his past behavior and requested Buddha to remain. However, Buddha declined his request, and shortly afterward, he and his sangha left. Buddha had no attachment to sponsors, no attachment to his own security and benefit. His purpose in staying in this kingdom had been fulfilled; he had inspired faith in the king and set him on the path of liberation. Now it was time to move on.

CHAPTER 38

To Give Up Harsh Words

> 34. Harsh words disturb the minds of others
> And spoil your own bodhisattva conduct.
> Therefore, to give up harsh words
> That upset others is the practice of bodhisattvas.

Words lack physical form, yet they can cut deeper than knives. There is nothing more destructive than harsh words when it comes to wounding someone's heart and mind. A few harsh words, directed at a sensitive spot, can slice someone's mind into a hundred pieces. Moreover, harsh words create enemies, conflict, and strife.

Harsh, or abusive, speech is not the conduct of bodhisattvas. The words, thoughts, and deeds of bodhisattvas should bring benefit and joy to others. At the very least, they should do no harm. As the bodhisattva Shantideva teaches in *Entering the Way of the Bodhisattva*,

> When talking, you should speak sincerely,
> Coherently, clearly, pleasantly,
> Without attachment or aversion,
> Gently and in moderation.[200]

Shantideva goes on to explain in detail the way bodhisattvas should comport themselves, from how they should look at others to their tone of voice to the way they should gesture with their hands. The bodhisattva's every movement of body, speech, and mind should be an expression of bodhichitta—the wish to benefit others, in both temporal and ultimate ways.

Of course, there are certain contexts when harsh words can be used for others' benefit, when spoken skillfully and with benevolent intent—for instance, when a parent scolds their child to impart a lesson to them or when a guru reproaches their student and exposes their faults for their own benefit. However, as Longchenpa states in his *Thirty Pieces of Heart Advice*, in this degenerate age, when students are riddled with such strong defilements, this can sometimes backfire:

> Pointing out faults to a short-tempered retinue
> In these degenerate times, even with the wish to benefit,
> Gives rise to negative states of mind.
> To speak peacefully is my heart advice.
>
> Giving advice with a wish to benefit and without
> self-interest,
> Or lovingly pointing out someone's hidden faults,
> We might be honest, but still it creates heartache.
> To speak pleasantly is my heart advice.[201]

There are many stories, from the past and present, that illustrate the karmic repercussions of uttering harsh words—stories of people being reborn as a hell being or hungry ghost, or with physical deformities and so on. One such story is that of Princess Dorjema, who lived during Buddha Shakyamuni's time.

Princess Dorjema was the daughter of King Sakya, one of the most powerful monarchs of the time. Princess Dorjema was born with what was considered in that culture at the time to be all nine marks of ugliness: a giant head, an enormous butt, rough skin, a large mouth, a crooked nose, protruding front teeth, and so on.

King Sakya was horrified to have such an ugly daughter. He was not heartless enough to abandon her, but he was too proud to show her to the public. He decided to keep her existence a secret, and so he provided her with nurses and maids, all sworn to secrecy, and kept her concealed in the innermost wing of his palace. The princess passed her days, months, and years in the confines of her royal quarters. Her physical needs were well taken care of—she was decked in the finest clothes and fed the most delicious food—but she was deprived of company and of the stimulation of the outside world. When she reached late adolescence, she began to feel the stirrings of desire. She told her father, King Sakya, that she wanted to marry. She threatened to take her own life if he did not find her a husband.

The king was now in a real quandary. He was determined to fulfill his daughter's wish but did not know how. Being of royal birth, the princess was required to marry someone of equal standing, but with her physical defects, he did not think he could find a worthy suitor for her. After all, most people did not even know of her existence. The king pondered the matter for some time then finally landed upon an idea.

His most devoted and trustworthy minister had a son who was not yet married. So, one day the king called this young man to him and, swearing him to secrecy, told him of the situation. He commanded him to marry his daughter. He vowed to reward him with wealth, rank, and whatever else he desired. In return, he made the young man promise to never expose the princess to others and to never talk about her appearance. The king would have him killed if he did so. The young man had little choice but to fulfill the king's command. And so, the couple were married in a private ceremony and installed in a mansion with seven walls and seven doors. Here, Princess

Dorjema continued to live in confinement, hidden from the world behind the seventh, innermost wall.

The young groom's friends heard about his low-key wedding and were curious to meet his bride. When he avoided all their questions about her, this only made them more curious. In the meantime, Princess Dorjema had learned about Buddha Shakyamuni from one of her maids. Ever curious about the outside world, she was always asking her maids and helpers what they had seen, heard, and done. When her maid told her about Buddha and his teachings, the princess was overwhelmed with wonder and faith. At the same time, she became more dejected than ever by her own situation.

It would be better if I were rid of this body, she thought, *better if I had the body of a bird, a common person, or even a dog. At least then I would be able to meet Buddha, to see his face and hear his voice. Instead, I am a princess imprisoned in her own palace by her father's pride. What wretched karma I have to be born with such an ugly body and be barred from Buddha's presence in this way.*

When the princess's husband continued to evade his friend's questions, they concluded that there were only two possible reasons for his secrecy: either his wife must be so incredibly beautiful that she was being kept hidden for fear of other's envy or she was so ugly and deficient that she was being kept hidden to protect the monarchy's reputation. One day, when they were all together, they brought out some alcohol. Pretending to drink, they all remained sober while getting their friend very drunk. Once he had fallen into a drunken stupor, they took his keys off him and ran to his mansion. They unlocked all seven doors, one after the other, and when they finally stepped into the innermost quarters, they could not believe their eyes.

Before them stood a woman of indescribable beauty and splendor. All they could do was stand there looking at her with slack jaws. The princess had grown so downcast with her situation and so full of faith in Buddha, that she had resolved to end her life once and for all. She was determined to break free of the confinement of her body and, taking another rebirth, to look upon Buddha's face with her own eyes. But the very moment she was ready to kill herself, peals of thunder filled the air. Buddha appeared in the space before her. She prostrated at Buddha's feet and wept with amazement, relief, and joy. As she looked upon Buddha's golden form, he met her gaze and embraced her with his boundless wisdom and love. Instantly, her body with its nine marks of ugliness was transformed into a body so divine that she outshone the beauty of all other women on earth. Her husband's friends were spellbound.

As they stood before her, her husband woke from his drunken sleep. He immediately put his hands to his belt, and when he did not find his keys there, he leaped to his feet. He raced to his mansion, his heart pounding in his chest. The king had not been joking when he had sworn him to secrecy at the cost of his life. He ran through the first open door, the second open door, the third open door, all the way into the princess's secret quarters, only to find his friends staring at the most beautiful woman he had ever seen and his wife, Princess Dorjema, nowhere to be seen.

"Where is my wife? What have you done to her?" he screamed. The beautiful woman turned to him and said, "My husband, your wife is right here." The princess then told her husband what had happened—how Buddha had graced her with his presence and how, through the power of his blessings and her faith, her body had been transformed.

When the king learned of her transformation, he was awash with amazement and disbelief. Later on, the king asked Buddha what past karma had been the cause of the princess's earlier body with its nine marks of ugliness. Buddha explained that many eons ago the princess had taken rebirth as the daughter of a householder. One day, she was offering a meal to a pratyekabuddha with an ugly demeanor, and in the folly of her youth, she insulted him.

"Ugh, what a vile man you are! You have all nine marks of ugliness!" she said. As a result of this sinful karma, she was afflicted for many lifetimes with the same nine signs of ugliness. The pratyekabuddha, aware of the grave karma this woman was creating by insulting a noble being, immediately displayed miracles by flying in the sky, emitting fire and water from his body, and so on. Seeing this, the young woman was inspired by faith, and regretting her abusive speech, she confessed her error before him.

"I was that pratyekabuddha," Buddha said. "Due to that karmic connection, the princess has met me again in this life, and through the merit of her past confession, her body was transformed upon seeing me. As a result of the merit gathered from offering to a pratyekabuddha, she was reborn in this life as the daughter of a king." Upon hearing this, the king was filled with faith in the Buddha and unshakable trust in karmic cause and effect.

Such are the karmic repercussions of harsh words. Therefore, it is the practice of bodhisattvas to give up harsh words and to always speak gently, honestly, and meaningfully, with the wish to benefit beings and avoid harming them at all costs.

CHAPTER 39

How to Be Rid of the Afflictions

> 35. When emotions become habit, they are hard to avert
> with antidotes.
> Therefore, with mindfulness and vigilance, to seize the
> weapon of the antidote
> And crush the afflictions of attachment and the rest
> The very moment they arise is the practice of bodhisattvas.

Everything is a matter of habit and familiarity—our emotions, outlook, behavior, and so on. For instance, people who are strongly habituated to anger have an angry disposition. If they deepen this habit, they will become even more aggressive. This applies likewise to the other emotions, such as attachment, jealousy, and the rest and to positive qualities, such as compassion, patience, and diligence. As Shantideva said,

> There's nothing at all that is not easy
> If you are used to it.[202]

In India, in the past, there was a group of fishermen. They lived with the smell of fish from morning to night, seven days a week, so they had long grown used to it. One day, there was a festival nearby, so they took some time off work and went to watch the performances. They were so engrossed by the show that they completely lost track of the time. When the sun began to set, they realized they better hurry home. They quickly set off, but before they could get very far, the sky grew dark. Their path home passed through an area of dense forest where wild lions and leopards roamed, so they all agreed it would be safer to seek shelter for the night and continue their journey in the morning.

There were no houses nearby, but they saw a temple in the distance, so they decided to sleep there. Inside, the temple was immaculate. Not only was it clean and tidy but the air was sweet with the smell of incense and the altar was full of fresh offerings and an abundance of fragrant flowers. The fishermen lay down, but, try as they might, none of them could fall asleep. Weary and restless, they sat up and asked each other, "What is going on? Why can't we sleep?!"

"Surely it is the stench of those flowers. Who on earth could sleep with such a foul smell?!" one of them said. They all agreed this was the problem.

"Well, do we have one of our baskets?" (These were the baskets they used for storing fish.)

"Yes, I have one," one of the fishermen said. They filled the basket with water to release its smell, wafted it around the temple, and then, with a sigh of relief, they all fell sound asleep.

This story illustrates the power of habit. We feel comfortable with what we are familiar with, no matter how unwholesome it might be. These fishermen preferred the smell of fish guts to the smell of fresh flowers not because fish guts smell good but because that was what they were used to. As sentient beings, we have grown used to disturbing emotions over the course of countless lifetimes, so these emotional habits run very deep. They are so ingrained in us that we cannot discard them immediately. Nevertheless, now that we have encountered Buddha's teachings and met genuine spiritual teachers, we can begin to undo these habits bit by bit by training on the path.

Mindfulness is necessary to accomplish even the simplest of mundane tasks. No need to mention its importance when accomplishing the sacred Dharma, from the vehicle of characteristics up to the Great Perfection, the pinnacle of vehicles. Here, in this context, mindfulness is the recollection of what is to be adopted and what is to be avoided. Thus, with mindfulness, the bodhisattva recalls the faults of the afflictions and the excellent qualities of bodhichitta. They recall that the afflictions have been torturing them and all mother-beings for countless lifetimes until now. With vigilance—the constant examination of the state of one's body, speech, and mind—the bodhisattva keeps track of what they are thinking, doing, and saying. They ask themselves, *Are my words, thoughts, and deeds in accord with the way of the bodhisattvas or not?*

It is when people lack vigilance that they make the most mistakes. This is especially the case these days, since most people focus their attention outward, instead of looking in at themselves. They concern themselves with others' business, things that are really not their concern, and they fail to turn their gaze inward and examine their own behavior, their own state of mind. From a lack of vigilance comes many downfalls. From the presence of vigilance comes a wealth of good qualities.

Maintaining mindfulness and vigilance is likened to taking up weapons. If you are armed with a sword or a gun, and you keep your weapon in your hand, no one will dare attack you because you are ready to strike back. Even if someone does dare to attack, you will easily fend them off. Similarly, when the bodhisattva arms themselves with the weapons of mindfulness and vigilance, they can notice the emotions as soon as they rear their heads, and then they can immediately crush them with the antidote. Thereby, they prevent the emotion from taking root in their mind. This is the meaning of *burjom*, of crushing (*jom*) an emotion the moment it arises (*bur*).

For instance, if you see a spark of fire land on a patch of dry grass and set it alight, it is easy to put the fire out. But if you fail to extinguish that first lick of flame and allow the fire to spread, you can end up with a devastating forest fire that no one, not even hundreds of firemen, can extinguish.

Similarly, you might have a table whose surface is held down by four nails, one in each corner. If one of the nails starts rising up but you hammer it down immediately, no harm will be done. However, if you do nothing, the nail will continue to rise up, and then the wood will start to warp. Eventually, the other nails will also rise up and the table will be damaged beyond repair. Another example is a loose thread in a vest. If you do not cut the loose thread and sew the small hole up, but you keep pulling the thread, the whole garment will fall apart.

Therefore, when you notice an emotion arising, you should immediately recall bodhichitta, both relative and ultimate. Bodhichitta is the supreme antidote. By recollecting the great kindness of all mother-beings, by generating the wish to repay their kindness, and so on, reinvigorate your relative bodhichitta. At the same time, remind yourself that all phenomena are empty of reality, that their appearance is an illusion, and thereby cultivate ultimate bodhichitta. In this way, the bodhisattva crushes emotions the moment they arise.

Once, the accomplished Kadampa geshe Ben Kungyal was invited to a sponsor's house to perform a ceremony on their behalf.[203] At some point during the day, the sponsor and their family went outside, and Ben Kungyal was left in the house on his own. As he was nearing the end of the ceremony, he remembered he had run out of tea, and from where he was sitting, he could see his sponsor's bulging tea bag.

Maybe I should take a portion of their tea, just a little bit, while they're not here. Surely there would be nothing wrong with that, he thought.

He looked around to make sure the path was clear, then he stood up, walked quickly into the kitchen, and put his hand into the tea bag. As soon as his hand touched the brick of tea, he came to his senses and was filled with remorse. Without a second thought, he started shouting out, "Help! Help! There's a thief! There's a thief in the house!" The lady of the house came rushing inside.

"Where are they? What's happened?" she gasped.

"They're right here. The thief is me!" Ben Kungyal said. He confessed his negative intentions, then said, "Please, get a knife and chop off my thieving hand right now!"

Geshe Ben flagged his negative motivation as soon as he noticed it. (That said, most likely he did not intend to steal at all but simply acted as if he did as a lesson for us all. For instance, Buddha Shakyamuni once said he had a headache, that he was in pain from a thorn piercing the sole of his foot, and so on. The buddhas and bodhisattvas often display such deeds for the benefit of disciples out of their compassion and skillful means.) If we were to find ourselves doing something shameful like stealing, we would hide it as best we can. After all, that is what we do: We conceal our faults. We bury ourselves in pretense. But look how Ben Kungyal identified his negative emotion and then cut through it right then and there. This is the unmistaken practice of bodhisattvas. Imagine the great stores of merit Geshe Ben must have gathered that day.

CHAPTER 40

Training in Accomplishing Others' Good with Mindfulness and Vigilance

> 36. In short, wherever you are, whatever you do,
> With constant mindfulness and vigilance
> That ask, "What state is my mind in?"
> To accomplish others' good is the practice of bodhisattvas.

The previous verse taught how the bodhisattva uses mindfulness and vigilance to relinquish the afflictions. This verse teaches how the bodhisattva uses these same two qualities to benefit others. This is such a precious verse. It opens with "In short," which tells us that it is a summary of all that has been taught above: relative bodhichitta, ultimate bodhichitta, how to generate these two types of bodhichitta initially, how to strengthen them through training in meditative equipoise and post-equipoise, and so on and so forth. As Sakya Pandita says in his *Treasury of Valid Cognition*,[204]

> When teaching the Dharma, be skilled in detailed
> exposition.
> When practicing the Dharma, condense all into
> a single point.

What is that single point? It is what is taught here in this verse. No matter what you might be doing, no matter where you might be, no matter what time it is, no matter what circumstance you might be in, it is the practice of bodhisattvas to continually examine the state of their mind with mindfulness and vigilance.

All Buddha's teachings are contained in the scriptures of the three pitakas and the practice of the three trainings. Every single one of these thousands of teachings is intended to tame the mind. As Buddha himself said,

> Commit not a single misdeed,
> Cultivate a wealth of virtue,
> And completely tame your mind—
> This is Buddha's teaching.

The most powerful method for taming the mind is bodhichitta, and yet bodhichitta is something intangible. A nuclear bomb can destroy an entire continent, but it cannot destroy negative emotions. The emotions dwell as habitual imprints in the all-ground consciousness—the most basic level of mind that is the ground of all samsaric experience—and consciousness is intangible; it cannot be destroyed by substance or material form. Bodhichitta is more powerful than material substance. Bodhichitta can purify the mind of all emotions and obscurations and lead one to liberation from samsara and the ultimate happiness of buddhahood. As it is taught,

> More crucial than generating bodhichitta is the dawning of bodhichitta.

To begin with, we must generate bodhichitta intentionally. It is unavoidable that our bodhichitta is contrived. However, this must eventually lead to the spontaneous dawning of uncontrived bodhichitta. And once uncontrived bodhichitta has dawned in us, our every action will automatically be of benefit to others. Until we reach this point, we should aspire that our every action of body, speech, and mind—the movement of our hands, the turn of our head, or the utterance of a single word—may benefit all beings, directly and indirectly, and be a cause for their temporal and ultimate happiness.

As Khenpo Chokhyab Rinpoche would say to us, through study and practice we need to be transformed. Just as wool turns red when soaked in dye, we need to let the Dharma sink into us and bring about deep change. Ideally, we will be completely changed, like white wool turning the deepest red. If that can not happen straight away, we should at least turn a light red. At the very least, we should take on a reddish hue.

Bodhisattvas are dedicated to benefiting others. To this end, they constantly examine their mind with unceasing mindfulness and vigilance. "Others" includes all countless beings, and from among all countless beings, bodhisattvas place a special emphasis on their enemies. They regard their enemies as especially important and especially kind. Many people flinch when they hear this. Some people even say it is impossible, but with bodhichitta we can make the impossible possible.

In the past, there lived a couple who lived happily and harmoniously together, until one day the husband died. His wife was so bereft that she could not bring herself to dispose of his corpse. She performed no cremation, no burial. Instead, she carried her husband's corpse around with her wherever she went. Everyone begged her to dispose of the corpse, but she would not be reasoned with. She took it with her everywhere, immune to its putrid stench.

Nearby there lived a bodhisattva named Keshawa. He saw the anguish this woman was going through, and he also saw that teaching her verbally would be of no use. One day, he walked over to her, carrying a woman's corpse on his back. He told her that this woman was his late wife. She was so surprised. Here was someone in the same situation, someone who understood what she was going through. From then on, the two of them stuck together. They went around with their rotting corpses and shared with each other their happy memories of their deceased husband and wife. They reminisced for hours at a time about how loving their late spouses were, how harmonious and fulfilling their marriages had been.

They passed several days in this way. Then, one day they arrived at the bank of the Karnali River and settled there for the night. The woman slept beside her husband's corpse, and the bodhisattva slept next to the corpse of his supposed wife. The bodhisattva got up in the night while the woman was asleep, threw both corpses in the river, and let them be carried away. Then the bodhisattva began to shout, and the woman woke up with a start.

"What is going on? What's happening?!" she said.

Turning to her, the bodhisattva said, "You said your husband was a faithful man, but look what he has done! He has run off with my wife!"

"No, that's not possible. He would never do that!" the woman said.

"Well, look for yourself. He's not here, is he? And nor is my wife!" The woman looked around, and indeed, neither her husband nor the bodhisattva's wife were anywhere to be seen. She was shocked and horrified. At the same time though, her attachment to her husband began to wane. Shortly afterward, she was able to let go of him and start living again.

Such are the lengths a bodhisattva will go to in order to help a single being. As bodhisattvas in training, we need to do whatever we can to help others. We should help in whatever capacity we can. If you are wealthy, you can help those in financial need. If you have the time and resources, you can make a meal for a neighbor who is sick. We should not dismiss the value of small gestures. As Buddha taught in *The Sutra of the Wise and the Foolish*,

> Do not take lightly small good deeds,
> Believing they can hardly help:
> For drops of water one by one
> In time can fill a giant pot.[205]

Pema Rangdrol was a disciple of the nineteenth-century master Do Khyentse Yeshe Dorje. His mother had died several years before, and one day, in the middle of a teaching session, Do Khyentse suddenly turned to him and said, "Pema Rangdrol, you need to go to India! You need to go and save your mother's life. Get up, get up! You must leave right now!"

This was no small journey, as it would take many months to travel from Kham to India. He would have to travel the whole way on foot, and through dangerous, unfamiliar lands. Still, with the compassionate wish to repay his mother's kindness, and with trust in his teacher, he left at once. First he made his way to Lhasa, and from there he crossed the border to India. Do Khyentse had not told him exactly where to go, so all he could do was wander from place to place, searching for his mother's rebirth with an open heart.

One day he saw a young girl about twelve or thirteen years old. She had been married off to an older man who had recently died. According to this country's custom, a widow was destined to be burned alive with the corpse of her husband, unless another man took her as his wife or unless she left the country, never to return. This young girl was petrified. She was crying and shaking uncontrollably. Pema Rangdrol thought, *Maybe this is my mother. Maybe this is her*. The timing certainly matched; it was twelve or thirteen years since his mother had died. He quickly announced his intentions to marry this girl and thereby saved her life. He then headed back to Tibet, with the young girl by his side. When they reached Lhasa, he took her to Shukseb Nunnery where she took ordination as a nun and became an outstanding practitioner. Pema Rangdrol then returned to Do Khyentse Yeshe Dorje in Kham, a journey that took him many more months. Such are the efforts the bodhisattvas go to for the benefit of a single mother-being.

CHAPTER 41

Dedicating the Virtue to Perfect Buddhahood

> 37. To dedicate to buddhahood
> All virtue gained through making effort in these ways,
> With wisdom pure of the three spheres,
> So as to dispel the suffering of all infinite beings is the
> practice of bodhisattvas.

The practice of dedication is unique to the Buddhist tradition, and it is a fundamental part of the Great Vehicle practice of the three excellences: the excellent preparation of bodhichitta, the excellent main part free of concepts, and the excellent conclusion of dedicating all virtue to the awakening of all beings. In Longchenpa's *Wish-Fulfilling Treasury*, Patrul Rinpoche's *Words of My Perfect Teacher*, and other texts, the function of the three excellences is described in the following way: The excellent preparation of bodhichitta infuses roots of virtue with skillful means, the excellent main part free of concepts makes roots of virtue invincible, and the excellent conclusion of dedication makes roots of virtue further and further increase. From among these three, the excellent preparation was taught with verse 10 and the excellent main part with verse 22. This concluding verse teaches the excellent conclusion, the bodhisattva's practice of dedication.

It is important to understand the difference between dedication and aspiration: Dedication consists of pledging one's virtuous deeds to the awakening of all beings, whereas an aspiration is simply the wish that beings attain awakening. Dedication must be preceded by a meritorious action; you need something to dedicate. This is not the case with aspiration prayers.

There's so much to say about these three excellences. You can learn much more about them from other texts. Simply speaking, if you maintain bodhichitta, all three excellences will automatically be present. This is the crucial point—to maintain bodhichitta in the beginning, middle, and end.

When you dedicate your virtue to awakening, the virtue becomes inexhaustible. It will not be spent until it ripens into the consummate fruition of perfect buddhahood. Furthermore, dedication makes virtue immune to the destructive forces of anger and so on. *The Questions of Sagaramati* says,

> Just as a drop of water that falls into the ocean
> Will never disappear until the ocean runs dry,
> Merit totally dedicated to awakening
> Will never disappear until awakening is reached.[206]

On the other hand, when we fail to dedicate virtue to awakening, it can easily be destroyed, and even if it remains intact and ripens, it will ripen just once and then it will be spent.

By striving diligently and ceaselessly in these practices, the bodhisattva gathers a vast wealth of virtue. They dedicate all this virtue to the awakening of all countless beings of the six classes so that they might be freed from all suffering and established in lasting, ultimate happiness. The bodhisattva does not dedicate virtue to mundane, short-term goals, such as good health, long life, and rebirth in the god or human realm. Such dedications bring no lasting benefit. They only perpetuate beings' suffering. With the wisdom that is pure of the three conceptual spheres of agent, action, and object, the bodhisattva dedicates their virtue to all beings. Free of attachment, they give it all away. As Longchenpa teaches in *The Wish-Fulfilling Treasury*,

> The great waves of the Great Vehicle's virtue are embraced by
> The preparation of bodhichitta, the main part beyond concepts,
> And the conclusion of dedication. These three excellences
> Are cherished treasures for those traveling liberation's path.

Although this final verse of *The Thirty-Seven Practices* primarily teaches the excellent conclusion of dedication, it also contains the excellent preparation and main part: "So as to dispel the suffering of all infinite beings" describes the excellent preparation of bodhichitta, and "with wisdom pure of the three spheres" describes the excellent main part, free of reference points.

In the kingdom of Magadha in ancient India, there lived an illusionist named Bhadra.[207] He was famed far and wide for his conjuring skills. He could produce illusions so convincing that they fooled even the wisest of men. One day he thought, *If only I can fool Buddha Shakyamuni with my magic. Then I will be crowned the king of illusionists and my fame will be etched into history!* He then went to see Buddha and invited him and his community of monks to lunch the following day. He reasoned that if Buddha were omniscient, as people said he was, he would decline the invitation to avoid looking like a fool. So when Buddha accepted the invitation, Bhadra thought with delight, *Well, it seems Buddha is not omniscient after all!* He returned home and got to work.

With his conjuring skills, Bhadra emanated an enormous marquee draped in gorgeous fabrics and decorated with flower garlands and jewels. Inside the marquee, he emanated a majestic throne for Buddha and beautiful seats for his monks. Then he conjured a lavish feast of all kinds of aromatic, mouth-watering food. The locals were awestruck by this marvelous spectacle. Looking around at his handiwork, Bhadra rubbed his hands in glee. He really had outdone himself this time. Now all he had to do was wait for Buddha to arrive.

Shortly before noon, Buddha appeared on the horizon, walking tranquilly along the path to Bhadra's village, followed by a great entourage of monks. Bhadra welcomed them graciously and ushered them into the marquee where he requested them to take a seat. Once they were all comfortably seated, a group of waiters filed in and filled Buddha's alms bowl and the bowls of all the monks with the most delicious-looking food.

Everything was going perfectly to plan. Bhadra could not help feeling excited that his crowning moment was just seconds away. He planned to snap his fingers just as Buddha raised the first handful of food to his mouth and dissolve the entire illusion, leaving Buddha empty-handed and sitting in the middle of a field on the dusty ground. Buddha would look like such a fool. And since the Buddha and his monks only ate at lunchtime, they would have to return to their hermitage with empty stomachs and nurse their hunger through the night.

As Buddha raised his first handful of food to his mouth, Bhadra snapped his fingers. But nothing happened. Buddha and all the monks were chewing the magical food as if it were real. Bhadra snapped his fingers a second time, then a third, then a fourth, but no matter how hard he tried, he could not dissolve his illusion. He looked around aghast as the Buddha and monks sat calmly and quietly in the magical marquee, eating their magical lunch. Of course, Buddha had been aware of Bhadra's intentions all along, and with the power of samadhi, he had blessed the magical food to be edible. By the end of the meal, Bhadra was flushed and sweating. He did not know what to do with himself.

Finally, when they had all finished eating and it was time to dedicate the merit of the meal, Buddha said,

> Just as the giver and the recipient
> And also the gift are not seen,
> May this equal act of generosity
> Be fully perfected for Bhadra![208]

With these words, Buddha dedicated the merit of the illusory offering, free of the three conceptual spheres. The giver, Bhadra; the recipient, Buddha and his monks; and the gift, the lavish feast are not seen—or rather, they are seen to be emptiness. May the virtue of this equal act—this gift of equality, beyond concepts and reference points—be perfected in the illusionist Bhadra, and likewise in all sentient beings. In this way, Buddha dedicated the merit to awakening, creating a great wave of virtue for all beings. It turned out that Buddha was the king of illusionists, and not Bhadra after all.

Many Tibetan scholars believe that the best compositions are those adorned with poetic language. In contrast, the twentieth-century scholar Gendun Chopel argued that the best compositions are those that can be understood clearly at first glance, like watching a film. The second-best compositions, he said, are those that can be understood after a little bit of reflection, and the worst are those that need to be deciphered like puzzles. Gendun Chopel's opinion was very unconventional, but it seems he was ahead of his time. These days, especially in the modern West, clarity and accessibility seem to be regarded as important literary qualities. In this sense, *The Thirty-Seven Practices of Bodhisattvas* is the best type of composition. You do not need to be a scholar to understand it; the words speak for themselves. At the same time, the text is incredibly profound.

Having made this gesture of humility, Gyalse Tokme assures us that his composition is authentic and unerring. He does this to prevent future students from questioning the veracity of the text and falling prey to the obstacle of doubt. When we engage in practice, we must do so with certainty, free of ambivalence or the two-pointed mind of doubt. When you have doubt, it is as if your mind is looking in two directions at once. Doubt dilutes the power of your practice. It obstructs realization and the development of noble qualities. Therefore, Gyalse Tokme is assuring us that, since it is based on the teachings of Buddha and his accomplished followers, *The Thirty-Seven Practices of Bodhisattvas* is indeed an authentic teaching. These bodhisattva practices are the indispensable path to awakening, without doubt.

The Virtuous End

The Conclusion

CHAPTER 42

How and For Whom This Text Was Composed

> Based on the teachings of the sutras, tantras, and treatises,
> And following the instructions of the sublime ones,
> I have arranged these thirty-seven practices of bodhisattvas
> For those who wish to train on the bodhisattva path.

Bodhisattva Gyalse Tokme based his composition on the teachings found in the sutras, tantras, and treatises. This includes sutras such as *The Heap of Jewels* and *The Stem-Array*, which pertain to the vehicle of characteristics. Tantras are teachings of the Vajra Vehicle of Secret Mantra. Although *The Thirty-Seven Practices of Bodhisattvas* is not a tantric teaching, since the basis and essence of the tantric path is none other than bodhichitta, we can say that this teaching is based on, or connected to, the tantras. We can also understand the word *tantra* in a wider sense as referring to teachings of definitive meaning, such as the *Uttaratantra*.

The sutras and tantras are the direct words of Buddha, whereas the treatises are works composed by Buddha's accomplished and learned followers. In this instance, "treatises" refers to Shantideva's *Entering the Way of the Bodhisattva*, Regent Maitreya's *Ornament of Clear Realization*, and so on, which describe the stages of realization, and Noble Nagarjuna's

Root Stanzas of the Middle Way and so forth, which explain the essential meaning of emptiness. In short, Gyalse Tokme's composition is rooted in these sacred scriptures. In addition, Gyalse Tokme has followed the instructions of the sublime ones, the great masters of past and present, including his own gurus, which draw on their personal experience and profound realization. All together, these make up the most perfect possible basis for a composition. This is how this text was composed.

For whom was it composed? For those who wish to follow the bodhisattva path. It is for their benefit that Gyalse Tokme set down these thirty-seven practices, which make up the entire bodhisattva path. As explained earlier, in this context we should understand the term *bodhisattva* (*gyalse*) to include the buddhas as well. These thirty-seven practices are the highway traveled by all the buddhas and bodhisattvas of the three times—past, present, and future. The bodhisattvas must engage in these trainings in order to traverse the path to buddhahood. Then, having attained perfect buddhahood themselves, they send forth a ceaseless stream of emanations that, in the perception of sentient beings, continue to display these practices in order to guide them on the path.

CHAPTER 43

The Unerring Nature of These Practices

> Since my intellect is only feeble and I have studied
> but a little,
> This is not a composition likely to delight the
> connoisseurs.
> But, since I've relied upon the sutras and what the
> saints have taught,
> I feel these are indeed the genuine trainings of the
> buddhas' heirs.

Gyalse Tokme begins this verse with a gesture of humility, saying his intellect is feeble and his composition is poor, but of course this is not true. This expression of humility is a sign of his bodhisattva qualities. It is an instructive gesture made for our benefit.

In Tibet, there is a long-standing tradition of formal poetry using analogies. For instance, rather than simply saying "the sun," a poet would say "the sky bindu," "the splendor of seven horses," and so on, and only those who had studied poetics would know what is meant. This figurative speech can be beautiful, but it can also make a text very cryptic and inaccessible. Gyalse Tokme is saying that his composition lacks such sophisticated poetics and linguistic frills.

CHAPTER 44

Demonstrating Humility and Requesting Forgiveness

> Still, the great waves of the buddhas and bodhisattvas' activities
> Are difficult for someone unintelligent like me to comprehend.
> So, I must beg the forgiveness of all the sublime ones
> For any contradictions, irrelevancies, or other flaws this composition may contain.

In the previous verse, Gyalse Tokme says he is confident that this text is unerring and that it teaches the genuine path of bodhisattvas. Still, with this verse he is requesting forgiveness for any possible mistakes that might have slipped in or for anything that might be incomplete. Of course, since the author is someone like Gyalse Tokme, it is impossible for there to be faults in this text. Gyalse Tokme was one of the most outstanding masters of his time. He was perfectly learned and accomplished and had many thousands of students. Nevertheless, in making this prayer for forgiveness, he is displaying one of the bodhisattva's noble qualities—humility. This is the conduct of bodhisattvas.

There are said to be two principal benefits to displaying humility. First, it demonstrates to others that one is a bodhisattva. Second, it prevents others from developing pride. Once we have seen exalted bodhisattvas like Gyalse Tokme displaying such humility, there is no way that we will be so presumptuous as to feel pride in our learning or accomplishments. Similarly, at the beginning of *Entering the Way of the Bodhisattva*, Shantideva writes,

> I won't say anything not said before,
> Nor have I any skill in poetry.
> Thus I have not intended this for others—
> I've written it to cultivate my mind.[209]

When we see these holy beings, our forefathers and teachers on the path, acting so humbly, it punctures our own pride. We dare not put on airs and think of ourselves as having qualities that our teachers themselves claim they lack.

The compassionate activities of the buddhas and bodhisattvas are like great waves; they are incredibly far-reaching, varied, and vast. Although the essence of these activities is one and the same—bodhichitta—the forms they take are literally limitless. Therefore, Gyalse Tokme says, it is possible that there are points of bodhisattva conduct that I have not yet heard or understood.

For instance, in the past there was a bodhisattva student called Sucandra who went to see Regent Maitreya. As he sat before Maitreya, numerous accounts of how Maitreya had trained in his past lives as a bodhisattva, enduring all sorts of hardships for the sake of buddhahood, appeared before his eyes. Sucandra saw that in some lifetimes Maitreya had sacrificed his beloved spouse, in some he had given away his cherished children, in others his status, property, wealth, even his arms and legs, even his life. It seems that Bodhisattva Sucandra's experience was something like being surrounded by hundreds of video screens each playing a video of a different activity or different lifetime. Maitreya created this display for Sucandra to help strengthen his bodhichitta resolve.

This is but one example of the great waves of the buddhas and bodhisattvas' activities. Another example is Buddha Shakyamuni's past lives as described in the Jataka Tales, which recounts the five hundred pure rebirths Buddha took as a bodhisattva and the hardships he embraced for the sake of buddhahood. Each lifetime has a slightly different taste, texture, and approach.

Since the heart of all the buddhas and bodhisattvas' activities is bodhichitta, these thirty-seven practices are not missing anything in essence. They are perfect and complete. However, Gyalse Tokme humbly says that since their activity is so vast and varied, it is possible that, in terms of approach and presentation, something could be incomplete. He says, "I must beg the forgiveness of all the sublime ones," meaning the buddhas and their bodhisattva heirs. "Contradictions" refers to anything that is in discord with the bodhisattva trainings, while "irrelevancies" refer to things that are not connected to the subject matter. As explained above, it is not actually possible for such flaws or any "other mistakes" to be present in this text. Nevertheless, Gyalse Tokme makes this humble request for forgiveness as a demonstration of humility.

CHAPTER 45

Dedicating the Merit of Composing This Text to Buddhahood

> Through whatever merit has here been gained, may all beings
> Generate sublime bodhichitta, both relative and ultimate,
> And through this may they become equal to Lord Avalokiteshvara,
> Transcending the extremes of existence and peace.

"Through whatever merit has here been gained" refers to the merit gained through the composition of this text. Indeed, the merit gained is exceptionally vast. Think of the impact this text has had from Gyalse Tokme's time until now. It has touched and transformed so many people over the centuries. It continues to be taught and practiced by all four major schools of Tibetan Buddhism. They all revere it as a crown jewel. It has guided so many people on the bodhisattva path. This is a truly transformative text.

In my own experience, from among all the many texts I have studied—the many volumes of philosophical and esoteric works—it is *The Thirty-Seven Practices of Bodhisattvas* and *The Words of My Perfect Teacher* that have really touched my heart and helped me transform. I received detailed teachings on *The Words of My Perfect Teacher* from Khenpo Dazer Rinpoche in Gangtok, and, after that, I received teachings on *The Thirty-Seven Practices* from Khen Rinpoche multiple times. Receiving these teachings was one of the greatest fortunes of my life. Likewise, this text has touched and transformed countless other people, so the merit it has generated is truly vast.

Gyalse Tokme dedicates this merit so that all beings may generate sublime bodhichitta and thereby attain the level of Lord Avalokiteshvara. Avalokiteshvara is often depicted in the form of a tenth-bhumi bodhisattva, standing next to Buddha Amitabha, but in fact Avalokiteshvara is a perfectly realized buddha. For instance, when illustrating the three-kaya buddhas, the dharmakaya Buddha is Amitayus, from whom appears the sambhogakaya buddha, Avalokiteshvara, from whom appears the nirmanakaya buddha, Guru Rinpoche. The state of perfect buddhahood transcends the two extremes of existence (the suffering of samsara) and peace (the partial awakening that is the nirvana attained by the shravaka- and pratyekabuddha-arhats). These two extremes are transcended, or surpassed, in perfect buddhahood, the peerless state of Lord Avalokiteshvara.

CHAPTER 46

The Colophon Endowed with Four Perfect Qualities

> The monk Tokme, a teacher of scripture and reasoning, composed this text in Jewel Cave (Rinchen Puk) in Ngulchu for his own and others' benefit.

The colophon is the last line of the text and the last of its five concluding points. It is "endowed with four perfect qualities," the what, why, who, and where of the composition, all of which are explained succinctly in this closing line. What has been composed? This text, *The Thirty-Seven Practices of Bodhisattvas*. Why? For what purpose? For benefit of oneself and others. By whom? By the monk Gyalse Tokme, who was a teacher of both scripture and reasoning. Where? In Jewel Cave in a place called Ngulchu in Central Tibet.

By tending the seedling of bodhichitta
And transcending the extremes of existence and peace,
May we become wellsprings of benefit and bliss for all.
May we embody bodhichitta, the most sublime!

May the teachers live long and the teachings endure,
May all beings follow the way of the bodhisattvas,

May the purpose of self and other be effortlessly fulfilled,
And may the three worlds be flooded with virtuous
auspiciousness!

This was written by Pema Rigtsal Dorje on the eleventh day of the twelfth month of the Wood Dragon year of the Tibetan calendar (February 1, 2025). Virtue!

Structural Outline

I. The virtuous beginning: The introduction
    A. The opening homage
        1. The concise homage
        2. The expanded homage
    B. The author's commitment to compose
II. The virtuous middle: The main body of the treatise
    A. The preliminaries: Entering the Dharma
        1. Making meaningful these freedoms and advantages that are so difficult to attain
        2. Abandoning your native land, source of the three poisons
        3. Adhering to solitude, source of good qualities
        4. Reflecting on impermanence and thereby renouncing the concerns of this life
        5. Avoiding the adverse condition that is bad company
        6. Relying on the conducive condition that is the spiritual friend
        7. Taking refuge, the gateway to the Buddhist teachings
    B. The main part: The paths of the three types of beings
        1. The path of lesser beings: Avoiding sinful actions in fear of the suffering of the lower realms
        2. The path of middling beings: Detaching yourself from samsaric pleasures and redirecting your efforts toward liberation

3. Generating the motivation of supreme bodhichitta: The path of greater beings: Freeing yourself from the extremes of existence and peace by training in the natural unity of emptiness and compassion
    - a) Generating the motivation of supreme bodhichitta
    - b) The application: Cultivating the two types of bodhichitta
        - (1) Cultivating relative bodhichitta
            - (a) In meditative equipoise, training in the exchange of self and other
            - (b) During post-equipoise, using adverse circumstances on the path
                - i) Using the four unwanted circumstances on the path
                    - (I) How to use loss on the path
                    - (II) How to use suffering on the path
                    - (III) How to use disgrace on the path
                    - (IV) How to use slander on the path
                - ii) Using on the path the two things that are difficult to bear
                    - (I) How to use on the path being wronged in return for kindness
                    - (II) How to use disparagement on the path
                - iii) Using poverty and prosperity on the path
                    - (I) How to use poverty on the path
                    - (II) How to use prosperity on the path

iv) Using anger and attachment on the path
 (I) How to use objects of anger on the path
 (II) How to use objects of attachment on the path

(2) Training in ultimate bodhichitta
 (a) In meditative equipoise, training in simplicity free from fixation
 (b) In post-equipoise, discarding fixation on the reality of objects of attachment and anger
 i) Discarding fixation on the reality of objects of attachment
 ii) Discarding fixation on the reality of objects of anger

c) Training in the bodhichitta precepts
 (1) Training in the six paramitas
 (a) Training in generosity
 (b) Training in discipline
 (c) Training in patience
 (d) Training in diligence
 (e) Training in meditative concentration
 (f) Training in wisdom
 (2) Training in the four practices taught in the sutras
 (a) To scrutinize your own confusion and give it up
 (b) To give up speaking of bodhisattvas' faults
 (c) To give up attachment to the households of sponsors
 (d) To give up harsh words

(3) How to be rid of the afflictions
(4) Training in accomplishing others' good with mindfulness and vigilance
(5) Dedicating the virtue to perfect buddhahood

III. The virtuous end: The conclusion
A. How and for whom this text was composed
B. The unerring nature of these practices
C. Demonstrating humility and requesting forgiveness
D. Dedicating the merit of composing this text to buddhahood
E. The colophon endowed with four perfect qualities

Notes

1. The monastery has expanded in recent years. There are currently more than three hundred and fifty monks residing at the monastery and more than one hundred and fifty nuns residing at the nunnery, which was founded in 2017.
2. The Sanskrit word *puja* means to worship and pay homage and refers to all acts of prayer and offering to the divine. The puja offered on the tenth and twenty-fifth lunar days of the month at Tulku Pema Rigtsal Rinpoche's monastery and nunnery is the profound practice of Troma Nakmo of the Dudjom Tersar lineage.
3. Guru Rinpoche, also known as Padmasambhava (the Lotus-Born), is the tantric master who established the Vajra Vehicle of Buddhism in Tibet in the ninth century. Chamara is one of the eight subcontinents surrounding Mount Meru, according to Buddhist cosmology. It is the location of the Glorious Copper-Colored Mountain, the terrestrial pure land of Guru Rinpoche.
4. A kata is a ceremonial scarf used in Tibetan culture as a symbol of pure intention, goodwill, and respect.
5. Rongzom Mahapandita, or Rongzom Chokyi Zangpo, was an eleventh-century translator, scholar, and author. He is one of the three major luminaries of the Nyingma tradition, alongside Longchenpa and Ju Mipham Rinpoche.

6. Nagarjuna (c. 150–250) is one of the six great commentators, known as the "Six Ornaments," of Buddha's teachings. Revered by all Mahayana Buddhist schools as an unsurpassed scholar, his teachings are the foundation of the Madhyamaka (Middle Way) school of thought. He is also esteemed as one of the eighty-four mahasiddhas and eight vidyadharas of India.
7. The Great Perfection (Dzogchen) is the final and ultimate teaching of Buddha. It refers to the system of practice that entails accessing innate awareness (*rigpa*) and to innate awareness itself. Because all phenomena are realized to be naturally perfect, or complete, within awareness, it is described as "perfection" and because it is the fundamental, all-encompassing nature of all things, it is said to be "great."
8. The four modes of natural rest (*chok bzhag bzhi*) are an aspect of Great Perfection practice that allow one's being to return to its innate awakened state.
9. Buddha described the body, speech, and mind as "gates" because it is through them that we function and accumulate positive, negative, and neutral karma. From among these three gates, mind is chief and body and speech are subservient.
10. A "vehicle" (*yana*) is a set of teachings that transports one to a specific fruition. Buddha taught a variety of vehicles in response to the needs and capacities of beings. These vehicles can be classified in various ways, one of the most common being the threefold classification of the Lesser Vehicle (Hinayana), the Great Vehicle (Mahayana), and the Vajra Vehicle (Vajrayana). The nine graded vehicles is the system employed by the Nyingma school of Tibetan Buddhism. The first three of the nine vehicles are the shravaka, pratyekabuddha, and bodhisattva vehicles. They are known as causal vehicles because they regard the path as the cause of the fruition of liberation and buddhahood.

They are followed by the three vehicles of outer tantra—kriya, upa, and yoga—and the three vehicles of inner tantra—maha, anu, and ati. The vehicles of outer and inner tantra are known as resultant vehicles, for they take the fruition as the path by seeing that buddhahood is our basic nature and training on the path is the act of unveiling this innate state.

11. Rongzom Chökyi Zangpo, *Entering the Way of the Great Vehicle: Dzogchen as the Culmination of the Mahāyāna*, trans. Dominic Sur (Snow Lion, 2017), 165.
12. Longchenpa (Klong chen pa, 1308-1364) is a great luminary of Tibetan Buddhism and a central figure in the Nyingma tradition. He systematized the Nyingma teachings in his *Seven Treasuries* and wrote extensively on the Great Perfection.
13. Khu nu bla ma bstan 'dzin rgyal mtshan, 1895-1977.
14. Patrul Rinpoche (Dpal sprul rin po che, 1808-1887) was one of the most illustrious teachers of nineteenth-century Tibet and author of *The Words of My Perfect Teacher*.
15. Do Khyentse Yeshe Dorje (Mdo mkhyen brtse ye shes rdo rje, 1800-1866) was the mind emanation of Jigme Lingpa. He was renowned as a mahasiddha and displayed many miraculous feats throughout the course of his life.
16. A feast offering (*ganachakra*) is a tantric offering in which oblations of food and drink are consecrated as the elixir of wisdom and offered to the mandala of deities and the mandala of one's own body.
17. A damaru is a small, round hand drum that is used in tantric rituals.
18. This refers to Yukhok Jadralwa Choying Rangdrol (G.yu khog bya bral ba chos dbyings rang grol, 1872-1952).
19. Approach and accomplishment (*bsnyen sgrub*) are two aspects of Secret Mantra practice. In this instance, they refer to stages of mantra recitation.

20. Tulku (Skt. *nirmanakaya*) is a title given to those who have been recognized as reincarnations of accomplished practitioners. Khenpo is a title given to monastics who have attained a high degree of knowledge in the traditional fields of Buddhist studies and are authorized to teach. It can also refer to a monastic preceptor and the abbot of a monastery. Henceforth in this book, *khenpo* has been translated as "scholar," except for when it is part of a teacher's name.
21. Se ra yang sprul rin po che.
22. A mind treasure is a divine revelation that arises spontaneously in the mind of a realized master.
23. Patrul Rinpoche, *The Words of My Perfect Teacher*, trans. Padmakara Translation Group (HarperCollins, 1994), 11.
24. The six paramitas are the transcendent perfections of generosity, discipline, patience, diligence, meditative concentration, and wisdom. They are "transcendent" because they are infused with the wisdom of emptiness.
25. Patrul Rinpoche, *The Words of My Perfect Teacher*, 16.
26. The three baskets (Skt. *tripitaka*) are the three collections into which Buddha's teachings are divided, so called because the palm-leaf folios on which the scriptures were originally written were collected and stored in baskets. The three baskets are the vinaya, sutra, and abhidharma.
27. In the Kadampa tradition, *geshe*, literally "virtuous friend," is a title given to a spiritual mentor. In the Geluk tradition, it is a title given to those who have completed the monastic curriculum.
28. The five genres of scripture are the five main subjects of Buddhist philosophy studied in the great monastic universities of India and Tibet:

    1. prajnaparamita (perfection of wisdom)
    2. madhyamaka (middle way)
    3. pramana (valid cognition)

4. abhidharma (phenomenology)
5. vinaya (monastic discipline)

29. Minyak Kunzang Sonam (1823–1905) was also known as Chokyi Drakpa. A full translation of his commentary is available in *Uniting Wisdom and Compassion: Illuminating the Thirty-Seven Practices of a Bodhisattva*, trans. Heidi Koppl (Wisdom, 2004).
30. The Nyingma, or Ancient, school of Tibetan Buddhism follows the teachings and translations introduced to Tibet up until the late tenth century. Central to the Nyingma tradition are the teachings of Guru Rinpoche. Ju Mipham Rinpoche (1846–1912) was one of the greatest Nyingma scholars and practitioners of the last century. His writings were instrumental in reinvigorating the Nyingma scholastic tradition.
31. Khenpo Kunzang Palden (Mkhan po kun bzang dpal ldan, 1862–1943), or Khenpo Kunpal for short, was a great scholar of the Nyingma tradition and a close disciple of Patrul Rinpoche. He was the main teacher of Botrul Rinpoche.
32. The term *mara*, meaning "demon" or "demonic force," refers to malevolent spirits or, symbolically, to obstacles on the path to awakening. Buddha spoke of four types of mara: the mara of the afflictions (the disturbing emotions of attachment, aversion, and so on); the mara of the aggregates (the five aggregates that are the basis for our mistaken belief in a personal self and that are the source of our suffering); the mara of death (death itself, which cuts short our precious human life, and the transience of all phenomena); and the mara of the divine son (the seducing forces of distraction and craving that hinder our attainment of liberation and awakening).
33. The bhumis are the levels, or stages, that describe a noble bodhisattva's journey to buddhahood. Typically, ten

bodhisattva bhumis are enumerated, with the eleventh bhumi being perfect buddhahood.

34. Shravakas and pratyekabuddhas are followers of the Lesser Vehicle. The shravakas (those who listen and proclaim) hear teachings, such as the four noble truths and the twelve links of interdependence, from the Buddha and, through reflecting and meditating upon them, attain the state of shravaka-arhat. Pratyekabuddhas are self-realized, or solitary, buddhas who, relying solely on their own insight and initiative, meditate on the twelve links of interdependence, thereby attaining the state of pratyekabuddha-arhat. The states of shravaka- and pratyekabuddha-arhat are partial awakenings that bring permanent freedom from samsara and its suffering.
35. Kunzang Pelden, *Nectar of Manjushri's Speech: A Detailed Commentary on Shantideva's Way of the Bodhisattva*, trans. Padmakara Translation Group (Shambhala, 2007), 34.
36. "All phenomena from form to omniscience" is a common phrase in Tibetan Buddhist literature. It refers to the entire range of classified phenomena from the coarsest (form) to the subtlest (omniscience) and everything in between.
37. Dharmachakra Translation Committee, trans., *The Heart of the Perfection of Wisdom Sutra, the Blessed Mother* (84000: Translating the Words of the Buddha, 2025), https://84000.co/translation/toh21.
38. Adam Pearcey, trans., *The Sūtra of the Heart of Transcendent Wisdom* (Lotsawa House, 2019), https://www.lotsawahouse.org/words-of-the-buddha/heart-sutra-with-extras.
39. The prajnaparamita (the perfection of wisdom) refers to the realization of profound emptiness, as well as the collection of sutras that expound profound emptiness. It can also refer to Maitreya's *Ornament of Clear Realization*, a commentary on the hidden meaning of the Prajnaparamita sutras.

40. Abhidharma is one of the three "baskets," or sections, of Buddha's teachings. These teachings are a form of metaphysics and focus on developing wisdom by analyzing the various elements of our experience. *The Treasury of Abhidharma* (*Abhidharmakosha*) by the Indian scholar Vasubandhu is one of the most widely studied abhidharma treatises.
41. Pramana is the study of valid cognition and forms a central part of the curriculum in most Buddhist colleges (*shedras*).
42. Madhyamaka (the middle way) is a Buddhist school of thought first articulated by the second-century Indian master Nagarjuna and elucidated further by Indian and Tibetan scholars, such as Chandrakirti, Shantideva, Aryadeva, Longchenpa, and Tsongkhapa, to name a few. The Madhyamaka is rooted in Buddha's teachings on emptiness beyond all conceptual extremes.
43. The vinaya is one of the three baskets of Buddha's teachings. These teachings focus primarily on monastic discipline.
44. 'Jigs med gling pa, 1730–1798.
45. Jigme Lingpa and Kangyur Rinpoche, *Treasury of Precious Qualities: Book Two*, trans. Padmakara Translation Group (Shambhala, 2013), 43.
46. The three realms are the desire realm, form realm, and formless realm. They encompass all possible samsaric states. The desire realm contains the three lower realms of hell beings, hungry ghosts, and animals, and the three higher realms of humans, demigods, and gods. It is called the desire realm because the beings inhabiting it are driven by sensual desire. The form realm consists of seventeen heavenly abodes. Beings in the form realm are not attached to coarse sensual pleasures but they remain attached to a subtle level of form. The formless realm consists of four meditative states and is so called because the beings dwelling here do not have coarse forms.

47. A yidam deity is a tutelary deity practiced in the Vajra Vehicle. An almost endless variety of yidam deities are found in the tantras. As manifestations of buddhas and bodhisattvas, or particular aspects of buddhahood, they may be peaceful or wrathful, male, female, or a third gender, as befits the nature and needs of the practitioner. Yidam deities are not worshipped as external deities but as expressions of one's original, awakened state.
48. "Omniscience" refers to perfect buddhahood, the fully awakened state that knows the nature of reality and all phenomena and how to benefit beings according to their needs.
49. "This Excellent Eon" refers to our current era, or cosmic cycle, so called because it was foretold that 1,002 buddhas would appear in the world during this time. Buddha Shakyamuni was the fourth of these buddhas and is the guide of the present age. Many years from now, the fifth buddha, Maitreya, will appear and once more turn the Dharma Wheel.
50. Chandrakirti (Zla ba grags pa) is a pivotal figure in the Madhyamaka tradition. Born in South India in the seventh century, he upheld the philosophy of Nagarjuna and elaborated on *The Root Stanzas on the Middle Way* with his treatise *Introduction to the Middle Way*.
51. Chandrakirti and Jamgön Mipham, *Introduction to the Middle Way*, trans. Padmakara Translation Group (Shechen, 2004), 59, with a minor edit by Laura Swan.
52. Karl Brunnhölzl, *Gone Beyond: Volume One* (Snow Lion, 2010), 237.
53. Jamgön Mipham, *A Feast of the Nectar of the Supreme Vehicle: An Explanation of the Ornament of the Mahāyāna Sūtras*, trans. Padmakara Translation Group (Shambhala, 2018), 15.
54. University of Calgary Buddhist Studies Team, trans., *The Questions of the Householder Vīradatta* (84000:

Translating the Words of the Buddha, 2025), https://84000.co/translation/toh72.

55. "NASA Animation Sizes Up the Universe's Biggest Black Holes," NASA, accessed May 28, 2025, https://www.nasa.gov/universe/nasa-animation-sizes-up-the-universes-biggest-black-holes/.
56. You can learn more about the extraordinary benefits of bodhichitta in chapter 1 of Shantideva's *Entering the Way of the Bodhisattva*, "The Excellence of Bodhichitta."
57. Patrul Rinpoche, *The Words of My Perfect Teacher*, 20.
58. "Obscurations" are the veils of confusion, and the negativity stemming from that confusion, that conceal the true nature of phenomena and prevent us from achieving buddhahood. In the case of hungry ghosts, obscurations manifest externally as a constant lack of food and drink; internally as tiny mouths, enormous stomachs, and the like, so that even if they acquire food and drink they can never satiate their hunger and thirst; and specifically as creatures feeding off their bodies and so on. See *The Words of My Perfect Teacher*, 72–75.
59. Patrul Rinpoche, 172.
60. Patrul Rinpoche, 25.
61. Dharmachakra Translation Committee, trans., *The Play in Full* (84000: Translating the Words of the Buddha, 2025), 25.3. https://84000.co/translation/toh95.
62. Thinley Norbu, *Sunlight Speech That Dispels the Darkness of Doubt: Sublime Prayers, Praises, and Practices of the Nyingma Masters* (Shambhala, 2015), 113.
63. These three types of human birth are discussed in chapter 1, verses 10–12 of Longchenpa, *Finding Rest in the Nature of the Mind*, The Trilogy on Rest 1, trans. Padmakara Translation Group (Shambhala, 2017), 7–8.
64. *Mala* is a Sanskrit word meaning garland. It refers to a rosary, or string of beads, used to count recitations of mantras and prayers.

65. Mgo log gser rta rin po che, also known as Pema Lungtok Gyatso (Pad+ma lung rtogs rgya mtsho, 1891–1964).
66. Pema Dechen Gyalpo (1873–1933), one of the main students of Dudjom Lingpa (1835–1903).
67. "To request a Dharma connection" means to request a minor teaching or transmission from a teacher in order to form a connection with them.
68. Trekcho (cutting through) and togal (direct crossing) are the two principal aspects, or paths, of Great Perfection practice.
69. The Sanskrit word *kaya* literally means "body" but also connotes "dimension" and "field." It is used to describe the multiple dimensions and manifestations of a buddha. In the Great Vehicle, these dimensions are typically categorized as the three kayas: the dharmakaya (reality body), sambhogakaya (enjoyment body), and nirmanakaya (emanation body). The nirmanakaya is the dimension, or manifestation, of awakening that can be perceived by ordinary beings. With their unconditioned and constant compassion, the buddhas and bodhisattvas emanate manifold emanation forms to bring temporal and ultimate benefit to beings.
70. The rainbow body is a phenomenon achieved by Great Perfection practitioners in which the physical body dissolves into a body of light, leaving little to no physical remains. Thirteen of Dudjom Lingpa's disciples attained the rainbow body by practicing the profound treasure teachings he revealed.
71. A pure land is a place or world manifested by a buddha or great bodhisattva. Once born into a pure land, one can progress toward buddhahood without the danger of falling back into samsara's lower realms.
72. Yeshe Tsogyal, *The Mahāguru Prayer*, trans. Rigpa Translations (Lotsawa House, 2014), https://www.lotsawahouse.org/tibetan-masters/pema-lingpa/yeshe-tsogyals-prayer, with minor edit by Laura Swan.

73. Shantideva, *Entering the Way of the Bodhisattva: A New Translation and Contemporary Guide*, trans. David Karma Choephel (Shambhala, 2021), 81.
74. Shantideva, 86.
75. A mahasiddha is a practitioner who has attained the supreme *siddhi*, or accomplishment—direct realization of ultimate reality. The eighty-four mahasiddhas were practitioners of the Vajra Vehicle living in India between the eighth and twelfth centuries. Many of them lived unconventional lives or held professions that are often regarded as incompatible with the spiritual path. See Donald S. Lopez, *Seeing the Sacred in Samsara: An Illustrated Guide to the Eighty-Four Mahasiddhas* (Shambhala, 2019).
76. "Mind training" (*lojong*) is a system of practical instructions for subduing the self-cherishing mind and developing the compassion and wisdom of bodhichitta. Rooted in the Great Vehicle teachings on the bodhisattva path, it was introduced to Tibet by Lord Atisha in the eleventh century and continued by the Kadampa masters.
77. Ati yoga is the third and highest of the three inner tantras and the pinnacle of the nine vehicles. It is synonymous with the Great Perfection.
78. The kusali offering is the practice of offering one's own body to other beings, using visualization techniques. See Patrul Rinpoche, *The Words of My Perfect Teacher*, 297–307.
79. Patrul Rinpoche, *The Words of My Perfect Teacher*, 57.
80. Dilgo Khyentse, *The Heart of Compassion: Instructions on Ngulchu Thogme's Thirty-Sevenfold Practice of a Bodhisattva*, trans. Padmakara Translation Group (Shechen, 2006), 126.
81. A noble being, or *arya*, is one who has directly realized emptiness, to some extent, and thereby transcended samsaric existence. There are four types of noble beings: shravaka arhats, pratyekabuddha arhats, bodhisattvas, and perfect buddhas.

82. Gampopa Sonam Rinchen (Sgam po pa bsod nams rin chen, 1079-1153/9).
83. You can read about what happened next in Dakpo Lhaje's hagiographies, Milarepa's hagiographies, and Milarepa's *One Hundred Thousand Songs.* See Jampa Mackenzie Stewart, *The Life of Gampopa* (Shambhala, 2004) and Tsangnyön Heruka, *The Hundred Thousand Songs of Milarepa: A New Translation*, trans. Christopher Stagg (Shambhala, 2017).
84. Vidyadhara of the Great Seal is one of the four vidyadhara (awareness holder) levels—a rubric of spiritual accomplishment used by the Nyingma tradition. Vidyadhara of the Great Seal is the third of these levels and equivalent to the path of meditation, from among the five paths. To attain this level is to achieve permanent freedom from samsara and to be close to the accomplishment of perfect buddhahood.
85. Patrul Rinpoche, *The Words of My Perfect Teacher*, 353.
86. Jigme Lingpa and Kangyur Rinpoche, *Treasury of Precious Qualities: Book One*, trans. Padmakara Translation Group (Shambhala, 2010), 41.
87. An arhat, literally "foe-destroyer," is someone who has attained permanent freedom from samsara by vanquishing the afflictions and their source—the mistaken belief in a personal self. The term is typically used to describe the partial enlightenment that is the final fruition of the Lesser Vehicle, but it can also be used more broadly to describe all levels of enlightenment.
88. Nagarjuna, *Nagarjuna's Letter to a Friend*, trans. Padmakara Translation Group (Snow Lion, 2013), 33.
89. Jigme Lingpa and Kangyur Rinpoche, *Treasury of Precious Qualities: Book One*, 48.
90. "Good Actions" are the bodhisattva's excellent actions of body, speech, and mind—actions that bring benefit to oneself and others and lead to liberation and buddhahood.

91. Rigpa Translations, trans., *The King of Aspiration Prayers: Samantabhadra's "Aspiration to Good Actions" (Zangchö Mönlam)* (Lotsawa House, 1996), https://www.lotsawahouse.org/words-of-the-buddha/samantabhadra-aspiration-good-actions.
92. Lochen Dharmashri (Lo chen d+harma shrI, 1654-1717) was a celebrated scholar of the Nyingma school.
93. "Parinirvana" means to fully transcend the sorrow of samsara. It is a term used to describe the death of Buddha and other awakened beings.
94. *The Chronicles of the Lotus-Born* (*Pad+ma bka' thang*) revealed by Yarje Orgyen Lingpa (Yar rje o rgyan gling pa).
95. Kunzang Pelden, *Nectar of Manjushri's Speech*, 81.
96. The conception of a personal self (*gang zag gi bdag 'dzin*) refers to sentient beings' erroneous perception of a truly existent self in their five aggregates of form, sensation, perception, conditioning factors, and consciousness—or more simply speaking, in their bodies and minds. The conception of a self of phenomena (*chos kyi bdag 'dzin*) refers to sentient beings' erroneous perception of true existence in all things. The conception of a personal self is subsumed within the conception of a self of phenomena. The conception of a personal self is the root of samsara. It keeps us trapped in the endless cycle of rebirth due to karma and emotions. Therefore, until we uproot this mistaken conception, we cannot attain liberation—a partial awakening that grants permanent freedom from samsara. And until we uproot the conception of a self of phenomena, we cannot attain omniscient buddhahood—the perfectly awakened state that is the perfection of wisdom and compassion and an inexhaustible source of benefit.
97. The personal liberation (*pratimoksha*) vows emphasize physical and verbal discipline and the avoidance of actions that would harm others. They are so called

because they are rooted in the Lesser Vehicle, whose followers strive for personal, as opposed to collective, liberation from samsara. The seven types of personal liberation vows are that of a fully ordained monk, a fully ordained nun, a novice monk, a novice nun, a female novice in training for full ordination, a male lay practitioner, and a female lay practitioner.

98. If you wish to take the analytical approach, you can refer to *In Praise of the Unique Qualities of the Bhagavan* and "Establishing the Teacher as Valid," the second chapter of Dharmakirti's *Commentary on Valid Cognition*.

99. These two figures are known in Tibet as Totsun Drubje (Mtho btsun grub rje) and Deje Dagpo (Bde byed bdag po), respectively.

100. *Khyad par 'phags bstod.*

101. The various aspects of refuge, such as its essence, etymology, divisions, benefits, and so on, are explained in detail in scriptures such as *Nectar of Manjushri's Speech* and, most importantly, the *Uttaratantra*. Moreover, having taken refuge in the Three Jewels, we need to observe certain precepts. These precepts were taught by Buddha himself and can be found in the sutras. They are also presented in treatises such as *Seventy Stanzas on Refuge*, in *Perfect Conduct* and other texts on the three vows, and in guidance manuals such as *The Words of My Perfect Teacher*. You can learn about these important details from these texts.

102. Rdo grub chen 'jigs med phrin las 'od zer, 1745–1821.

103. Rdo grub chen thub bstan phrin las dpal bzang po, 1927–2022.

104. "Liberation" refers to complete freedom from samsara, the cessation of suffering attained by the shravaka and pratyekabuddha arhats. It can also refer to the attainment of rebirth in one of the nirmanakaya pure realms, such as Buddha Amitabha's Blissful Realm (Sukhavati) or Guru

Rinpoche's Glorious Copper-Colored Mountain. However, the term most commonly refers to the fruition of the shravaka and pratyekabuddha arhats, while the term "great liberation" refers to perfect, complete buddhahood.

105. Patrul Rinpoche, *The Words of My Perfect Teacher*, 94.
106. Gendun Chopel (Dge 'dun chos 'phel, 1903–1951) is one of the most controversial and celebrated figures in the recent history of Tibet. He was a philosopher, historian, artist, translator, traveler, and a campaigner for the modernization of Tibet.
107. Gendun Chopel, *In the Forest of Faded Wisdom: 104 Poems by Gendun Chopel, a Bilingual Edition*, trans. Donald S. Lopez (University of Chicago Press, 2009), 69.
108. Khro phu lo tsA ba byams pa dpal, 1172?–1236?.
109. Chandrakirti and Jamgön Mipham, *Introduction to the Middle Way*, 59. Minor changes to the translation were made by the translator to the third and fourth lines.
110. Long-life pills are round pills made with substances that increase longevity and are consecrated with longevity mantras and so on. They are usually made with dough and rolled with the hands into neat balls. Rinpoche is using long-life pills as a metaphor for our perception of the self as a neat, self-sufficient entity that exists in and of itself.
111. The nonexistence of the personal self is realized by employing profound modes of reasoning, such as the sevenfold reasoning of the chariot. These reasonings are explained briefly in the discussion on ultimate bodhichitta in the commentary on verse 22, on p. 187.
112. The paths of accumulation and joining are the first two of the five paths that make up the journey to buddhahood. The path of accumulation is further subdivided into lesser, middling, and greater stages, and the path of joining is subdivided into the stages of warmth, summit, acceptance, and supreme attribute. See also note 131.

113. "The precious Jowo in Lhasa" refers to the Buddha Shakyamuni statue housed in the Jokhang temple in Lhasa, Tibet. It was brought to Tibet from China by Wengcheng Gongzhu as part of her dowry when she married King Songtsen Gampo in the seventh century. This statue is one of the most revered images in Tibet.
114. Jamgön Mipham, *A Feast of the Nectar of the Supreme Vehicle*, 53.
115. The full title of this section, as found in Minyak Kunso's structural outline, is "The Path of Greater Beings: Freeing Yourself from the Extremes of Existence and Peace by Training in the Natural Unity of Emptiness and Compassion."
116. Through the shravaka and pratyekabuddha paths of the Lesser Vehicle, one can realize the lack of a personal self, thereby attaining personal liberation from samsara, the extreme of existence in which one is trapped in an endless cycle of suffering. However, from the Great Vehicle perspective, or the perspective of bodhisattvas seeking perfect buddhahood, this peaceful state of liberation (*nirvana*) becomes yet another extreme—a state of peaceful cessation that is free of all suffering but limited in the depths of its wisdom and void of the enlightened qualities needed to effortlessly benefit beings. It is only with both the wisdom and compassion of the bodhisattva path that one can achieve complete awakening—perfect buddhahood that transcends the extremes of both samsara and nirvana, thereby fulfilling the benefit of oneself and all other beings.
117. Karl Brunnhölzl, *Gone Beyond, Volume One*, 237.
118. Jamgön Mipham, *A Feast of the Nectar of the Supreme Vehicle*, 15.
119. You can learn about these classifications from *The Words of My Perfect Teacher*, *Treasury of Precious Qualities*, and other Great Vehicle texts.

120. Shantideva, *Entering the Way of the Bodhisattva*, 5.
121. Dharmadhatu (the basic space of phenomena) is the true nature of all things; emptiness pervaded with awareness. It encompasses all phenomena—samsara and nirvana, the world and all beings.
122. Nagarjuna, *Nagarjuna's Letter to a Friend*, trans. Padmakara Translation Group (Snow Lion, 2013), 53.
123. The suffering of suffering is the blatant suffering of falling sick, feeling discontent, losing a loved one, and so on. It is what we ordinarily describe as "suffering." The suffering of change is the pain caused by the transience of things. For example, no matter how comfortable and secure your situation might seem, it is not reliable. Sooner or later, it will change, and what used to be a source of pleasure will become a source of pain. The all-pervasive suffering of conditioning is difficult to recognize but nevertheless colors every aspect of our experience. This third type of suffering refers to the five aggregates that are the basis of our experience; because the aggregates are conditioned, they are the nature and source of suffering.
124. Patrul Rinpoche, *The Words of My Perfect Teacher*, 74.
125. Patrul Rinpoche, 200.
126. For the training in application bodhichitta, consisting of the six paramitas, see chapters 29–34.
127. Shantideva, *Entering the Way of the Bodhisattva*, 100.
128. Shantideva, 99.
129. Shantideva, 99.
130. The Secret Mantra samayas are the sacred commitments, or vows, of the Vajra Vehicle.
131. *Commentary on Valid Cognition* (*Tshad ma rnam 'grel*) by the seventh-century Indian master Dharmakirti.
132. The maxim "Profit and victory to others; loss and defeat to myself" comes from Geshe Langri Tangpa's *Eight Verses of Training the Mind* (*Blo sbyong tshig brgyad ma*).

133. The journey to perfect buddhahood is described in terms of progression through the five paths of accumulation, joining, seeing, meditation, and no more learning. The first four constitute the path of learning, whereas the fifth path of no more learning is perfect buddhahood. The path of seeing is equated with the first bodhisattva bhumi, Perfect Joy. This marks the juncture at which one directly realizes emptiness, thereby transcending samsaric existence. On the path of meditation, one traverses the second to tenth bhumis, and when one reaches the path of no more learning, one attains perfect buddhahood—the eleventh bhumi, Universal Radiance.
134. A chuba is the traditional unisex Tibetan dress. It is a loose, ankle-length robe that is tied around the waist with a sash. The overlapping folds at the front of the dress create a pocket of sorts where personal items can be stored.
135. This story is also told in *The Words of My Perfect Teacher*, 121–22.
136. Thinley Norbu Rinpoche, *White Sail: Crossing the Waves of Ocean Mind to the Serene Continent of the Triple Gems* (Shambhala, 2001).
137. Dodrupchen Jigme Tenpe Nyima, *In Praise of Patrul Orgyen Jigme Chökyi Wangpo*, trans. Adam Pearcey (Lotsawa House, 2020), https://www.lotsawahouse.org/tibetan-masters/dodrupchen-III/patrul-praise.
138. Bla ma rig grol, 1943–2004.
139. This story is also told in Patrul Rinpoche, *The Words of My Perfect Teacher*, 231–34.
140. Shantideva, *Entering the Way of the Bodhisattva*, 49.
141. Patrul Rinpoche, *The Words of My Perfect Teacher*, 248.
142. The Sarma schools are the "new" schools of Tibetan Buddhism that follow the teachings translated and introduced to Tibet from the tenth century onward by

teachers such as Lotsawa Rinchen Zangpo, Lord Atisha, and others. The Sarma schools include the Sakya, Kagyu, Geluk, and other traditions.

143. Khenpo Jigme Phuntsok Rinpoche (Mkhan po 'jigs med phun tshogs, 1933–2004) was one of the most influential Nyingma teachers of the late twentieth century. He remained in Tibet after 1959 and, following the end of the Cultural Revolution, established Larung Gar in Serta, Golok, which has grown to become one of the largest monastic institutions in the world.

144. A "hand empowerment" refers to the traditional custom of a teacher transmitting blessings to a student by placing their hand on the student's head.

145. Patrul Rinpoche, 249.

146. Bod sprul mdo sngags bstan pa'i nyi ma, 1898/1900/1902–1959.

147. Shantideva, *Entering the Way of the Bodhisattva*, 49.

148. Shantideva, 34–35.

149. The thirteen major treatises (*gzhung chen bcu gsum*) are thirteen seminal Buddhist texts that have long formed the basis of the curriculum in many Buddhist colleges (*shedras*) in Tibet. The five major sciences are the secular sciences of craftsmanship, medicine, logic, and linguistics, and the inner science of Buddhadharma

150. The Fourth Dzogchen Rinpoche, Mingyur Namkhe Dorje (Rdzogs chen grub dbang mi 'gyur nam mkha'i rdo rje, 1793–1870.

151. Tulku Pema Rigtsal, *The Great Secret of Mind: Special Instructions on the Nonduality of Dzogchen*, trans. Keith Dowman (Snow Lion, 2012), 25.

152. Adam Pearcey, trans., *The Sūtra of the Heart of Transcendent Wisdom* (Lotsawa House, 2019), https://www.lotsawahouse.org/words-of-the-buddha/heart-sutra-with-extras.

153. Shantideva, *Entering the Way of the Bodhisattva*, 114.
154. This story found in chapters 85 and 86 of Gareth Sparham, trans., *The Perfection of Wisdom in Eighteen Thousand Lines* (84000: Translating the Words of the Buddha, 2025), https://84000.co/translation/toh10. A shorter version of the story is found beginning in chapter 73 of Padmakara Translation Group, trans., *The Perfection of Wisdom in Twenty-Five Thousand Lines* (84000: Translating the Words of the Buddha, 2025), https://84000.co/translation/toh9.
155. This is a reference to the Buddhist practice of saving the lives of animals from slaughter by buying them and setting them free. Before being freed, they are symbolically offered to the Three Jewels of Buddha, Dharma, and Sangha and blessed with sacred substances and mantras with the intention of sowing in their mindstreams the seeds of liberation and awakening. This brings immediate benefit to the animals in this life and enduring benefit in their future lives as well.
156. The present-day Deer Park in Sarnath represents only a tiny portion of the original sanctuary, which encompassed a vast tract of land.
157. This story is told in section 9.714 of *The Chapter on Medicines*, trans. Bhaiṣajyavastu Translation Team (84000: Translating the Words of the Buddha, 2025), https://84000.co/translation/toh1-6.
158. Karma Chakme (Karma chags med, 1613–78) is one of Tibet's most celebrated scholars and practitioners. "Mountain Dharma" (*ri chos*) is a genre of instruction given for those who wish to devote themselves to contemplative practice in solitude. Karma Chakme's *Mountain Dharma* (*Chags med ri chos*) is one of his most well-known compositions. See Khenpo Karthar Rinpoche, *Karma Chakme's Mountain Dharma: Volumes I, II, and III* (KTD, 2005, 2006, and 2008).

159. Nagarjuna, *Nagarjuna's Letter to a Friend*, trans. Padmakara Translation Group (Snow Lion, 2013), 29.
160. These three levels of discipline are discussed in detail in treatises such as Ngari Pandita's *Ascertaining the Three Vows* and Lochen Dharmashri's *A Cornucopia to Fulfill All Wishes, a Commentary on the Three Sets of Vows.*
161. The numbers of vows mentioned here are specific to the Mulasarvastivada tradition of vinaya that is upheld in Tibet. In other traditions of vinaya, such as the Theravada tradition upheld in Sri Lanka, Thailand, and so on, the numbers of vows are slightly different.
162. The manner in which a lower set of vows, such as the five precepts of a lay practitioner, is transformed and subsumed into a higher level of vow, such as the bodhisattva vow, is known as "the principle of upward containment of qualities" (*yon tan yar ldan gyi tshul*). See Ngari Panchan, *Perfect Conduct: Ascertaining the Three Vows*, trans. Khenpo Gyurme Samdrub and Sangye Khandro (Wisdom, 2015).
163. The appearance of bindus (spheres) of light at the time of death is regarded as an auspicious sign and an indication of the deceased practitioner's realization.
164. Ponda Khen Rinpoche (Sbom mda' mkhan rin po che), also known as Polu Khenpo Dorje (Spo lu mkhan po rdo rje, 1896–1970).
165. Kyabje Penor Rinpoche (Pad nor rin po che), or Kyabje Drubwang Pema Norbu Rinpoche (1932–2009), was the eleventh throne holder of the Palyul Lineage and the supreme head of the Nyingma lineage from 1993 to 2001. He established Namdroling Monastery in southern India, which has since become the largest Nyingma institute in the world.
166. These are just a few details of where and when Khen Rinpoche taught in Tibet, India, and Nepal. More about Khen Rinpoche's activities can be found in his

hagiography. See Tsultrim Gyatso (Tshul khrim rgya mtsho), *'Bras ljongs su deng rabs bod kyi bla ma rnams kyi mdzad pa dang rnam thar bsdus pa* [The abbreviated hagiographies of Tibetan lamas in contemporary Sikkim] (Namgyal Institute of Tibetology, 2008); and Lama Thinley Dorje, "Khenchen Dazer," The Treasury of Lives, July 2019, https://treasuryoflives.org/biographies/view/Dzogchen-Khenpo-Dawai-Ozer/TBRC_P8977.

167. The saffron Dharma robe is the sign of a fully ordained monk or nun. Thus, Khenpo Dazer Rinpoche is saying that his faultless observance of the monastic vows is his greatest accomplishment.

168. Dharmapalas (Dharma protectors) are nonhuman beings who have vowed to guard and protect Buddha's teachings and its followers. They can be emanations of buddhas and bodhisattvas or mundane spirits, gods, and demons who have been subjugated by a great master, such as Guru Rinpoche, and bound under oath. Followers of the Vajra Vehicle make regular offerings to the dharmapalas in request and thanks of their protection.

169. These offerings are profound Secret Mantra practices that enable the practitioner to gather vast stores of merit and wisdom and to purify obscurations (the veils of confusion concealing the awakened nature of all things) while bringing immediate temporal benefit to other beings. They employ deity visualization, mantra recitation, and meditative concentration to make immeasurable offerings to the buddhas, bodhisattvas, and all samsaric beings. The water-torma offering is an offering of water and grains dedicated primarily to wealth deities and hungry ghosts. The Tibetan word for smoke offering is *sang* (*bsang*), meaning "to cleanse and purify." This offering of fragrant smoke and other substances focuses on purifying beings' mindstreams and the environment. The *Mountain Smoke*

Offering (*Ri wo bsang mchod*) was revealed by Lhatsun Namkha Jigme and is one of the most widely practiced smoke offerings in the Nyingma tradition. *Sur* is a type of offering in which food is charred to release its scent. This scent is then offered to all beings—from the buddhas and bodhisattvas down to those suffering in the lower realms—and especially to bardo beings (those in the intermediate state between death and rebirth) and hungry ghosts.

170. Shantideva, *Entering the Way of the Bodhisattva*, 49.
171. In *The Ornament of the Mahayana Sutras*, and other texts, it is taught that the paramitas are set forth in sequence, with each paramita being more challenging, elevated, and of greater virtue than the paramita preceding it.
172. Shantideva, *Entering the Way of the Bodhisattva*, 49.
173. The term *emptiness* describes the lack of substantial reality that is the ultimate nature of all things. It is used at all levels of Buddha's teaching, from the Lesser Vehicle to the Vajra Vehicle. However, the implication of the term can vary significantly depending on the context. For example, in the Lesser Vehicle teachings, *emptiness* typically refers to the emptiness of the personal self, whereas in the Great Vehicle teachings, the term typically refers to the emptiness of all phenomena, of which the emptiness of the personal self is but one specific instance. In the context of this third type of patience taught in the Great Vehicle, "profound reality" refers not only to the emptiness of the personal self but to the emptiness of all things.
174. Hashang was a Chinese Buddhist master who visited Tibet in the eighth century and taught a nihilistic, and hence erroneous, form of Ch'an meditation. He was publicly defeated in debate by Kamalashila and henceforth banished from Tibet.

175. Shantideva, *Entering the Way of the Bodhisattva*, 69.
176. Mercury pills are a type of alchemical medicine, or *rasayana*.
177. Patrul Rinpoche, *The Words of My Perfect Teacher*, 246.
178. The generation and completion stages are two principal aspects of Vajra Vehicle practice. Trekcho and togal are two aspects of the practice of the Great Perfection, which is the pinnacle of the Vajra Vehicle.
179. The refuge vows and five precepts are the vows one receives when formally entering the Buddhist path by taking refuge in the Three Jewels of Buddha, Dharma, and Sangha as the teacher, the path, and one's companions on the path, respectively. These vows are the foundation of the path and the support for all other levels of vow, such as the bodhichitta vow and the Secret Mantra samayas. The refuge vows consist of three things to be abandoned, three things to be done, and three supplementary precepts. The five precepts are to avoid killing, lying, stealing, sexual misconduct, and intoxication. To learn more about these vows, see Patrul Rinpoche, *The Words of My Perfect Teacher*, 182–87.
180. Shantideva, *Entering the Way of the Bodhisattva*, 81.
181. Yeshe Tsogyal, *The Mahāguru Prayer*, trans. Rigpa Translations (Lotsawa House, 2014), https://www.lotsawahouse.org/tibetan-masters/pema-lingpa/yeshe-tsogyals-prayer, with a minor edit by Laura Swan.
182. Longchenpa, *Finding Rest in the Nature of the Mind*, 145.
183. For more detail, see Dilgo Khyentse Rinpoche, *The Sage Who Dispels Mind's Anguish: Advice from the Guru, the Gentle Protector Mañjuśrī, on the Means of Accomplishing the Yogas of Śamatha and Vipaśyanā*, trans. Samye Translations (Lotsawa House, 2008), https://www.lotsawahouse.org/tibetan-masters/dilgo-khyentse/sage-who-dispels-minds-anguish. This text is based on Mipham Rinpoche's *The White Lotus: Background*

Teachings on The Treasury of Blessings (*Thub chog byin rlabs gter mdzod kyi rgyab chos pad+ma dkar po*).

184. "The sixteen aspects of impermanence and so on" refers to the sixteen aspects of the four noble truths that are taught as remedies for the mistaken belief in permanence and so on. The four applications of mindfulness are the mindfulness of the body, sensations, the mind, and phenomena. The four noble truths and the four applications of mindfulness are well known as teachings and practices of the Lesser Vehicle, but they are also central to the Great Vehicle path.
185. Jigme Lingpa and Kangyur Rinpoche, *Treasury of Precious Qualities: Book Two*, 57.
186. Kun dga' dpal ldan, 1878–1944/1950.
187. O rgyan bstan 'dzin nor bu, 1841/1851–c. 1900.
188. Khenpo Shenga (Mkhan po gzhan dga') was also known as Shenpen Chokyi Nangwa (Gzhan phan chos kyi snang ba, 1871–1927).
189. "Cutting through to primordial purity" describes the practice of trekcho while "leaping over to spontaneous presence" describes the practice of togal.
190. In the Vajra Vehicle teachings, there are further divisions of the kayas.
191. Shantideva, *Entering the Way of the Bodhisattva*, 109.
192. Dilgo Khyentse Rinpoche, *Zurchungpa's Testament*, trans. Padmakara Translation Group (Snow Lion, 2006), 343.
193. Chandrakirti and Jamgön Mipham, *Introduction to the Middle Way*, 68.
194. Jigme Lingpa and Kangyur Rinpoche, *Treasury of Precious Qualities: Book One*, 26.
195. As taught in *The Nectar of Manjushri's Speech*, the four causes that exhaust virtue are (1) not to dedicate, (2) to dedicate awry, (3) to brag to others, and (4) to have regrets. See Kunzang Pelden, *The Nectar of Manjushri's Speech*, 394.
196. Shantideva, *Entering the Way of the Bodhisattva*, 26.

197. Patrul Rinpoche, *The Words of My Perfect Teacher*, 12.
198. Rgan rigs bzang rdo rje, 1902–1984.
199. "The Alchemy of the Siddhas," Rigpa Wiki, accessed May 28, 2025, https://www.rigpawiki.org/index.php?title=The_Alchemy_of_the_Siddhas.
200. Shantideva, *Entering the Way of the Bodhisattva*, 44.
201. Longchen Rabjam, *Thirty Pieces of Heart Advice*, trans. Daniela Hartmann (Lotsawa House, 2014), https://www.lotsawahouse.org/tibetan-masters/longchen-rabjam/30-stanzas-of-advice.
202. Shantideva, *Entering the Way of the Bodhisattva*, 51.
203. The following story is also told in Patrul Rinpoche, *The Words of My Perfect Teacher*, 127.
204. Sakya Pandita Kunga Gyeltsen (Sa skya pan di ta kun dga' rgyal mtshan, 1182–1251) was one of five founding masters of the Sakya tradition of Tibetan Buddhism. *Treasury of Valid Cognition* (*Tshad ma rigs gter*) is one of his most widely read works.
205. Patrul Rinpoche, *The Words of My Perfect Teacher*, 124.
206. Patrul Rinpoche, *The Words of My Perfect Teacher*, 326, with minor edit by Laura Swan.
207. This story is told in Kīrtimukha Translation Group, trans., *The Prophecy for Bhadra the Illusionist* (84000: Translating the Words of the Buddha, 2025), https://84000.co/translation/toh65.
208. *The Prophecy for Bhadra the Illusionist*, 1.105.
209. Shantideva, *Entering the Way of the Bodhisattva*, 3.

Bibliography

Bhaiṣajyavastu Translation Team, trans. *The Chapter on Medicines*. 84000: Translating the Words of the Buddha, 2025. https://84000.co/translation/toh1-6.

Brunnhölzl, Karl. *Gone Beyond: Volume One*. Snow Lion, 2010.

Chandrakirti and Jamgön Mipham. *Introduction to the Middle Way*. Translated by the Padmakara Translation Group. Shechen, 2004.

Chokyi Drakpa. *Uniting Wisdom and Compassion: Illuminating the Thirty-Seven Practices of a Bodhisattva*. Translated by Heidi Koppl. Wisdom, 2004.

Dharmachakra Translation Committee, trans. *The Heart of the Perfection of Wisdom, the Blessed Mother*. 84000: Translating the Words of the Buddha, 2025. https://84000.co/translation/toh21.

Dilgo Khyentse Rinpoche. *The Sage Who Dispels Mind's Anguish: Advice from the Guru, the Gentle Protector Mañjuśrī, on the Means of Accomplishing the Yogas of Śamatha and Vipaśyanā*. Translated by Samye Translations. Lotsawa House, 2008. https://www.lotsawahouse.org/tibetan-masters/dilgo-khyentse/sage-who-dispels-minds-anguish.

Dilgo Khyentse Rinpoche. *Zurchungpa's Testament*. Translated by the Padmakara Translation Group. Snow Lion, 2006.

Dilgo Khyentse. *The Heart of Compassion: Instructions on Ngulchu Thogme's Thirty-Sevenfold Practice of a Bodhisattva*. Translated by the Padmakara Translation Group. Shechen, 2006.

Dodrupchen Jigme Tenpe Nyima. *In Praise of Patrul Orgyen Jigme Chokyi Wangpo*. Translated by Adam Pearcey. Lotsawa House, 2020. https://www.lotsawahouse.org/tibetan-masters/dodrupchen-III/patrul-praise.

Gendun Chopel. *In the Forest of Faded Wisdom: 104 Poems by Gendun Chopel*. Edited and Translated by Donald S. Lopez. University of Chicago Press, 2009.

Jamgön Mipham. *A Feast of the Nectar of the Supreme Vehicle: An Explanation of the Ornament of the Mahāyāna Sūtras*. Translated by the Padmakara Translation Group. Shambhala, 2018.

Jamgön Mipham. *The Wisdom Chapter: Jamgön Mipham's Commentary on the Ninth Chapter of The Way of the Bodhisattva*. Translated by the Padmakara Translation Group. Shambhala, 2017.

Jigme Lingpa and Kangyur Rinpoche. *Treasury of Precious Qualities: Book Two*. Translated by the Padmakara Translation Group. Shambhala, 2013.

Khenpo Karthar Rinpoche. *Karma Chakme's Mountain Dharma*. 3 vols. Karma Triyana Dharmachakra, 2005, 2006, and 2008.

Kīrtimukha Translation Group, trans. *The Prophecy for Bhadra the Illusionist*. 84000: Translating the Words of the Buddha, 2025. https://84000.co/translation/toh65.

Kunzang Pelden. *Nectar of Manjushri's Speech: A Detailed Commentary on Shantideva's Way of the Bodhisattva*. Translated by the Padmakara Translation Group. Shambhala, 2007.

Longchen Rabjam. *Thirty Pieces of Heart Advice*. Translated by Daniela Hartmann. Lotsawa House, 2014. https://www.lotsawahouse.org/tibetan-masters/longchen-rabjam/30-stanzas-of-advice.

Longchenpa. *Finding Rest in the Nature of the Mind*. The Trilogy on Rest 1. Translated by the Padmakara Translation Group. Shambhala, 2017.

Lopez, Donald S. *Seeing the Sacred in Samsara: An Illustrated Guide to the Eighty-Four Mahasiddhas*. Shambhala, 2019.

Minling Lochen Dharmashri. *A Cornucopia to Fulfil All Wishes, a Commentary to the Three Sets of Vows*. Mindrolling, 2021. https://dharmacloud.tsadra.org/book/min-lc-004-a-cornucopia-to-fulfil-all-wishes/

Mipham Rinpoche. *The Treasury of Blessings: A Practice of Buddha Śākyamuni*. Translated by Rigpa Translations. Lotsawa House, 2023. https://www.lotsawahouse.org/tibetan-masters/mipham/treasury-blessings-practice-buddha-shakyamuni.

Nagarjuna. *Nagarjuna's Letter to a Friend*. Translated by the Padmakara Translation Group. Snow Lion, 2013.

Padmakara Translation Group, trans. *The Perfection of Wisdom in Twenty-Five Thousand Lines*. 84000: Translating the Words of the Buddha, 2025. https://84000.co/translation/toh9.

Patrul Rinpoche. *The Words of My Perfect Teacher*. Translated by the Padmakara Translation Group. HarperCollins, 1994.

Pearcey, Adam, trans. *The Sūtra of the Heart of Transcendent Wisdom*. Lotsawa House, 2019. https://www.lotsawahouse.org/words-of-the-buddha/heart-sutra-with-extras.

Pema Wangyi Gyalpo and Dudjom Rinpoche. *Perfect Conduct: Ascertaining the Three Vows*. Translated by Khenpo Gyurme Samdrub and Sangye Khandro. Wisdom, 1999.

Rongzom Chokyi Zangpo. *Entering the Way of the Great Vehicle: Dzogchen as the Culmination of the Mahāyāna*. Translated by Dominic Sur. Snow Lion, 2017.

Rigpa Translations, trans. *The King of Aspiration Prayers: Samantabhadra's "Aspiration to Good Actions" (Zangchö Mönlam)*. Lotsawa House, 1996. https://www.lotsawahouse.org/words-of-the-buddha/samantabhadra-aspiration-good-actions.

Shantideva. *Entering the Way of the Bodhisattva: A New Translation and Contemporary Guide*. Translated by David Karma Choephel. Shambhala, 2021.

Sparham, Gareth, trans. *The Perfection of Wisdom in Eighteen Thousand Lines*. 84000: Translating the Words of the Buddha, 2025. https://84000.co/translation/toh10.

Thinley Norbu. *Sunlight Speech That Dispels the Darkness of Doubt: Sublime Prayers, Praises, and Practices of the Nyingma Masters*. Shambhala, 2015.

Tulku Pema Rigtsal. *The Great Secret of Mind: Special Instructions on the Nonduality of Dzogchen*. Translated by Keith Dowman. Snow Lion, 2012.

University of Calgary Buddhist Studies Team, trans. *The Questions of the Householder Vīradatta*. 84000: Translating the Words of the Buddha, 2025. https://84000.co/translation/toh72.

Yeshe Tsogyal. *The Lotus-Born: The Life Story of Padmasambhava*. Translated by Erik Pema Kunsang. Rangjung Yeshe, 2004.

Yeshe Tsogyal. *The Mahāguru Prayer*. Translated by Rigpa Translations. Lotsawa House, 2014. https://www.lotsawahouse.org/tibetan-masters/pema-lingpa/yeshe-tsogyals-prayer.

Index